Reluctant Witnesses

RELUCTANT WITNESSES

*Survivors, Their Children, and
the Rise of Holocaust Consciousness*

Arlene Stein

OXFORD
UNIVERSITY PRESS

OXFORD
UNIVERSITY PRESS

Oxford University Press is a department of the University of Oxford.
It furthers the University's objective of excellence in research, scholarship,
and education by publishing worldwide.

Oxford   New York
Auckland   Cape Town   Dar es Salaam   Hong Kong   Karachi
Kuala Lumpur   Madrid   Melbourne   Mexico City   Nairobi
New Delhi   Shanghai   Taipei   Toronto

With offices in
Argentina   Austria   Brazil   Chile   Czech Republic   France   Greece
Guatemala   Hungary   Italy   Japan   Poland   Portugal   Singapore
South Korea   Switzerland   Thailand   Turkey   Ukraine   Vietnam

Published in the United States of America by
Oxford University Press
198 Madison Avenue, New York, NY 10016

Library of Congress Cataloging-in-Publication Data
Stein, Arlene, author.
Reluctant witnesses : survivors, their children, and the rise of the
Holocaust consciousness / Arlene Stein.
    pages cm
Includes bibliographical references and index.
ISBN 978–0–19–973358–3 (hardcover : alk. paper)   1. Children of Holocaust survivors.
2. Children of Holocaust survivors—Family relationships.   3. Holocaust
survivors—Family relationships.   4. Holocaust, Jewish (1939–1945)—Psychological
aspects.   5. Memorialization.   6. Holocaust, Jewish (1939-1945)—Influence.   I. Title.
D804.3.S748 2014
940.53′180922—dc23
2013044643

9 8 7 6 5 4 3 2 1
Printed in the United States of America
on acid-free paper

For David and Debbie, who know the whole story

CONTENTS

Reluctant Witnesses

Introduction

Our Holocaust

While nascent talk of the Holocaust was in the air when I was growing up, I was barely aware of it, even in New York City, which was home to a sizable Jewish population, some of whom were survivors. We did not learn about it in school in the 1960s and early 1970s—even in lessons about World War II or about the waves of immigration to America's shores—and there were no public memorials or museums to the murdered millions. There was barely a category of experience called "the Holocaust," and the genocide of European Jewry was generally subsumed under talk of "the war."

A patchwork memorial culture was gradually emerging as some religious leaders worked to incorporate the Holocaust into Jewish liturgy, synagogues constructed small-scale shrines, Jewish associations erected makeshift memorials at numerous cemeteries, and summer camps lit candles to remember the dead. But these efforts were modest, locally based, and not very visible aspects of Jewish communities, and they were generally seen as irrelevant to non-Jewish Americans. Survivors and their families tended to keep to themselves, forming their own organizations, or they did their best to block out the past.

Although I was keenly aware of the fact that my own history was intimately connected to a tragedy that occurred thousands of miles away and decades before my birth, I could not really name it or claim it as my own. My parents spoke about their losses only obliquely, and silence often prevailed outside the home. While my father was a survivor, he did not think of himself as such. If talk of the genocide circulated in intellectual publications and in magazines like *The New Yorker* (which carried Hannah Arendt's reportage from the 1962 trial of Nazi leader Adolf Eichmann), they were nowhere to be found in our lower middle-class Bronx household. Nonetheless, the experience of war and loss shaped nearly every aspect of my father's life, as well as the lives we made together.

From a very early age, I knew that his entire family—with the exception of an uncle who had come to the United States before the war, and a cousin who survived the war years in Russia, returning to her native Poland afterward—and most of my mother's extended family had been destroyed. (Her immediate family left Poland for England when she was a child, in the early 1930s.) Yet I possessed little embodied knowledge of these physically absent but psychologically present people, or of a place called Poland, once the home of a centuries-old vibrant Jewish culture.

My parents sometimes joked that had they met in Poland, they would never have had anything to do with one another. She was from a poor, highly religious family who lived in a small community outside Warsaw; he was from a large, somewhat acculturated family in the city, who were better educated and more urbane, though limited in their class aspirations by the anti-Semitism that surrounded them. But by the time they arrived in New York in the early 1950s, where they met, my mother had become known to others as an Englishwoman and my father as an American; both diligently tried to erase any association with Poland and the worlds they had lost.

My brother and I were born into a family that seemed curiously devoid of history and yet simultaneously steeped in it. Removed in time from tragic events, we had traces of the past—names mentioned in hushed tones, photographs retrieved from hidden boxes—hauntings and gaps. There was little context for understanding our family history. When our friends spoke about family gatherings with grandparents, aunts, and uncles, we remained silent, fearful of speaking about losses we barely understood, and knowing intuitively that they were not the subject of polite conversation.

But as I grew older, I watched with great interest, more than a little curiosity, and a good deal of relief as it became more acceptable to tell others about "our" tragedy. By the 1980s, the destruction of European Jewry, the subject of numerous documentaries and Hollywood films, was widely recognized as a universal moral touchstone. The United States Holocaust Memorial Museum, established in Washington, DC, the following decade, drew twice as many visitors as the White House; numerous states came to mandate Holocaust education; and the remaining survivors garnered large, attentive audiences when they spoke in high school auditoriums and public libraries across the nation. Our losses seemed much less private: now they had a name, and even a hulking museum in the center of our nation's capital. I no longer felt that I needed to guard my family's secret trauma, as it now seemed to belong to everyone.

This book began as a very personal effort to make sense of my traumatic inheritance and how it had shaped my relationship with my father. Who was Lawrence Stein, I wondered, and what was the world he came from like? How did his wartime experiences change him? And why was it so difficult for him to share this past with me? These are many of the same questions that other descendants of survivors have asked, and they are the same questions that writers of fiction, artists, and performers who share backgrounds like mine often explore in their work: we're history detectives, narrators of unspoken pasts, family genealogists and archivists.

As this project unfolded, it became a sociological endeavor as well, an investigation into the evolution of Holocaust memories in the United States, and into the aftermath of mass violence more generally. If for so many years the subject of the genocide could barely be uttered, something seemed to shift as I got older: the tenor of the conversation seemed to become much more public. How, I wondered, did we get from *there*—a time when speaking of the Holocaust was mainly a private activity, confined to certain groups, frequently accompanied by a great deal of trepidation, and which barely had a name—to *here*: the rise of a robust Holocaust memorial culture that has broad resonance?

This public reckoning was not simply due to the passage of time. It had to be organized, fought for, and created, particularly as there was so much working against it. Because the experience of genocide is traumatic—"outside the range of human experience"—and by its very definition shocking and disruptive, there is a tendency on the part of perpetrators, victims, and others to protect themselves and others from knowing about such events, which are often followed by denial.[1] "The ordinary response to atrocities is to banish them from consciousness," writes psychologist Judith Herman, describing trauma's tendency to hide—to retreat, to refuse narration, and to become buried in the psyche, only to be re-experienced through nightmares, flashbacks, physical symptoms and emotions that continue to haunt the victim after the fact—now labeled post-traumatic stress disorder (PTSD). A recent book about trauma is titled *The Unsayable*.[2]

Trauma stories are particularly difficult to tell when the surrounding society does not wish to listen. American soldiers returning home from war, for example, have often described their difficulties reconnecting with supportive people and new opportunities, and how they encounter stigma if they disclose lingering post-traumatic effects.[3] In the aftermath of floods and other natural disasters, survivors often feel cast off, and marked as different.[4] Former child soldiers in Nepal who returned to their villages after serving with the Maoist rebels during their country's 1996–2006 civil war were frequently stigmatized or ostracized by family members and local villagers.[5] Across societies, victims of sexual violence are often shunned by those around them. Because trauma has a tendency to hide and the traumatized are often stigmatized, the space for witnessing, recalling, and commemorating traumatic events must be won through struggle.[6]

Indeed, building a Holocaust memorial culture entailed a great deal of work on the part of many, many individuals. Some of this work was institutional, such as the development of educational curricula and the establishment of museums and memorials, mainly by Jewish communal organizations. Some of it was intellectual: teasing out the specific aspects of the Jewish genocide from other events of World War II, and recounting the experiences of those who were most affected by it. Here I tell a story of the rise of Holocaust memory in the United States that focuses on the private, informal acts of memory that took place among families of Holocaust survivors—but even these seemingly private acts were always shaped by the social and political environment that surrounded them, and the kinds of stories that were possible to tell.

Survivors had the most to gain—and also the most to lose—by recalling the destruction of European Jewry at a time when so much seemed to conspire to keep their stories private. To speak of what they had endured would bring the terrible past into the present at a time when they were trying to move on and create new lives. And yet not speaking made it nearly impossible to mourn their losses and to establish close relationships with others—including their own children. It's little wonder that collectively survivors were often deeply ambivalent about telling stories of the Holocaust. They wanted to be known by those closest to them but did not want to reveal information that was potentially damaging, and they wanted to protect their children. Their children, in turn, were curious about what their parents had endured, but fearful of knowing too much.[7]

So many ghosts seemed to share the dinner table. These ghosts were disruptive and also at times generative, leading many descendants, as they became older, on quests to gain knowledge about and come to terms with their parents' pasts, pushing their family stories into the public sphere. Facilitated by openings in the culture that challenged silences, overturned taboos, and blurred the private and the public, descendants came, over time, to coax their parents, the reluctant witnesses, to share their stories with them and with the larger world.

The writer Eva Hoffman, herself the daughter of Eastern European Jews displaced by the Nazis, describes this as the opposite of the trajectory that one expects in relation to historical events. The adult world asks first "what happened," and then tries to make sense of the "meaning of facts," she writes. But those who were born after the event "sense its inward meanings first and have to work their way outward towards the facts and the worldly shape of events."[8] Typically, information about the past tends to flow from older to younger generations, from grandparents and parents to children. But trauma creates silences, and encouraged descendants of survivors of the Holocaust to become coaxers and facilitators of their parents' stories, and eventually producers of Holocaust stories themselves.[9]

The trajectory of Holocaust consciousness in the United States roughly follows the rise of this pivotal "second generation." When this cohort was in its infancy and youth, in the 1950s and early 1960s, Holocaust consciousness was inchoate; the events of the genocide were not yet clearly separated from World War II, and not broadly recognized beyond local commemorative efforts in far-flung Jewish communities. For most Americans, there was a generalized desire to move on, reconstruct their lives, and not dwell on the past, and survivors followed suit. That would change when descendants entered puberty and young adulthood in the 1960s and 1970s, and began to assert their own autonomy, and when a series of cultural movements challenged many of the assumptions with which they grew up.

Even if they were not directly involved in the social movements sprouting all around them, survivors' children could not help but be shaped by many of the ideas those movements introduced into the cultural conversation. African Americans recalled the experience of slavery, and how it shaped black consciousness. Feminists redefined rape as an act of violence that was important to confront and publicize. Gays and lesbians made the "coming out" story a master narrative. Experiences of child abuse and drug and alcohol abuse were forced into the open, validating those who were brave enough to speak publicly.[10] If their parents saw Holocaust storytelling as mainly a private affair, their children were part of a cohort that transformed private pains into public stories, and claimed a sense of victimhood.[11] Armed with ideas from therapeutic culture, and influenced by identity politics, children of survivors formed a collective identity and began to reclaim their hidden family histories, coaxing the reluctant witnesses to speak.

SURVIVORS

Some 140,000 Jewish refugees from Europe's devastation arrived on American shores after the defeat of the Nazis. Generally between the ages of 15 and 35, they had spent years in concentration camps, hiding in forests, passing as Gentiles in Warsaw or Berlin, or exiled in Russia. Many were the sole survivors of their families, or nearly so.[12] They came from small villages and big cities. They were religious and they were assimilated. The "Holocaust survivor," as I use the term, is any Jew who lived under Nazi occupation during World War II and who was thus threatened by Nazi policies but survived. This includes those who were confined to ghettos, forced labor camps, concentration camps, those who were in hiding or living under false identities, refugees who left their families behind, those who fought with the partisans, those who were sent away in the *kindertransport*, and others.

While they were an extraordinarily diverse population, by virtue of the fact that they survived the Nazi onslaught, survivors were faced with many common challenges: they were forced to reconstitute, practically from scratch, essential aspects of lives—their livelihood, their families—in material as well as emotional senses. Refugees, immigrants, and migrants who lose their place in historical and generational continuity, their native language and country, as well as the very physical space of home and community, must try to preserve identity in the face of radical historical change.[13] Survivors of genocide, whose worlds have been radically depopulated, experience acute discontinuity. Some successfully reconstruct their lives, to be sure, while others are less successful. But even those who are outwardly successful grapple with emotional challenges. Growing up, I knew survivors who worked around the clock to provide for their families, but whose efforts often seemed like desperate attempts to flee from the memories that gnawed at them. In my own family, and others like mine, the calm of daily life was often punctuated by strange yells in the night.

Little of this seemed to show up in either social science or journalistic accounts of the experiences of survivors in the early postwar years, which tended to emphasize their great flexibility and resilience when confronting the challenge of rebuilding their lives after the war. Dorothy Rabinowitz's *New Lives*, published in 1976, contrasted individuals' wartime experiences in concentration camps, in displaced persons camps, and in hiding, with the relative tranquility of their American lives. The author interviewed 108 survivors living in 11 cities and found individuals who were haunted by their wartime experiences, but who had nonetheless adapted well to their new lives, becoming more or less prosperous in their adopted land. We learn that each treasured, above all else, "the freedom they find" and "the generosity of spirit," and that despite the odds, they carried on, making families, careers, and livelihoods.

That book, and others like it, celebrated the opportunities the United States offered for reinvention and economic success, emphasizing survivors' apparently extraordinary capacities for adaptation and assimilation. It pictured America as the antithesis of European fascism, and more subtly, of communism as well, and as a bulwark against tyranny, savior of the remnants of European Jewry. But such claims were overstated and were based on a fundamental sampling flaw, over-representing those who were willing to speak publicly about their lives, and who were better equipped to transcend their traumatic experiences. Rabinowitz's book also obscured its ideological agenda: to affirm Jewish and, indeed, American upward mobility and success. It reflected the dominant view of survivors, that having been rescued from death by American troops and offered a second chance, they took their place among other immigrants to the United States and thrived in their adopted home.[14]

Thinking of survivors simply as immigrants, albeit immigrants who faced additional challenges, reinforced the ideology of American individualism. From Horatio Alger's notion that anyone, with a little bit of will, can pull himself up by his bootstraps, to Dale Carnegie's recipe for success, *How to Win Friends and Influence People*, to the current obsession with unlocking the formula for "happiness"—positive thinking is pervasive in our culture. It is one of the—dare I say—*positive* aspects of being American. Collectively, we are forward-looking and pragmatic. We refuse to dwell in the past. But there's a dark side to that sunny cultural disposition, which Barbara Ehrenreich calls a "massive empathy deficit."[15] A culture that seeks comfort, consolation, and reassurance distances itself from hardship and pain.

Contrasting with this focus on resilience is a voluminous psychological literature that pictures survivors very differently: as damaged individuals. Early psychological accounts detailed the overwhelmingly intense feelings of guilt that survivors suffered when so many of their loved ones perished. The concept of "survivor guilt," first coined in relation to Holocaust survivors, became central to the psychological approach. "If I had done this or that, perhaps he or she would be alive today," went the survivors' internal conversation, according to this literature. "Survivor guilt" led many survivors to feel emotionally unworthy of the memory of the millions who perished; some believed their own lives had been saved by the deaths of innumerable others, and that only those who suffered the most extreme forms of victimization had the right to be heard.[16] In the early 1960s the concept of "trauma," defined in relation to the tragic event and its traces, began to make its way into psychiatric accounts of survivors.[17] Psychiatric journals began to publish articles documenting survivors' ongoing problems, suggesting that trauma might be a permanent injury that could reshape personal identity. Derived mainly from clinical samples, their diagnoses were skewed toward those who had sought out psychological help.

Neither the popular focus on survivors' capacity to transcend the past, nor the psychological literature on guilt and ongoing trauma, fully grappled with the contexts into which survivors were thrust after the genocide. They arrived in countries like the United States, where they were often received grudgingly, where anti-Semitism persisted, where the survivors constituted a relatively small group compared with other immigrant populations, and where there was generalized apprehension about confronting survivors' wartime experiences. Eventually, sociologically oriented psychologists described a "conspiracy of silence" that emerged after the war, in which survivors encountered audiences that were unwilling to listen, and they were told not to speak. One study of 300 survivors noted that during their early days in the United States, "most immigrants quickly learned not to talk about the war, often rationalizing their reluctance by saying that the stories were too horrible to be believed."[18]

Psychologist Yael Danieli found that "no one, including mental health professionals, listened to [survivors] or believed them when they attempted to share their Holocaust experiences and their related, continuing suffering" and so they "bitterly opted for silence." She described the indifference, avoidance, repression, and denial that enacted this silence. "Survivors' war accounts were too horrifying for most people to listen to or believe. Their stories were therefore easy to ignore or deny," she wrote. "Even people who were consciously and compassionately interested played down their interest, partly rationalizing their avoidance with the belief that their questions would inflict further hurt." That is, beyond the inability to hear the stories of survivors, there was also an inability to comprehend a catastrophe that was without precedent.

While this was a much-needed rejoinder to the individualistic thrust of both popular and psychological studies, the notion of a conspiracy of silence was too intentional, too deliberate. In *The Drowned and the Saved*, Primo Levi described a landscape filled with betrayal and destruction, in which humanity turned its back on its own.[19] He describes survivors' sense of shame, the failure of recognition that, in the words of psychologist Silvan Tomkins, occurs when "one is suddenly looked at by one who is strange, or...one wishes to look at or commune with another person but suddenly cannot because he is strange...or unfamiliar."[20] Indeed, survivors' accounts of interactions with distant family, neighbors, and others in the United States in the postwar years suggest that those who survived the Nazi war on the Jews felt widely misunderstood, unrecognized, and even stigmatized—shamed.

They often felt doubly betrayed: first during the war, by their home countries, and the bystanders in their midst, and then afterward, in their adopted countries, when they tried to interact with those around them, and attempted to share their wartime experiences. While many survivors were undoubtedly stricken with feelings of guilt, the extent of their feelings of shame has been understated. To recognize such feelings would implicate their host societies, including the United States, for failing to adequately respond to survivors' needs for empathy and understanding.

For many survivors, feelings of shame and fear percolated below the surface, and silence filled the gap between what could and couldn't be said, even with closest family members. Largely unrecognized at the time, except perhaps in clinical settings, these feelings disappeared from social analysis, and were mainly invisible in the surrounding culture.[21] They coexisted with what Geoffrey Hartman calls "antimemory"—a stance toward the Holocaust that "tries to ward off the resurgence of deeply unsettling, intolerable memory," seeking premature closure on the past, comfort rather than confrontation.[22]

There was also great ambivalence about claiming ethnic and religious difference. In the postwar era, although collectively Jews achieved to a remarkable extent the freedom that eluded them in Europe, they continued to be haunted by their outsider status. Anti-Semitism persisted and was widely internalized by Jews themselves. In the world of my youth, 1970s New York City, mixed messages abounded: be true to your Jewish roots, keep the faith, don't flaunt your Jewishness—but don't trust the *goyim*, the Gentiles. "Fix" your noses, straighten your hair, don't be "too Jewish"—but don't marry outside the faith. The most popular icon of postwar American girlhood, Barbie, was created by a Jewish woman working through her own ambivalence (and exhilaration) about being in a land that was both welcoming and strange. Descendants of survivors grew up in this context, at a time of ambivalence about speaking openly about the genocide—and indeed about being Jewish.

DESCENDANTS

A quarter of a million American children grew up with parents who had survived the Nazi onslaught upon European Jewry.[23] They were, like their parents, a diverse group, but by virtue of the fact that they were members of families who were forced to reconstitute themselves after the war, and also members of a distinctive baby boom generation, they shared many things in common. They grew up with parents who had often endured tremendous suffering, whose extended family networks had for the most part been extinguished, and where the past continued to exert a shadowy presence.

But they were, at the same time, members of the rebellious, sometimes narcissistic baby boom generation. They had one foot in the aftermath of a traumatic history that was formative in their parents' lives but which they had little direct knowledge of, and the other foot in a generation steeped in a series of social movements that were roundly questioning the wisdom of their fathers—and mothers.

While I did not particularly think of myself as a member of a club comprising other survivors' children, I knew that I possessed terrible, unspeakable secrets that I dared not share with others. The Holocaust was a taboo subject in my world, even in the heavily Jewish north Bronx of my youth. There did not seem to be a language to describe the experiences of our parents, or the will to try to describe them. And yet thanks to the efforts of feminists and gay and lesbian activists, I had a keen understanding of why I felt compelled to suppress my same-sex desires as I was growing up, and a name for why this seemed necessary: homophobia. But why, I wondered, did I find it so difficult to talk about something like the fact that my relatives had been murdered, and why did I feel that it was something I so zealously needed to hide from others?

When I began to look around at what had been written about people who grew up in families like mine, years later, I found a voluminous psychological literature about the impact of trauma on subsequent generations. Clinicians and memoirists showed how little knowledge children of survivors possessed of their parents' wartime (and frequently, prewar) experiences. In general, parents made an unspoken pact not to speak of the atrocities, so as not to burden their children. And yet they unconsciously transmitted trauma to their children. In an extensive literature on the "second generation," psychologists described the blurring of boundaries separating parents and children that led children to internalize their parents' trauma-based anxieties. Fearful parents clutched their children too closely, and children over-identified with their parents' painful experiences. But the opposite was also true: children pulled away from their parents, missing opportunities for intimacy, and practicing cold detachment. They suppressed their anger and resentment toward their parents for fear of hurting them.

Many observers described the second generation as wounded, as characterized by absences. Psychoanalyst Dori Laub used the metaphor of an "empty circle" to describe what he termed the "inner objectlessness" of descendants. Describing one woman's inability to confront her familial losses, he notes, "perhaps it was not the gory details from which she had to look away, but the empty circle itself, the 'absence' hidden behind all the stories she had lived and told."[24] "For children of survivors," he writes, "these 'wounds without memory' may compellingly find expression as the very shape of their lives—as a sense of void, terror, woundedness, and loss that defies all comfort—and may paralyze their ability to have a family of their own." Others wrote similarly of the "phantom pain" felt by children of survivors, their inability to come to grips or witness the losses that figure so largely in their lives, the persistence of "absent memory" and inability to testify to what cannot be remembered.[25] Finding evidence of intergenerational trauma, a vast literature describes this cohort as depressed, angry, fearful, mistrustful, cynical, and over-identified with their parents, characterizing its melancholia as a suppressed and ambivalent alternative to mourning.[26]

While such diagnoses may be useful in clinical settings, they tended to generalize from clinical samples, offering value-laden judgments of psychological health that were at times pathologizing. Focusing on the issue of what individuals did and didn't know, and how knowledge of the past was transmitted within families, it seems to me, is a more productive path to pursue. What do those who come after traumatic events know about the world of their parents? What don't they know? How does this shape relationships between parents and children, and how does it influence the ways in which children come to understand themselves? If the first generation knew very clearly what it is had lost, the second generation, one step removed from these losses, was shaped by trauma's afterlife.[27] While children of survivors were not directly traumatized, they "know" trauma. Shaped by their parents' losses, they also lived at a remove from these losses. This distance, coupled with the fact that they came of age in a different moment from their parents, created a very different relationship to traumatic memories.[28]

Descendants often spoke of a palpable anxiety, a vague feeling that "all was not right with the world," which informs as well as shapes their subsequent life experiences, their sensibilities, outlook, and affect. Before they could speak, anxiety—along with love and concern—was communicated by parents in nonverbal and verbal ways. Children picked up information about their parents' pasts through untold stories, gestures, and mysterious envelopes. These traces of the past—"hauntings, ghosts and gaps, seething absences, and muted presences," in Avery Gordon's words—lived on in ways that are often not immediately knowable but which nonetheless profoundly shape children's self-understandings.[29] At times, the taboo nature of knowledge of the traumatic past made it even more salient in their lives than it normally would be; the fact that parents tended to hide a great deal from them amplified their affective charge. Children imagined the worst, developing fantasies about their parents and grandparents' experiences, or they blocked out the past, refusing to linger on painful memories.

Collectively, they felt a tremendous sense of loyalty to their parents, and a feeling that it was up to them to redeem their losses through their own successful lives. Descendants also expressed resentment toward their parents: for being different, for not being like other "normal" American parents, for their traditional ways, and for being the bearers of terrible knowledge about "man's inhumanity to man." How could they define a sense of self that is separate from their parents, while living up to their responsibilities? It was a difficult balancing act. They struggled with these conflicted feelings for their parents and the huge gaps in their knowledge about them, and with an ambivalent, ambiguous sense of loss, which was at times generative. The second generation—the descendants—grew up, in Marianne Hirsch's terms, "dominated by narratives that preceded their birth," whose "own belated stories are displaced by the powerful stories of the previous generation."

These powerful stories, stories that speak of traumatic events, often resist understanding and integration, propelling descendants on a search for an understanding of that which came before them.[30] There are wounds, gaps, and losses, but there are also possibilities. Those who grew up amid silence may develop a tremendous desire for knowledge about the past; a sense of loss can spur individuals to undertake emotional memory work to make sense of these absences, to order them, and to build bonds with their parents.

It was no coincidence that as the descendants moved into adulthood in the 1970s and 1980s, stories of the Jewish genocide, which circulated for much of the postwar period in the private enclaves of families and within survivor communities—the terrain that Avishai Margalit calls "thick memory"—migrated into the public sphere, the world of strangers, and of "thin memory."[31] Descendants reached early adulthood in the 1970s, precisely at the moment when a host of political and cultural movements were making talk about the Holocaust more and more possible. Survivors of rape and incest transformed their private memories into public speech, descendants of African slaves invoked the history of the Middle Passage, and outposts of therapeutic culture offered new scripts and incitements for speaking.[32]

THE RISE OF HOLOCAUST CONSCIOUSNESS

Today, Americans learn about the Holocaust in their middle school curricula, watch films about it on television, and visit massive museums dedicated to preserving its memory. As my son moved through high school, he consumed a regular diet of novels and history lessons documenting the genocide of European Jewry. Looking around at this evidence, someone coming of age today might imagine that commemorations of the Holocaust were always part of the postwar American landscape. And yet there was a great deal of reticence about speaking of the Holocaust for at least two decades after the war's end among Jewish Americans, as well as among non-Jews, described by some as a "conspiracy of silence." More recently, the historian Hasia Diner has declared that this silence is a myth: American Jews began building a commemorative culture swiftly and with a great deal of determination.[33]

But while numerous small-scale efforts to memorialize the murdered Jews of Europe made their way into Jewish communities during the immediate postwar period, it took several decades for consciousness of the Holocaust to consolidate, and for an understanding of the genocide of European Jewry to cohere into a meaningful category of experience, and one that deserved broad recognition. While there were annual commemorations commemorating Jewish wartime resistance in New York at least since the 1960s, for example, it was not until the 1980s that we see the emergence of a widespread "Holocaust consciousness" that encompassed a number of linked developments: the consolidation of the idea of a "Holocaust," understood as the genocide of European Jewry; the growing cultural salience of institutions such as memorials and museums dedicated to its memory; the formation of collective identities of survivors and their descendants, some of whom told their stories in public; and the expansion of audiences for Holocaust stories beyond Jewish communities. Cumulatively, these developments made the Jewish genocide a prominent part of the American cultural landscape. Today, over three-quarters of Jewish Americans believe that remembering the Holocaust is essential to their sense of Jewishness, while less than one-fifth say that observing Jewish law is important.[34]

Sociologists tell us that memory, especially the collective memory of societies, is not like a light switch that one can turn on or off. The formation of collective memories, particular trauma memories, is frequently a protracted process, requiring the efforts of different "carrier" groups to make claims on public space and attention. For example, it took the efforts of black intellectuals to represent the experience of slavery and to articulate its importance for subsequent generations before African Americans could claim the legacy of slavery as a salient part of its collective identity.[35] Similarly, when some writers, activists, and intellectuals called for the importance of remembering the murdered Jews of Europe in the early postwar period, they initiated a process that took several decades to play out, and which required the participation of groups of individuals who were not intellectuals, or indeed very elite—including the vast majority of survivors and their children.

Today, when there are those who claim that heightened consciousness of the murder of European Jewry is fundamentally a conservative development, one that was engineered by well-connected elites because it was politically and financially beneficial for them to do so, this history has largely been forgotten. For example, historian Peter Novick and others have charged that American Jews built a Holocaust memorial culture—establishing museums and memorials, lobbying for the teaching of Holocaust history, and incorporating Holocaust memory into Jewish ritual—in order to mobilize guilt, stave off Jewish collective assimilation, and curry sympathy for the Zionist project. In doing so, he argues, they were abandoning the liberal, ethical strain of Jewish culture that had been ascendant in America, in favor of a muscular nationalism, anchoring a collective Jewish identity in the agony of European Jewry.

For at least two or three decades after the war, writes Novick, the genocide of European Jewry was not widely discussed because as a group struggling for integration into the mainstream, American Jews did not wish to see themselves as victims and could see few benefits in embracing Holocaust memory. That began to change in the 1960s, as the Eichmann trial and the 1967 Six Day War re-sensitized American Jews to existential threats posed to the Jewish people, and the publication of Elie Wiesel's *Night* (in 1960) helped bring the term "Holocaust" into public discourse. At that moment, according to Novick, "a series of choices by Jewish leaders, tacitly ratified by their constituents" transformed the genocide into the signal event of modern Jewish history.[36]

But as many American Jews will tell you, national communal organizations do not necessarily speak for us all. The conversations that occur in Jewish communities about so many different things—such as intermarriage and Jewish continuity, the continued Israel-Palestine crisis, or the meaning of the Holocaust today—is closer to a cacophonous mix of discordant voices than a harmonious chorus.[37] Those who would claim to speak for the collective conscience of American Jewry are representing only a particular segment of a diverse array of voices. And so it is with Holocaust memory, too. Holocaust memories have undoubtedly served conservative ends at times, enabling power brokers in this country and elsewhere to mobilize guilt in the service of their own particularistic commitments. Yet claims that Holocaust memorial efforts were orchestrated entirely by Jewish elites for self-serving political ends fail to appreciate that the urge to remember the genocide came from the grassroots, too. An important group of constituents for commemoration were those who were most affected by it: survivors and their children, who for many years and for a variety of reasons felt that they could not speak openly about their experiences.

Thus, in many respects, Holocaust consciousness represents a democratization of culture, and a growing willingness on the part of many Americans to confront traumatic memories and catastrophic histories. The processing of traumatic events requires a listening space, but this space was not granted automatically: it had to be fought for. In the 1970s and 1980s, American culture became more receptive to these efforts, transforming the figure of the victim from a pitied or shamed figure into a heroic subject: a survivor. Children of Holocaust survivors were influenced by these cultural currents and their cross-fertilization with feminism, therapeutic ideas, and the movements of racial and ethnic minorities; they formed support groups and online forums, participated in heritage trips to Poland and Hungary and other far-flung places, and coaxed their parents to speak, finally, about the past. This was rarely a simple process, or one that was free of conflict.

From a very early age I learned to assiduously keep the past at bay, to avoid books and movies that incorporated Holocaust themes, and to skirt around the topic with my parents. This ambivalence carried over to my own relationship with my father, a somber man whom I loved deeply, but who always seemed out of place, and whose Polish accent, strange way of dressing, and lack of familiarity with American culture embarrassed me. I hated him for the way he shouted in his sleep during nightmares about being chased by dogs. I resented him for exposing me to the fact that people do terrible things to one another—though he rarely spoke explicitly about it. And I developed an intense, vicarious identification with the struggles of African Americans, devouring *Black Like Me*, *Native Son*, and scores of books about blackness in America, as if to try to better understand the experience of collective trauma and marginality from a safer distance.

But when I moved into my early twenties, something shifted: I felt a growing need to know about my father and where he came from, and how the Holocaust legacy impacted our lives together. I joined a support group for children of survivors in Berkeley, California. There I began to speak about my family's Holocaust legacy with others for the first time. Fifteen years later, shortly after my father's death, I found myself on a bus hurtling through the streets of Warsaw, looking for traces of the world he had lost. Art Spiegelman's *Maus*, which brilliantly documented a descendant's telling of his survivor father's story, had recently been published. And still, I was barely aware of the fact that thousands of other children of survivors were embarking on similar quests for memory, passionately seeking answers to questions.

Over time, I began to realize that the "second generation" was a kind of social movement that deserved sociological reflection. Nearly two decades after I first attended a descendants' support group, I became a participant-observer in an electronic mailing list, or listserv, organized by and for children of survivors, in which we discussed our parents' lives, our relationships with them, and what it meant to be descendants and inheritors of the legacy of the Holocaust. Later, I analyzed oral histories with survivors and their children conducted by the United States Holocaust Memorial Museum, and interviews conducted by a group of Philadelphia psychologists in the 1990s. From among these archived interviews, I randomly selected 24 in-depth interviews with survivors, and 28 interviews with children of survivors to analyze (see Appendix: Methodological Notes for additional discussion). I conducted an additional series of in-depth interviews with 14 children of survivors living in the New York area, several of whom were publicly active in the "second generation" movement. I also read numerous memoirs written by children of survivors, discerning common themes, and considered my own family's story—weaving recollections, photos, and fragments into this mix of data.

As my research proceeded in fits and starts, over a 15-year period, it became clear to me that this would be a book about storytelling, about how we tell and sometimes hide difficult stories in the hope of making our world mean something beyond ourselves. Who tells stories, who listens, who does not, and why? It begins with the insight that storytelling is a social process; we do not tell our stories in isolation, and we do not make up stories out of whole cloth. For example, there are a limited number of narrative styles, or templates, that we use to tell stories, and some are more socially valorized than others.[38] Storytelling also requires willing storytellers and audiences. The storytellers must envision, to some degree, the frames that listeners bring. How will others understand the story I am telling? Will they understand it at all? A story is less likely to be told if the potential tellers believe that it will be misunderstood. Sometimes it takes an intermediary to convince the potential storyteller that there are interested and sympathetic audiences.[39]

In this book, we meet a number of different participants: the producers of stories, those who provide life histories for archives, memoirs that are published, or increasingly, who tell stories online, in Internet discussion sites; the coaxers, coaches, and coercers, who provoke stories from people, and who become listeners and questioners who probe, interview, and interrogate, such as oral historians, journalists, doctors, and therapists; and finally, the consumers, readers, and audiences who consume the stories and interpret and make sense of them.

While telling stories is certainly a social process, it is a deeply personal, emotional one too—especially when the stories are so fraught, and so difficult to tell, as trauma stories often are. As a sociologist trained to elicit interviews that focus on the conscious, cognitive realm, understanding the internal lives of my subjects has been one of the great challenges of this project, particularly as I analyze interviews that have been done by others, sometimes reading through the lines to discern what is not said.[40] Much of what goes on in social life, including the telling of stories, is not at all deliberate or consciously organized. To the extent that I am able to do so, I am mindful of the ways that people talk about their experiences, the meanings they attribute to them, and the ways in which meanings are explicit as well as implicit, conscious as well as unconscious. I have tried to listen to the stories "in between"—the "noisy silences and seething absences"—being attentive to the power of feelings, and to the meanings of gaps and silences.[41]

After trauma, we know there is typically a period in which silence and fragmented speech prevail. A central theme of the book is the powerful role that shame played in the lives of many survivors, and in their children's lives as well. If massive trauma interrupts people's lives, severing the ties that bind them to one another, shame forecloses the possibility of recognition.[42] People protect themselves by covering up these shameful feelings, driving them underground. To find evidence of shame, one must be an empathetic listener, analyzing what people tell us, as well as what they do not say. Having lived with survivors, I know what shame looks like, and I understand many of the feelings associated with it.

While my own story reflects many of the experiences of my cohort of descendants, it is at the same time a very particular story of one person, and one family. While cultural contexts frame individual experience, we respond in varied ways. My own brother's relationship to our familial history, for example, has been different from mine. While it has undoubtedly affected him profoundly, he has chosen to work through it differently, more privately. Even within the same family, there is a great deal of variation: for some individuals, this traumatic legacy is highly salient; for others, it is less so. While we may have a great deal in common by virtue of the fact that we grew up with parents who experienced tremendous loss and disruption, different families have different emotional economies, and we process our experiences in individual ways.

And still, there is a social, collective story to be told about survivors' and descendants' efforts to tell Holocaust stories, and how it changed over the course of a few decades. This book is about the evolution of that storytelling. It is not a work of history per se, but a psychosocial account of the transformation of Holocaust consciousness, told largely from the perspective of survivors and their descendants. It traces the unfolding of Holocaust storytelling at different moments: from the time the survivors came to the United States and interacted with distant family members and neighbors, and ending with the stories their children told when their parents were no longer capable of speaking.

ORGANIZATION OF THE BOOK

Placing survivors and their families at the center of the story of the rise of Holocaust consciousness, I focus on the kinds of narratives that were tellable at different periods. This book is organized around critical turning points that led existing meanings of the past to be re-examined, reshaping understandings of victimhood and survival. Each chapter focuses on a different moment, or historical turning point, showing how it facilitated certain ways of speaking about the Holocaust. It proceeds in roughly chronological order.

Chapter 1 begins in the immediate postwar period, the late 1940s and early 1950s, when the survivors first arrived in the United States and were just beginning to establish families. It was a time of "moving on," of celebrating American victory, when victimhood was not yet associated with either compassion or virtue. Since being a victim suggested weakness and vulnerability, few wished to be identified with it. The Cold War years encouraged conformity, and made expressing "negative" feelings in public taboo. Survivors considered the "real" victims to be family members, friends, and neighbors who had perished. Their identification with them, and their guilt for having survived when so many did not, made it difficult to see themselves as victims too; so did the shame they experienced in relation to others. In public, they told stories that emphasized heroism, resistance, and overcoming—restitution.

In the second chapter, we move on to the 1950s and early 1960s, when children of survivors were young, and were just beginning to process the Holocaust legacy. In the families they created, survivors told stories filled with silence and gaps, frequently transforming tragic recollections into stories of heroism. And still the past lived on, shaping the interactions between parents and children. Although psychiatrists during this period began to notice the enduring effects of trauma, survivors were hesitant to embrace these illness narratives. It would take the rise of the "second generation" into adulthood, as well as a series of shifts in American culture—the rise of the counterculture, feminism, identity politics, the ethnic revival, and therapeutic culture—for survivors and their descendants to claim their tragedy.

As a quarter of a million descendants of survivors moved into adulthood in the 1970s, some began to coax their parents to tell their stories. Paradoxically, their quest to separate from their parents often made them more able to listen to them. Empowered by a collective identity, they coaxed their parents to share their stories, reframing the meaning of victimhood into a more affirmative category. Descendants, as we see in Chapter 3, helped push their parents' stories, which had circulated for much of the postwar period in the private enclaves of families, into the public sphere.

Thanks in part to these efforts, by the following decade survivors gained the moral authority to bear witness, commanding an increasingly important presence in Jewish communities and beyond, as we see in Chapter 4. In the 1980s, many survivors addressed audiences of schoolchildren, unknown individuals who might listen to their audiotapes or see their video testimonies, as well as their own children and grandchildren, and so many of the stories that were previously hidden, or difficult to understand because they were told in fragments, began to circulate in different crevices of the culture, making their ways through families and communities and into the halls of museums and memorials. Once they began to tell their stories to dispersed publics, the notion that they were "survivors"—victims who possessed a sense of agency—began to coalesce.

In Chapter 5, we meet descendants in middle age, and in the new millennium. The passage of time deepened the kinds of memory work they participated in. In search of stories that would situate their parents' lives in the larger context of prewar Europe, they traveled alone or in groups to their parents' places of origin; they conducted oral histories with surviving relatives; they produced films and memoirs that narrated their parents' biographies, and they searched for documentary objects such as letters and photographs. As the remaining original tellers of Holocaust stories rapidly pass away, the coaxers, the second generation—along with their children— became key Holocaust storytellers, transforming their ghosts, finally, into ancestors.

This is a story of progress of sorts, in which a group of people who had previously been unrecognized and misunderstood managed to find its voice, and it is my story, too. Today, memories of the destruction of European Jewry are a very visible aspect of American culture—the subject of Hollywood films, national museums, and high school curricula. It is also a moment when a sense of fatigue seems to have set in, leading growing numbers of American Jews to resist Holocaust talk, and to suggest that it is time to move on. Yearning to be an ethnic and religious group, like Italian or Irish Americans, one that is defined by distinctive foods and ritual customs, rather than by the legacy of pain and suffering, some claim that Holocaust memory is crowding out other sources of Jewish meaning and diminishing the possibility of joy and celebration. Reflecting upon the moment we find ourselves in, I conclude, in Chapter 6, by asking: Is there too much Holocaust memory?

CHAPTER 1

Interrupted Lives

To survive was to escape fate. But if you escape your fate, whose life do you then step into?
Anne Michaels, *Fugitive Pieces*

They spoke a variety of different languages—Russian, Polish, German, Greek, Yiddish, and more—and had as many different conceptions of what it meant to be a Jew. They were the adherents of great Hassidic rabbis in small towns in Poland, the Ukraine, and Hungary, who sought to reconstruct their shattered religious communities in the New World, and encouraged their flocks to do the same, settling in communities like Borough Park, Brooklyn, where they reconstituted their shtetls to the best of their ability. And they were atheists, former prostitutes, products of mixed marriages, and others who were only nominally Jewish, who wished to remake their lives and their ties in a fashion that was more compatible with a pluralist society and a secular world. What they shared was the experience of destruction, of having their once-familiar worlds ripped apart and torn asunder, and the challenge of reconstituting their lives.

In this chapter, I draw upon oral histories with survivors to show how, in interactions with family, neighbors, and others in the United States in the early postwar years, they felt widely misunderstood and unrecognized. The late 1940s and early 1950s, when the survivors arrived, was a time of "moving on," of celebrating American victory. Victimhood was not yet associated with either compassion or virtue. The Cold War years encouraged conformity, and made expressing negative feelings in public taboo. While discussions of the emotional lives of survivors have often focused on the intense feelings of guilt that accompanied survival when so many of their loved ones had perished, in interviews with survivors conducted decades later, it is shame rather than guilt that appears so salient. Strangers, neighbors, and even family members averted their eyes, say survivors, leading them to feel awkward, self-conscious, apologetic, embarrassed, and sometimes even ridiculous, degraded, or humiliated.[1]

Nesse Godin was born in 1928 into a highly religious family in Lithuania. Her mother, Sara, owned a dairy store and her father, Pinchas, worked at a shoe factory. She had two brothers. In 1941, Nazi Germany occupied her town and required all members of the Jewish community to wear a yellow Star of David. Jewish children were prohibited from attending school, and Jewish businesses were confiscated. In 1941, Nesse and her family were forced to move into a ghetto. In 1944, the few Jews remaining in the ghetto, including Nesse, were deported to the Stutthof concentration camp, where she was separated from her mother and brother. In the camp, Jewish women looked after Nesse, protecting her and advising her on how to survive. She was transferred to four other slave labor camps and then, in January 1945, she was sent on a death march with a group of 1,000 female prisoners.

After surviving ghettos, forced labor, a concentration camp, and a death march, Nesse was 17 and near death when Russian soldiers found her huddled in a barn in a small village at war's end, "all skin and bones," suffering from typhus and a high fever. When she looked in the mirror she did not recognize herself. She traveled to Lodz, Poland, and heard from someone who was in a camp with her mother that she was still alive, having survived Auschwitz. It took them weeks to find each other, but they were eventually reunited, and soon learned that Nesse's brother was also alive, in a displaced persons (DP) camp in Germany.

At the DP camp, Nesse recalled, survivors set up schools and small manufacturing operations, supported one another, and began to make sense of what they had endured. They may have hesitated about dwelling on the past, and even feared talking about it, but when they got together, for visits, for cups of tea, for walks, they talked. They compared their suffering. They talked about where they were during the war. They talked about what they did to survive. "It was like counseling," said Nesse, "because you poured out and you found out, gee, I wasn't the only one, there was others and others and others." At the camp, Nesse met a man, another refugee, and they were quickly married.

In 1949, Nesse and her mother received permission to immigrate to the United States, where her mother's sister lived, and they settled in New York. Her relatives helped them settle and adapt to life in the United States, and they put Nesse and her husband up in their small house. "They were very kind, they were very supportive, they were very sweet," she said of her relatives. But, she added, "they didn't want to hear anything about a Holocaust." As Godin recalled, her aunt told her "she had enough pain losing two sisters and two brothers" and didn't want to "diminish the joy of having a sister, a niece and her family." So she avoided asking questions about what Nesse had endured. Nesse wanted to share her experiences with her relatives, and she felt an obligation to do so, to witness the suffering of others who did not survive. When she had been hungry, cold, and huddled in a barn with a group of older women, she recalled, they had told her: if you survive, you must tell others of our fate. She often tried to share her story, she said. But few people wanted to listen. "They didn't want to know," she said of those she encountered in the United States after the war. "Even my aunt who loved me, who helped me, my cousins that were dear to me, they always said, you suffered enough, don't talk about it."

Dorianne Kurz, who was liberated from Bergen-Belsen by Russian troops when she was nine, also speaks of landing in a strange place, where few understood what she had endured, or even tried to understand. Dorianne's family fled from Austria to Amsterdam in 1940. Her father was deported to Auschwitz. After their mother was seized, Dorianne and her brother hid with Gentiles. The three were reunited at Bergen-Belsen, where they were deported via Westerbork. They were liberated during the camp's 1945 evacuation. She returned to Amsterdam after the war with her mother and brother. Her mother was severely ill with typhus and eventually died, and her uncle arranged for her and her brother to immigrate to the United States.

When Dorianne and her brother arrived in Brighton Beach, Brooklyn, in 1946, she recalls that when they arrived, "nobody talked about it"— not even in New York, the city that had welcomed more refugees from war-ravaged Europe than any other. Speaking of her uncle's family, who took her and her brother in, Dorianne said: "They did not try to draw me out about the experiences during the war. Once in a while I would mention something, but they didn't try to get me to talk about it." Perhaps her relatives felt that talking about her experiences would lead Doriane to re-experience trauma. Perhaps they wanted to protect themselves from knowing what had happened to her and their extended family.

Although we cannot know their relatives' reasons for not inquiring about their prewar experiences or about the fate of their missing relatives, we can see from these oral histories that Nesse, Dorianne, and other survivors were confronted in the early postwar period with the task of figuring out how to present themselves to others, and how to share stories of enormous loss and disruption, at a time when Americans possessed little knowledge about their experiences and were often reluctant to know more.[2] In light of the fact that American troops fought against the Nazis and were among the liberators of the concentration camps, one might have expected survivors to elicit considerable public sympathy after the war. In fact, survivors often relied on the kindness of strangers, social workers, Jewish resettlement agency workers, and family members when they first arrived in the United States. But most survivors suggest that they could share their experiences with non-survivors only in very limited ways, and they grappled for words to describe their experiences in an environment where few seemed eager to listen. Survivors say again and again that they rarely, if ever, spoke of their wartime experiences during the first two decades after World War II to relatives already living in this country, or with friends and acquaintances they met when they arrived. They tended to arrive with few or no resources, and were beholden to their relatives for emotional and material support; they were dependent on others, and could not rock the boat.

Ruth Kluger, in her memoir *Still Alive*, tells a similar story. Arriving in the United States after the war, she and her mother spent their first Thanksgiving with relatives on Long Island. After dinner, she recalls, "they took us home in their large and showy new automobile. While we sat in back in the dark, snug and comfortable, my aunt at several removes lectured me." She told her: "You have to erase from your memory everything that happened in Europe. You have to make a new beginning. You have to forget what they did to you. Wipe it off like chalk from a blackboard." Kluger recalled that her aunt gestured as if wiping a board with a sponge. "I thought," she wrote, "[my aunt] wants me to get rid of the only thing that I own for sure: my life, that is, the years that I have lived. But you can't throw away your life like old clothing, as if you had another outfit in the closet. Would she want to wipe away her own childhood? I have the one I have—I can't invent one for myself that's more respectable. Struggling with foreign words that seemed to lurk behind seven veils, I told her why I had to reject this invitation to betray my people, my dead. The language was recalcitrant. My aunt hardly listened to my alien gibberish."[3]

Kluger described the difficulties she and others faced in integrating their experiences into everyday speech, and the ways in which many of their experiences were indescribable to others. There was not yet something called "the Holocaust." The murder of European Jewry was conflated with the larger war. The genocide, she writes, did not yet have a name, and hence it "wasn't even an idea, only an event: among the other disasters of the Second World War, a lot of Jews had died." Kluger reflects upon the consequences of this: "A concept without a name is a like a stray dog or feral cat. To domesticate it, you have to call it something."

Although narratives of the ghettos and camps appeared in the mid-1940s, it took time for these materials to be translated, and understanding trailed far behind. The concept of "genocide," of the deliberate destruction of whole categories of people, was not yet widely known or understood.[4] Because of its enormous scale and unprecedented nature, and the frequent conflation of the Jewish genocide with World War II, it was impossible to grasp its meaning and scale. The term "Holocaust" first circulated during the war, mainly in Jewish circles, but did not appear in the popular press until 1959, and was not widely used to discuss the genocide of Europe's Jews until the late 1960s, when the Holocaust became the Holocaust, in a conceptualization that separated the experiences of Jews from others under Nazi rule, such as political prisoners or gypsies (Roma).[5]

The emergence of the term shaped the kinds of conversations that were possible, marking the experience of Europe's Jews from the larger experience of "the war," and made the experience of the Holocaust, known also as Shoah, describable in a way that it had not previously been. It universalized the experiences of Jews across different nations, melding them into a unified whole, and offered a kind of religious interpretation of the genocide as a "burnt offering," a kind of spiritual martyrdom. It suggested, against the American tendency to imagine the Holocaust as a universal instance of "man's inhumanity to man," in a move that would later become a source of great controversy and debate, that the genocide of Europe's Jews was unique and incomparable to anything that had come before. And it made possible the robust transnational Holocaust memory culture of today that includes Israel, Europe, and Australia, along with South Africa and Argentina, although North American cultural formations tend to dominate.[6]

But in the first two decades after the war, the stories of survivors were stories of chaos, of lives interrupted—senseless stories that often appeared crazy, lacking in temporal ordering, and devoid of meaning. They were confusing and often unintelligible to others. While it was difficult for survivors to tell these stories, it was often impossible for those around them to listen to them. Few survivors had a comprehensive understanding of what they themselves had endured, or a larger cultural context in which to make their stories intelligible to potential audiences. When David Boder, an American psychologist, traveled to Europe's displaced persons camps in 1946 to conduct the first interviews with survivors, he found that while they could talk about their own experiences, they lacked a bigger picture of what had happened in Europe during World War II. The horrors were too overwhelming, complex, and seemingly irrational to put into words; there was not yet a vocabulary or a way of describing them.[7]

Survivors' potential audiences—relatives, acquaintances, neighbors, members of Jewish communities in the United States, and others—had not been primed to hear such stories, which were often considered so extreme as to be unbelievable. Lacking a suitable frame for sharing Holocaust stories, or willing audiences to listen to them, during the early postwar period, from the mid-1940s through the 1950s, survivors narrated their stories in ways that downplayed their chaotic nature, transforming them into more palatable tales of resistance and integration—or they kept silent.

WHO WOULD BELIEVE US?

As Thomas Blatt recalled of this period, "Who would believe us?" The stories seemed unbelievable at the time, and each story was more unbelievable than the next. "Nobody," he said, "understood us." Blatt was 16 when he escaped from Sobibor, the notorious death camp, where his entire family was killed. Of more than 300 who escaped, most were captured by the Germans and killed. He hid at a nearby farm. When the farmer tried to kill him, he escaped and went off to another village, where a friend of his father's gave him a note to deliver to a farmer in the next village. When he did that, the farmer sent him with a note to another village.

At 16, Blatt found himself working as a courier for the peasants' battalion, an underground resistance group, hiding his identity, and even attending church at times. He told a story about how a farmer stole his shoes and tried to kill him, and killed others in the underground. After the war, to try to get his shoes back, he sent a note with a few *zlotys* to the farmer, hoping he would return them. The farmer told him to meet him in the forest at a particular time, and that he would bring his shoes. The exchange was made, and the two went their separate ways. In retrospect, Blatt said, it was stupid to have contacted the farmer again; he could have been killed. A few days later he returned to the farmer's house with two other underground members, hoping to take the farmer into custody, or possibly to shoot him on the spot, but he had already left town, fearing reprisals.

Every survivor had her own version of stories like this one, which spoke of experiences that were often beyond belief—that were so outside everyday experience that they were often difficult to comprehend. Harry Alexander, who was originally from Germany, described the ways that Americans distanced themselves from the survivors and their experiences, anticipating that "they will make a joke or forget about it." Alexander arrived in the United States after spending three years in a concentration camp in the desert in North Africa. He was captured by the Gestapo in Nice, France, and was sent to a camp outside Algiers. In the camp he and other prisoners worked 10 hours a day building train tracks through the dessert. They worked in 110-degree heat with only two cups of water a day, and at night had no blankets in bitter cold weather. Fifty people slept in tents made for ten, and desert rats, snakes, and scorpions were frequent visitors. The camp commander was a sadist who picked out 10 men, tied them to a pole naked, and beat them with his horsewhip. When he was released, a British officer told Alexander, "in England you will start a whole new life. The war is over." Harry replied: "the war may be over for you, the war isn't over for me. And as far as starting a new life, how do you do that? How do you start with no family, no home, no country, no money, no trade, no skill, no education?" As he recounted this exchange, Alexander's anger was palpable. "How do you start a new life? They had taken all this away from me and they haven't given [any of it] back. How do you start a new life?"

In his first years in the United States, Alexander never spoke with anyone about his experiences of spending three years on the brink of starvation and going for days on end without water. He chose not to, he said, because he "just wanted to keep busy." Dwelling on the past was too painful, reminding him of the overwhelming nature of their losses. So he deliberately drove his difficult memories inward, keeping them to himself: "I suppressed these feelings and these memories and these experiences and this hurt and this pain for so long, for so many years." Alexander renounced his belief in God after the war. There is shame in his voice as he speaks of his feelings of betrayal and hopelessness, and his loss of a sense of agency and personal meaning.

As his story suggests, survivors' sense of estrangement was often primed by their own experiences of dehumanization, betrayal, and loss of trust in others during the war years. But what was so disturbing to so many of them, as they described it 40 years later, when they were interviewed at the behest of the United States Holocaust Memorial Museum, were their continued feelings of betrayal upon arriving in the United States, when they interacted with others and encountered reluctant audiences for their stories. Survivors wanted to be known by others; they wanted to tell their stories, at least in limited ways. To tell one's story is to share one's past, and to develop bonds of mutual recognition. After the war, however, many of those closest to them refused to listen, averting their eyes, refusing to see their faces.

Alexander describes living a quiet life after the war, of being devoted to his family, and having little to do with organized social activities, Jewish or otherwise. "My mother was Jewish, [we had a] kosher house, my father, what did it get them?" he scoffed. "I said to the Rabbi, he came to my house, he said, come to *shul* (synagogue), and I said when you give me the answer to my question, to my satisfaction. Give me one good reason why I should go to *shul*. To empty my conscience of guilt? I have done nothing wrong in my life that I have to ask forgiveness. God has nothing to forgive me for, but I have plenty to forgive him for. Straighten that out and I'll come to *shul*. Convince me that there is a God and I'll go. The only thing I believe in is me. That's the only thing. If I don't keep myself alive, nobody will. If I don't work and make a living, nobody will pay my bills. I'll be in the street. That's all I know."

Like many other survivors, particularly those who had experienced the war years in isolation, fighting alone for their survival, Alexander lost his trust in the world. The postwar years seemed like a double betrayal. As he recalled, "I didn't have a place, any place to go, I had no body to talk to. At least in the army, you have some people, some friends. Here I had no one. I was all on my own, all alone in a strange land. A land that didn't even want me. Let's face it. If you don't speak English like the English do, you're an outsider. They don't like you and they show it. I had no other place to go, what could I do? I got into a lot of fistfights. I was bitter. I was disappointed. I was hurt. Inexperienced to stand on my own two feet. For a year, I wandered around. Did odd jobs. And then I decided I'd go to America."

When Alexander arrived in the United States, he brought with him this sense of broken trust, feelings of alienation, and lack of faith. This betrayal was reinforced by the responses of many of those he met. To describe this as a deliberate disavowal or distancing on the part of others is probably incorrect. Rather, such distancing was the product of fear, confusion, and lack of information, and probably an unconscious wish to protect oneself. Few Americans had a way of understanding who the survivors were, or what they had endured. Psychiatrists and social workers were similarly baffled; these survivors did not fit into their prior understandings and frameworks. Few survivors, moreover, accepted a definition of themselves as victims—victimhood carried with it connotations of weakness, which few wished to identify with. The public expression of negative emotions—sadness, melancholy, grief, guilt—was widely considered to be socially unacceptable. Those who had survived the genocide tended to believe that the "real" victims were family members, friends, and neighbors who had perished; their identification with them made it difficult to see themselves as victims as well.

Erwin Baum, who was born in Warsaw and was a young teenager when the war broke out, empathized with the strangers he met when he arrived in the United States, who could not understand what he had endured. "If you tell your story to somebody, it's to the other person, it's just like reading a book," he said. "It doesn't affect you very much because you did not live it." Baum was thirteen when the Nazis invaded Warsaw, was raised in a ghetto orphanage, and was deported to several concentration camps, including one in which airplane parts were fabricated. He recalls being subjected to physical torture in the camps. Upon being liberated, he was sent to Luxembourg and eventually moved to Israel, Belgium, and Canada, and settled, finally, in the United States.

At the time of the interview, conducted in 1994, Baum was 68. "You see, us, survivors, you know? I'm talking to you and somehow I cannot touch upon the, the feeling that it happened to me, you know? Because it was so tragic, so awful, what I went through, that it's just humanly impossible to comprehend, you know? So it's just like reading a book about somebody's experience. So you cannot expect anybody to have any feelings about it." This was true, he believed, even of American Jews.

In the late 1940s, Americans were just beginning to hear about the strange refugees from Hitler's destruction arriving on their shores. The genocide was not yet widely recognized as the Holocaust, signifying the genocide of European Jewry, distinct from the events of the war. The term "Holocaust," from the Greek *holokaustos*, meaning burned whole, or a sacrificial offering on the altar, was first used to describe the systematic program of Jewish extermination in the November 1942 issue of *Jewish Frontier*, but it was not yet in widespread use. Before the genocide, the term commonly referred to large fires, earthquakes and other disasters. Destruction of this magnitude had never before occurred in "civilized" Europe, and Turkey's genocide of Armenians during World War I was not widely known or discussed. American journalists who covered the liberation of the concentration camps tended to emphasize the nationalities of those who had been imprisoned, rather than their Jewishness. At the liberation of Dachau, one journalist characteristically described a "seething, swaying crowd of Russians, Poles, Frenchmen, Czechs and Austrians...cheering the Americans in their native languages."[8] What Americans knew about the survivors came primarily from ghoulish newsreel footage of the liberation of the concentration camps broadcast in cinemas at the end of the war.

But over the next several years, images of living, breathing survivors emerged. These media depictions tended to focus on how survivors arrived hopeful about the future, and how quickly they adapted and made contributions to their adopted country. There were stories about sisters who, separated during the war, hadn't seen each other for years, only to discover they were living a few blocks from each other in New York City. And there were stories of survivors celebrating Thanksgiving at "refugee" hotels. The survivors, Americans were told, were like any other immigrant group, and were successfully adapting and making new lives. Idealized depictions such as these transformed a tragic story into one designed to inspire, console, and uplift. To guard against discomfort, such "restitution narratives" emphasized the possibility of overcoming one's past and assimilating into the American grain. They sought to restore order out of disruption, offering stories of redemption that emphasized progress.

While American Jews were deeply affected by the destruction of their European counterparts, and many had lost family members, collectively they were often ambivalent about their relationship to the survivors, who were reminders of the worlds many had struggled to leave behind. In a 1944 essay, Hannah Arendt traced the importance of Jewish thinkers to the status of Jews as a "pariah people" who were essentially outsiders in Western culture. Social climbing "parvenu" Jews, in contrast, traded their Jewish identities for social acceptance.[9] In the United States, in the decades before World War II, in inner-city Jewish settlements a host of styles of Jewishness and Jewish politics—socialists, communists, anarchists, and their Yiddishist, Hebraist, and Zionist variants, from atheistic communism to various types of orthodoxy—had flourished. By World War II, most American Jews had come to strongly identify with their adopted nation, downplaying ethnic particularity in favor of a more universalistic conception of Americanness, distancing themselves from the "Old Country."

After the war, the classic urban experience of American Jews in the densely settled Jewish sections of New York and other Eastern cities, rapidly gave way to a mass movement to the suburbs—the antithesis of the shtetl. Jews were "becoming white folks," anthropologist Karen Brodkin has suggested, aided by programs like the GI Bill, which helped push the children and grandchildren of southern and Eastern European immigrants into the middle classes.[10] As they moved to the suburbs and into the middle classes, Brodkin and others have argued, American Jews distanced themselves from the inner cities, from their own history of immigrant hardship and struggle, downplaying their Jewishness in the public sphere so that they could advance socially. Of course, a desire to escape from persistent anti-Semitism certainly played a role, too.

And still, many Jews expressed their Jewishness through their Americanness, and frequently did not see the two as being in conflict with one another; assimilation was redefining mainstream America as much as it was redefining the lives of American Jews. As historian Yuri Slezkine writes, the United States was the "only modern state in which a Jew could be an equal citizen and a Jew at the same time." America offered "full membership without complete assimilation."[11] Indeed, Philip Roth described Jews in wartime Newark as "needing no larger terms of reference, no profession of faith or doctrinal creed, in order to be Jews. Their being Jews issued from being themselves, as did their being American."[12]

Today, in the age of multiculturalism, when difference is a source of pride and diversity is recognized as resistance to the conformity of the "melting pot," many Americans see this bargain as a bad one, as the product of the relative powerlessness and self-hatred of American Jews at a time of virulent anti-Semitism. Assimilation has become a dirty word.[13] But at the time, race, not ethnicity, was becoming the "paradigmatic problem of America," and Jews, as a whole, were "only too happy to shed their marginal status."[14] Most American Jews shared the experience of immigration, and many maintained ongoing connections to their European cousins before World War II severed those linkages. One can imagine how painful it was for them to learn of the mass murder, particularly those who had immigrated most recently, who lost close family members in Europe. After the war, American Jews raised millions of dollars to provide food, clothing, and housing to resettle the survivors, and lobbied for a relaxation of immigration restrictions; yet because they were fearful of being identified with victimhood, or wanted to distance themselves emotionally from the destruction, many played down the Jewish nature of the tragedy, turning away from the survivors.

In one frequently mentioned incident of the late 1940s, some prominent Jewish New Yorkers proposed to erect a genocide memorial in New York City, only to be rebuffed by the American Jewish Committee, the Anti-Defamation League, and the American Jewish Congress, among others, on the grounds that such a monument would be a "perpetual memorial to the weakness and defenselessness of the Jewish people" and was "not in the best interests of the Jewry." Edward Shapiro writes: "During the 1950s, Jewish communities did not sponsor Holocaust commemorations, the Jewish lecture circuit did not feature speeches on the Holocaust, no Holocaust centers existed in the United States, and there was little public discussion among Jews regarding the fate of European Jewry."[15] There was little consensus about whether the destruction of European Jewry should even be publicly memorialized.

While there were numerous small-scale memorial efforts in Jewish communities, there was not yet an understanding of the destruction of European Jewry as an event that was of great significance beyond Jewish communities. And even within these communities, ambivalence often prevailed.[16] Some American Jews no doubt felt guilty for having been able to do little to save their European counterparts; others believed the survivors were pointing an accusatory finger at them for not saving them. Many people found survivors' very presence threatening—there was at this moment a great deal of stigma attached to the very act of surviving. At times, Jewish neighbors even prevented their children from playing with child survivors because, recalls Lisa Derman, "Many people thought that those who had been in a concentration camp survived, I don't know doing what. Eating other people's flesh, or they were terrible."

Derman was born in 1926 in Raczki, Poland, and fled with her family to a forest, where they witnessed the massacre of Jews, including her mother. She was sheltered by Christians and returned to the ghetto to find her father and brother, who had survived the massacre. There she met a man, Aron, who was involved in the underground movement, with whom she joined a partisan unit, and eventually married. When they arrived in the United States after the war, Lisa and Aron Derman encountered the pervasive belief that survivors had actively or passively participated in their own destruction by "going like sheep to the slaughter."

To identify with the survivors and truly empathize with them would require American Jews to imagine that they themselves could have experienced the unimaginable. Perhaps that was too difficult, or too unbearable, for them to do so—clashing with a culture that was eager to move on, that prized self-reliance, and that believed in the possibility of self-transformation. In their early days in the United States, survivors tested audiences to see how much information they could share with others; what they found frequently was that the answer was very little.[17] Those around them often diverted their eyes, turning away from them. But the opposite was also true: some individuals became the focus of intense, unwanted curiosity, which was at times no less challenging.

IT WAS EASIER TO SAY I CAME FROM FRANCE

At war's end, Esther Adler, who was originally from Germany, came to the United States, married a man who worked in the television industry, and moved to Connecticut. "I didn't want to live in the past, I didn't want to talk about what happened to me and in fact I very seldom talked about it. Most of our friends didn't know I was a survivor," she recalls. She proceeded to try to live a "normal" life, which for Esther meant presenting herself as a French immigrant to others, even to her husband Jim. "As far as they knew I came from France and that was it, I was learning the language, I was learning the customs, I was becoming Americanized, but they did not know I was a survivor. In fact Jim knew very little about it, but I never talked about it and he didn't quiz me about it, so I very seldom talked about it and I did not search out any other survivors."

Why did Esther not share her past with others? "It would have been too complicated telling my life story to everybody who asked me where I was from," she says. "It was easiest to say I came from France because I spent quite a few years there and I went to school there and I liked France," she recalled. "I really liked it, so it was very easy for me to say, I grew up in France, but I was born in Germany and that's usually what I tell people and it's pretty accurate. You know...I cannot tell them all the detours I made, it's just too many when you start with one...so how come you were there and how come you were there. It would be very difficult for me to explain that without telling my story to everybody and I don't like to do it."

Accounting for her decision to cover her identity, passing as French rather than as a German Jew, Esther says it was "easier" to present herself as French. At a time of persistent anti-Semitism, being French and deracinated was a more favorably viewed immigrant status rather than that of an abject Eastern European Jew. Her French accent deflected attention from her Jewishness—and even more important, from her survivor identity, which was fine for her. She did not want to arouse curiosity.

Those who settled in small towns and cities where there were few Jewish residents, and where they were less likely to know other survivors, faced particular challenges. After Sylvia Green was liberated from Bergen-Belsen, she settled in Lexington, Kentucky. Her neighbors were aware of the existence of survivors, though they had never met one before. At the time Sylvia and her sister were the only survivors living in Lexington. Curious neighbors came to see her at the department store where she worked, and gawked. "They just wanted to see me, like I was a novelty." They did not ask her about her past, but just looked and stared. Would she have shared her past with them? She said that even if they had asked, she would "not have been ready to talk [about] what happened to me." She did not yet have the vocabulary, or the distance she needed, to share her story with others, she said. "It took years and years before I was able to talk."

Laura and Daniel Simon were refugees from Hungary who met after the war. Laura survived Auschwitz and Daniel was imprisoned in labor camps in the Soviet Union. After the war, they described themselves as "Hungarians." As their son Mel recalled, "they never used the term 'survivor.'"[18] "You know, that wasn't something they liked to really think or talk about," he said. "I mean, they lost a lot of family and they had a lot of terrible experiences. They certainly weren't proud of it, or they could easily have done without it. It wasn't a special status." His last point is key. To identify as a "survivor" is to claim distinction on the basis of having suffered. But in an individualistic culture geared to self-advancement and achieving against the odds, there was little dignity in such suffering.

Suffering was the mark of an identity that was, in sociologist Erving Goffman's terms, "spoiled."

When strangers come into our presence, we draw a set of assumptions about who they are on the basis of their appearance. In the process, evidence can arise of their "possessing an attribute that makes them different from others" and "of a less desirable kind," wrote Goffman.[19] He provided a compelling analysis of how stigma shapes everyday interactions, creating the sense among some people that they are unworthy of love and respect. Among the stigmatized, he wrote, were those with physical deformities, such as individuals who walk with a limp, those possessing "blemishes of individual character," such as those with addictions, and those possessing "tribal stigmas" of race, nation, or religion—namely, racial and ethnic minorities. If they are "discredited," if their stigmatized trait is not concealable, the stigmatized are compelled to manage tensions that arise when they interact with others. If their stigma is concealable, and they choose to conceal it, they must manage their identities to minimize a sense of difference. He described the dance in which individuals try to control the reactions of others by manipulating what they reveal about themselves.

Curiously, Holocaust survivors are absent from his analysis, perhaps because of their relative invisibility, and also because many American Jews in the 1950s (including perhaps Goffman himself) minimized their Jewishness in exchange for social acceptability.[20] Nonetheless, Goffman's understanding of how individuals manage "spoiled identities" provides a useful lens through which to understand survivors' recollections of their initial contact with strangers and acquaintances in the United States in the 1940s and 1950s. What Goffman suggests is that stigma and shame are pervasive in modern life, becoming particularly insidious at certain moments and in certain places. While stigma is an attribute of the individual that is "out of place," what is considered out of place (or deserving of shame) varies across time and place. In other words, what is considered discreditable in one society may be tolerated, or even valued, in another. So while Holocaust survivors are now widely revered, or at least are seen as deserving of sympathy and understanding, this was not always the case.[21]

Survivors' oral histories speak not only of their past suffering, but also of their subsequent status as objects of curiosity. Since their "spoiled" identities were generally not immediately apparent to others, they describe incidents in which they manipulated what they revealed to others, learning to read the requirements of particular places in order to best present themselves to the "normal" world in a fashion that minimized social tensions. They employed different normalizing strategies: some disguised their stigma, and passed as non-survivors, and even as non-Jews, creating entirely new biographies that bore little resemblance to their old ones. Others adopted a "cover" that emphasized less stigmatized aspects of their identities—a French origin, for example, rather than their Polish-Jewish one—a strategy that required the cooperation of allies such as family members and social workers, who helped them buy new clothing, to dress in keeping with American styles, to learn English, and to cover up any identifying signs of stigma.

Still others retreated "backstage" into their families, to worlds comprised nearly entirely of other survivors, or to their own private worlds, avoiding social contact as much as they possibly could. In fact, many survivors engaged in all of these practices, which were not mutually exclusive. One could pass completely at one point in one's life, and then chose to cover. One might pass during the workday, but then retreat backstage at night, withdrawing into one's family, or remaining with other survivors. What this suggests is that appearing normal in public was not a simple accomplishment: it required a great deal of work.

Some attribute their decision to cover their identities to their experiences of anti-Semitism in the United States. Even in New York City, Eva Edmands recalls, some landlords refused to rent to Jews, and certain hotels were off limits. After the German annexation of Austria in March 1938, Eva's family left Vienna for Paris and were trapped in the occupied area of France. Trying to find refuge in Switzerland, they were caught by the French police, and they survived the war under the protection of a priest. After the liberation of France in 1944, Eva and her parents returned to Paris. In 1946, they emigrated to the United States. Having believed that "we left all of that behind," Edmands was shocked by her encounters with anti-Semitism in the United States. Although anti-Jewish attitudes were fading in the postwar era, anti-immigrant sentiment fused with anticommunist fervor, leading to the imposition of immigration quotas on those arriving from communist countries. Many Jewish survivors, who hailed from countries of the Soviet bloc, often became suspect as enemy aliens who were potentially subversive of American national interests.[22] In response to these attitudes, Edmands said, she began to revert to her wartime practice of covering her identity.

"A strange thing happened at this point, I was really almost ashamed of having a Jewish background and so I didn't tell anybody," said Edmands. "I told them I was French but I didn't tell them about my background of being a survivor or anything like. I just determined I wasn't going to tell people. I told them I was French but I didn't tell them about my background of being a survivor or anything like that because the Germans had done such a good job of propagandizing and making you feel like you were the scum of that earth, that so, it is so insidious that after a while, you're being told, you know, over these years, you're scum, you're scum, you wind up believing. I said, well maybe I am inferior, maybe I'm not [as] good as anybody else. And so I just determined I wasn't going to tell people." Here we can see how feelings of stigma and inferiority may have begun years before, perhaps during the war itself. As Edmands suggests, silence was sometimes an intentional act designed to exercise agency, to avoid being defined by one's victimhood.

For those who had been tattooed at Auschwitz, whose status as survivors was written on their bodies, identity management was a particularly daunting task. Goffman describes stigma symbols, which were originally bodily signs deliberately inflicted to indicate some low moral status. The word "stigma" derives from the Greek, and refers to a kind of tattoo mark that was cut or burned into the skin of criminals, slaves, or traitors in order to visibly identify them as blemished or morally polluted. The concentration camp tattoo as stigma symbol appeared in an early Philip Roth short story, "Eli the Fanatic." In the story, Leo Tzuref, a survivor in black hat and Hasidic dress, arrives in Scarsdale, New York, a formerly Gentile bastion, and the upper middle-class Jews who are living there are demoralized. From the moment he encounters Tzuref, whose very name evokes, in Yiddish, *tsuris* (trouble), Eli Peck feels off balance. He decides that Leo must be persuaded to shave off his beard, conceal his tattooed numbers, and trade in his black hat and coat for a Brooks Brothers suit. In this story, Roth captures the ambivalence of many American Jews toward the survivors, and the ways those who had been tattooed carried their stigma on their bodies.

After the war, those numbers became resonant symbols of persecution. Some survivors were defiant in their refusal to erase the past, resenting the expectations of others that they would conceal potentially unsettling information. Thomas Buergenthal recalls that immediately after the war in Germany, people noticed his mother's concentration camp tattoo and often remarked on it, and yet she defiantly wore short sleeves. When someone said, "Don't you think you should have this tattoo removed?" she replied: "This is a badge of honor, I would never remove this." Buergenthal was born to German-Jewish/Polish-Jewish parents who had moved from Germany to Czechoslovakia in 1933, and grew up in the Jewish ghetto of Kielce, Poland, and was later sent to concentration camps. He emigrated from Germany to the United States in 1951. Buergenthal recalls that despite powerful pressures to conceal their bodily marks, his mother and others chose to reveal them, partly out of loyalty to those who were killed by the Nazis. Most, however, reported feeling ashamed of their tattoos.

Child survivor Irene Hizme was only two when the war broke out. She and her twin brother, Rene Slotkin, were born in 1937 in Czechoslovakia, and were deported with their mother to Theresienstadt, then Auschwitz, where they were subjected to medical experiments. After the war was over, her tattoo was a bitter reminder of what she had endured. "I was so totally ashamed of my tattoo because I felt that this was a mark of some sort that I had committed some great grievous sin for which I had been adequately punished, but I certainly didn't want anybody to know that I was in a concentration camp. I mean that was like, my God, I would sooner die than have someone know."

Some survivors feared that the identifying marks, if revealed, would force them to talk about their experiences. One woman recalled that at a dance in San Francisco a man stared curiously at her from time to time; finally he came over, introduced himself, and confessed that he had seen the numbers on her arm. "I was wondering," he asked, "why you were wearing your laundry numbers on your arm?" What were they really, he wanted to know, some sort of decoration? She told him, "No, that's my telephone number." Faced with unwanted attention, some described how they covered, removed, or otherwise tried to obscure those marks.

When Hizme entered school in New York City, even though her teachers knew she was a survivor, she says that they never gave her a sense that they empathized with or truly understood her situation. "I always had a certain sadness and memories that just kept haunting me," she recalled. "It didn't help that nobody ever asked me anything or wanted to even know. Even at school and though I'm quite sure that all the teachers were perfectly aware that I was their one and only...survivor student. No teacher ever befriended me especially or tried to help me especially. They just kind of let me be...I felt very outside all the time. I never kind of quite got into the fun of the activities at school."

In winter Irene wore long sleeved shirts; during the summer, her mother bought pancake powder and mixed it to match her skin. "Every morning, " Irene recalls, her mother "would get this waterproof stuff and she'd mix the color to be exactly right and we'd feather it and powder it and I thought it was really quite good, but in all honesty, anybody who had any eyes would have seen that there was something on my arm that I was covering, but no one ever asked. In fact, it's strange, I remember overhearing a teacher in my school point to me and say 'she's the little girl that came from the concentration camps.' And another teacher said to me, "No. It couldn't be. No children survived the concentration camps."

At times, survivors tried to have tattoos removed by those who were ill-qualified for such a task. One woman attended nursing school in Cleveland after the war, where student nurses wore short-sleeved uniforms, and a number of Jewish doctors commented on her tattoo, encouraging her to have it removed. As she was about to marry an American and wanted to erase the past, she agreed, and in 1949, a surgeon excised the numbers from her left forearm. But the wound did not heal in the usual way and an abnormal scar developed, raised and reddened, and did not begin to subside for many years—which she saw as a symbol of her failed attempt to become an American, and of the difficulty of erasing history.[23]

A small but significant minority of survivors tried to pass in all aspects of their lives, avoiding other survivors, changing their public appearance, their names, even their identities, denying their Jewishness and raising their children as Christians. This was more common among those who stayed in Europe after the war, who were also more likely to marry Gentiles and to embrace communism's universalistic claims.[24] But passing also took place with some frequency in the United States. Sometimes it occurred among those who wished to assimilate and downplay their Jewishness; at times it was a carry-over from their wartime experiences. In her memoir *After Long Silence*, Helen Fremont, daughter of a survivor, describes how her mother "had invented herself a hundred times over by the time the war was over." It was nothing, she said, "to sew a new identity onto the old ones and present it to an unsuspecting America."[25]

In order to pass, in addition to changing one's name, religious identity, and at times one's personal appearance, one also had to compose a false autobiographical story—a reinvention that was, for many survivors, a familiar process. They had hidden in different countries in Europe during the war, inventing and reinventing themselves at different moments, always fearing that others would find them and hand them over to Nazi occupiers. Compared to their wartime "passing" among Russians, Poles, Ukrainians, and Italians, some survivors suggested that passing in America was much easier. Americans, they remarked, had far less understanding of ethnic and other distinctions; in a more diverse and geographically mobile society, it was easier to hide. Still, those who chose to pass completely were faced with the anxiety that everyone really knew, and they had a permanent feeling of being watched. Close relationships had to be avoided, biographies had to be maintained and managed as unique and coherent. The stigmatized needed to be constantly alert. Much as stutterers monitor their speech for forthcoming difficult words, and gay people historically have carefully checked their homes for any signs of homosexual literature in order to discourage visitors' curiosity, some tell deliberate lies. Foreign accents, which provoked the question, "where are you from?" could become emotional minefields.

Esther Adler recalls an incident when she attended a rally for presidential candidate Adlai Stevenson in Queens with her husband Jim. She looked across the arena and saw a young woman whom she knew from her former life, and blurted out, "I knew her in Bratislava," to her husband. This revelation pierced the façade she had created, forcing her to reveal more of her story. What this suggests is that identity management was successful only if one surrounded oneself with others who knew nothing of one's past, or those who are willing to be complicit in one's new identity story. But this was not always possible.

Adler, who arrived in the United States via Czechoslovakia, Germany, and France, describes herself as a "very reluctant Jew" who downplayed her Jewishness and her survivor status after coming to the United States, for fear that these attributes would stigmatize her, and because she felt that they had little meaning for her. Other survivors, when they arrived, joined orthodox religious communities. Those on the secular Left, who had little place for God, tended to affiliate with socialists, Yiddish speakers, or with no one at all. Most, however, tried to adapt to American ways and American Jewish life, integrating their Jewishness, and their status as survivors, into their lives as best they could.

The mutual concealing of troubling information was a kind of dance, in which survivors revealed something of their past, waited to see how others responded, and then backed away, often retreating into silence. Eva Hoffman, the daughter of survivors who grew up in Poland and England, writes: "Survivors did not think their status was going to be enhanced by radical vulnerability. Aside from shame, there was the fear—and the reality—of stigma. The survivors may have spoken of what they had endured among themselves. But among strangers who had not lived through similar things and might not credit those who had, among those who, even if they did credit the stories, might misunderstand or were almost certain to do so, the survivors kept silent. They passed for normal."[26]

During the early decades after the war, survivors often experienced themselves as shunned by those around them, or as objects of extreme curiosity. Both of these roles were uncomfortable: the first caused others to avert their eyes, and failed to recognize the survivors at all; the second placed them on a pedestal, or positioned them as objects of pity, failing to see them as fully human. As a group, only those who had actively fought in the wartime resistance, who were feted in American Jewish communities and venerated by other survivors, managed to elude this stigma and its attendant shame.

Among survivors, those who were resisters, who had fought back against the Nazis, were held in high esteem. A cult of the hero was pervasive in Europe, the United States, and Israel during the immediate postwar decades. Focusing on acts of wartime heroism was a common "restitution narrative" that circulated in popular culture, and American Jewish communities accorded recognition to those who actively defended the nation or combatted fascism, including ghetto fighters and partisans, who were seen as warriors and heroes.[27] Resisters seemed to elude the stigma that they were mentally imbalanced, that they survived by eating the flesh of others, or that they had willingly marched to their deaths—replaced by the heroic narrative of the ghetto fighter defending his or her people.

Lisa and Aron Derman had been partisans during the war, living in the woods under the command of the Soviets, and fighting against the Nazis. Aron lost three sisters and his mother; Lisa lost a younger brother, and was eventually saved by a Gentile in the ghetto near her town, narrowly eluding capture. When they arrived in the United States, they stayed with Lisa's relatives: two uncles and an aunt, who asked them who had survived among their immediate relatives. "We only told them that," recalled Lisa. And then they shut the door on the discussion, avoiding, in particular, any discussion of atrocities they had witnessed. "They did not ask about atrocities, they were afraid to touch that." Imagining what was going through her relatives' heads, she surmised, "they thought that if we talked about it, they didn't know how we were going to act." So, she said, "They didn't touch it."

Little by little, recalled Lisa, "we revealed some of it, but they didn't press." She admits that she and her husband "weren't so anxious to tell them all the details." There was, in other words, an implicit compact between the two sides, a compact born of the desire to protect one another from knowing too much. Her relatives did not inquire, and Lisa and Aron "only told them as much as they asked. But we did not tell them in detail." Lisa believed her American relatives wanted to protect them: "They were afraid for our feelings. They thought we had suffered so much, why remind them? They kept on saying: this is America, things will be different here, things will be good."

Their relatives threw them a shower, and people brought them all sorts of gifts so that they could create a household. They dressed them, took them on drives to Coney Island, and tried to show them a good time. Lisa recalls that she and her husband "were taken over by the greatness of the city," and every night they were hosted and "treated royally everywhere we went." Friends and distant relatives imagined that they had endured a series of events too horrible to discuss, and steered conversations to less unsettling matters. But the Dermans never encountered stigma, they said: "Everywhere we went, we were the elite of survivors, because we resisted." In keeping with American individualism, they were accorded status for "doing something"—for their ability to act, to think creatively, and on some level, however limited, their ability to be independent.

The Dermans' story suggests the ways in which some survivors' tragic stories were transformed into "restitution" narratives that emphasized survival and overcoming. These narratives downplayed the tragic nature of what survivors had endured, transforming chaos, interruption, and loss into more coherent, forward-looking narratives of progress. While focusing on heroism helped to temper the horror of the events, it was bound to be highly conflicted, elevating some to the status of active agents of history, and plunging others into feelings of shame and guilt. As psychologist Bruno Bettleheim, himself a survivor, suggested: "the depiction of survivors as active agents responsible for their survival is a completely misleading distortion." He and others challenged efforts to link survivors with resistance, action, or heroism.[28]

Founded in 1962, the Warsaw Ghetto Resistance Organization, which honored the 1943 insurgency in which hundreds of young Jews held off their Nazi attackers for several months, was among the most public of the survivor organizations, sponsoring an annual commemorative program in New York City. Each year, its public program began with a cantor singing the national anthem, and continued with a Hebrew prayer and the singing of ghetto songs. A host of dignitaries—senators, Israeli representatives to the United Nations, governors, mayors, and rabbis—spoke and lit six memorial candles, chanted the *kaddish*, the memorial prayer, and recited the last words of the commander of the ghetto uprising. Finally, at the end of the event, the crowd sang the Partisan Hymn, written by a young poet and partisan in the Vilna Ghetto when he heard about the Warsaw Ghetto Uprising. "This song was written with our blood and not with lead," it proclaimed. "This is no song of free birds flying overhead. But a people amid crumbling walls did stand. They stood and sang this song with rifles held in hand."[29]

By commemorating the ghetto uprising, survivors affirmed those who had stood up to the Nazis—rather than the vast majority who escaped by going into hiding, or had survived by sheer luck, and sometimes even by betraying those around them. Such commemorations elevated resisters to heroes, framing them as soldiers and war heroes who exercised valor and agency. Since all but a few resisters were eventually killed, this focus was bittersweet. While affirming pride in the bravery of others, this "restitution narrative" distanced itself from the full extent of the tragedy, playing into many survivors' sense of powerlessness. Why, many asked themselves, were they not able to resist? The focus on resisters may also have inadvertently intensified the sense of guilt that survivors felt about having survived while other family members, friends, and neighbors did not, thus contributing to their public silence. As few survivors had the capacity to resist, the preoccupation with resisters during the first two decades after the war failed to give those who fell outside this category a position from which to speak and bear witness.

Hollywood films and Broadway plays of the early postwar years also emphasized themes of valor and redemption. Anne Frank's diary, published in the United States in 1952, was marketed as "the universal story of a young girl." When the play appeared on Broadway, it ended with Anne pronouncing her faith in the goodness of all people. Her story found wide acclaim, said Bruno Bettleheim, because "it denies implicitly that Auschwitz ever existed. If all men are good, there was never an Auschwitz."[30]

Ludwik Szlifersteyn was neither a resistance fighter nor a concentration camp internee. He spent the war years in Soviet-occupied Poland and later in Russia, having fled Warsaw immediately after the Nazi invasion on September 1, 1939. In Russia, he worked as a teacher and was eventually sent to a labor camp in Siberia. Later, he was drafted into the Red Army, fighting at the Romanian front. At war's end, he was among 180,000 Jews who were repatriated from the Soviet Union. When he returned to Poland to look for surviving relatives, with the exception of a cousin who had also spent the war years in Russia, he found no one.

After war's end, Ludwik sat in limbo, waiting in deportation camps, wandering from country to country, barred by restrictive immigration policies from entering the United States. He spent five years in transit: first in Sweden, and then in Cuba. His family, or what was left of it, consisted of his uncle Joe and Joe's wife Tola. Joe had left Poland, immigrating to America on the eve of the war, and had changed his name from Szlifersteyn to Stein. Ludwik did not know his uncle's address, so he sent the letter to "Joseph Stein, Brooklyn, New York"; thanks to an intrepid mail carrier, it reached his uncle, who arranged for him to obtain an American visa.

In 1951, when he landed in New York, Ludwik rented a room in the apartment of a Polish refugee couple he had met in Cuba while awaiting entry to the United States. The Washington Heights neighborhood in upper Manhattan, which had earlier been dubbed "Little Berlin" because of the large German-Jewish population, became a home to yet another wave of Jewish immigrants in the 1940s and 1950s: survivors. There were so many survivors, in fact, that Poles, Germans, and other groupings constituted small subcultures with their own religious and communal institutions. There he became Lawrence Stein.

Because Lawrence, who was my father, spent the war years outside Nazi-occupied territory, eluding the ghettos or concentration camps that were the fate of most Jews, he occupied a liminal position in the universe of survivors. His experience suggests an additional set of explanations for why it was difficult, if not impossible, for many victims of Nazi persecution to speak on their own behalf: they did not conform to normative understandings of who was a "survivor." My father's experience was not officially recognized by the agencies entrusted with distributing reparations to Jewish victims of Nazi policy, or even by Jewish organizations that sought to represent the survivor community in the postwar period. Within the survivor population, the distinctions among concentration camp internees, those who were trapped in the ghettos of Warsaw, Lodz, and other cities, and those who lived outside Nazi occupation, were blurrier. As my father would say, referring to those who had endured camps, "others had it much worse than I did."

Was my father a survivor? If we use an expansive definition, he certainly was.[31] But in the immediate aftermath of the war, survivors were often defined by official agencies as those who had been held in ghettos and interned in concentration camps and in lands under Nazi occupation, categories that excluded people like my father.[32] My father had lost his family, his home, his nation—everything but his life. As he was on the run for most of the war, and in the Soviet Union, where he was eventually imprisoned in a labor camp, his story did not fit into emerging restitution narratives that defined heroism as fighting back.

The only formal survivors' organization he ever participated in was the annual Warsaw Ghetto Resistance Organization commemoration in New York. After his death, I found a program for the 1979 "Memorial Service for 6,000,000 Jewish Martyrs" (Figure 1.1) among my father's most precious possessions, along with treasured family photographs and letters from scattered friends and relatives in Argentina, Russia, Cuba, and beyond. By attending an annual rite focused on resistance and martyrdom, he linked himself to a heroic moment in the history of the war, a moment in which he himself could not rightly claim a role, but with which he nonetheless deeply identified. Stripped of power during the war, and having no recognized heroic role after the war, he attended this commemoration alone, never with friends or family. As he saw it, he was neither a victim (the "true" victims were all dead) nor a survivor (if that term signified the experience of being directly persecuted by the Nazis), nor a resister (in the sense of taking up arms against the Nazis, as symbolized by the Warsaw

Figure 1.1:
The Warsaw Ghetto Resistance Organization (WAGRO), one of the earliest and longest-running survivor organizations, holds annual commemorative ceremonies in New York.

Ghetto Resistance Organization and other associations of resistance fighters). He was a marginal man, unable to speak openly about his experiences.[33] He never spoke of himself as a "victim," however.

During the first two decades after the war, the "victim" label was used almost exclusively to refer to those who had perished during World War II. Those who survived did not refer to themselves as victims—in homage to the dead, because they wished to distance themselves from the "real" victims, or because they identified with them. If my father did not identify as a victim, neither did he ever use the term "survivor." When he gathered with others who had survived, he and others described themselves as "political prisoners," as "deportees," as having endured "death marches," "the war," or, using a term that predated the idea of a singular Holocaust, "the catastrophe." Together, they shared stories of their wartime experiences and memorialized the dead; they revisited their histories, reinterpreted the past, and developed a collective sense of themselves and spaces for storytelling that afforded a sense of biographic continuity. Estrangement may have led to a loss of confidence and trust, but it also spurred a search for new forms of community made up of "others of like mind."[34]

Within Jewish communities, nascent efforts to build a Holocaust memorial culture began to take shape during the first decades after the war, and some survivors attended these memorial events, at times sharing their stories. Against those who have said that American Jews silenced survivors, historian Hasia Diner has argued that American Jews "did not beg them to be quiet but listened to their public testimonies."[35] Still, one wonders about the extent of survivors' involvements in such commemorations, and indeed, more generally, about how well they were integrated into organized Jewish communities. In interviews, few survivors speak of being aware of such commemorative events; and even fewer speak of participating in them. What this suggests is that even though they often came together religiously, American Jews and survivors tended to live in separate worlds. As Elie Wiesel recalled of this time, "survivors were understood by survivors alone."[36]

Torn from their families, homes, and sense of identity, survivors were faced with remaking their lives in both a practical and psychic sense. Yet there was little place for them to express their grief, either collectively or individually. What stands out in their accounts is the shame of telling a story that must appear unbelievable and entirely out of tune with surrounding society.[37] After enduring unspeakable experiences, they often felt unrecognized or misunderstood by social workers, family members, and others they encountered when they first came to the United States. They spoke of intense loneliness, the belief that no one really knew them—or wanted to know them. As Primo Levi wrote of survivors, many "remember a dream which frequently recurred during the nights of imprisonment they had returned home and with passion and relief were describing their past sufferings, addressing themselves to a loved person, and were not believed, indeed were not even listened to."[38] Too often, it seemed, that dream came true.

So while their traumatic experiences and their inability to speak of them may have created an impassable gulf between survivors and non-survivors, these experiences became the basis for identification among survivors, who developed support networks and created surrogate families, forming organizations with names like "newcomers club," "1939 Club," "New Americans Club," and "Central Club," or referring to each other as "greenhorns," the "newly arrived," or other cryptic references to a history that seemed too overwhelming to name. In large Jewish population centers in the United

States, there were organizations for those who had been spirited out of Europe on the *kindertransport,* or those who had served in the resistance, and synagogues whose membership was composed entirely of other survivors and their families.

Leftist Yiddish speakers, known as Bundists, found others like themselves, and highly religious Jews formed enclaves, as did German-speaking Jews. Some of these networks had their origins in displaced persons camps; others were rooted in existing hometown social clubs, which were formed in the late nineteenth century by Jewish immigrants, organized around common geographic and cultural ties.[39] In these groups, distinctions blurred; camp internees mixed with resisters and those who had spent the war years in hiding; those sharing a common national origin and language found each other.

Many survivors describe their social world as composed almost entirely of other survivors. If the surrounding world did not understand what they had endured, these collective bonds were a source of strength and solidarity. As survivor Lily Margules recalls, "I never talked about [my wartime experiences]. I never talked about it. The only time that I talked, I had a lot of friends that were survivors, when we used to meet a lot. We used to entertain each other, you know, I had a very good social life. We clung to each other because we had no families, so like, friends were families. Very few had families. And so we clung to each other. Whenever we came together, we used to talk about all kinds of things, we used to talk politics and what movie did you [see], but we always ended with our, what we went through. This one was talking about it, and this was the end. And so, so it was in United States."

These affiliations permitted survivors to revisit their histories and reinterpret the past, developing a collective sense of themselves, and it offered a space for storytelling. Thomas Buergenthal recalls that when survivors gathered, there was both pleasure and pain: "Things would come back and you would talk about this or that and another thing that is so interesting, people often think that when people get together from a camp, all we'd talk about were all these terrible things that happened. The truth of the matter is that we often laughed about things in retrospect, about things that happened that were funny, about this or that. You couldn't take all of this if it were only reminiscences about all the terrible things." Often, they became surrogate extended families, affording a feeling of continuity, however partial, between their past and present lives.[40]

Most accounts of the early postwar years emphasize survivors' great flexibility and resilience when confronting the challenge of rebuilding their lives after the war, portraying their experiences as a narrative of liberation, redemption, adjustment, and smooth integration. Collectively, we prefer modernist stories of restitution that suggest that despite moments of chaos and interruption, life goes on; yesterday I suffered, but today I endure. But survivors of traumatic disruptions are wounded storytellers. Their stories are exceedingly difficult to tell, and also difficult to listen to. There are cultural taboos against such stories, which seem senseless to those outside their universe, and lacking in temporal ordering and meaning. Such individuals tend to protect themselves by not speaking, and audiences protect themselves by not listening to them. Survivors described the sense of being strange, unfamiliar to those around them, and unable to share their stories. To tell one's story and to admit victimhood invited negative judgments from neighbors, family, and others.

While they wished for others to recognize their losses, they did not want to be defined as victims, and many individuals were ambivalent about whether they were in fact victims at all. The "real" victims, they believed, were dead. For lack of a suitable frame for sharing their stories, or willing audiences to listen to them—outside those who had suffered similarly—survivors narrated their stories in a fashion that downplayed their chaotic nature, transforming them into more palatable tales of restitution and heroism.

So at a time before widespread Holocaust consciousness, and before "post-traumatic stress disorder," when America was preoccupied with reintegrating returning soldiers, when the melting pot ideal made American identity synonymous with submerging group differences, survivors expended a great deal of energy rebuilding their lives, making livelihoods and new families, and faced enormous challenges in making themselves understood by others—including, as we will see in the next chapter, those closest to them.

CHAPTER 2

Desperately Seeking Normality

Childhood was a strange place to find oneself after so much history.
Helen Fremont

We weren't like *Leave it to Beaver*.

Ann, *child of survivors*

M y parents busied themselves with being normal, refusing to dwell on "the war" in public. After years of dislocation, they saw ordinariness as a refuge, and had little interest in being exceptional, in rising above everyone else. They wanted to put down roots, have a family, and live their Jewishness without shame or persecution. Our family photographs, which speak of this yearning to be normal, were emblematic of my parents', particularly my mother's, finely orchestrated attempts to construct a surface happiness. They are heavily skewed toward birthdays, family gatherings, and summer outings, and are highly stylized, conveying less about the actual content of our lives than about how my parents wished to think about themselves: as jovial and sociable.[1]

As in albums of many other families, excessive attention is lavished on the first-born child, and there are an extraordinary number of photographs from the year of my birth: photos of my parents happily clutching me as a baby, always in a similar pose, holding my head upright, tightly against their bodies, photographs of me eating, sleeping, smiling for the camera, crying. In these images, one sees evidence of how children were thought of during that era: as little princes and princesses. My mother clothed me immaculately: the child as reflection of the adult. I was to be a streamlined extension of my mother, but with all the opportunities that had been denied to her. In many of the photographs we look genuinely happy. Indeed, these

MAR 1960

Figure 2.1:
Pearl and Lawrence Stein, with the author as an infant, Long Island, New York, 1960.

are some of the few existing photographs that show my father smiling (see Figure 2.1).

All family photograph collections are highly stylized, and idealized, representations of domestic lives. Ours similarly picture a formal world of fathers who wore neckties at family gatherings, mothers who were well coiffed, and a universe in which appearances were extraordinarily important. They suggest that my mother spent a great deal of time and effort polishing her appearance, stretching a limited clothing budget with ingenuity and the help of Loehmann's bargain basement; like many women of her generation, she never left home unless she was perfectly made up and nicely dressed. She went to great lengths to establish our normality for others, conjuring a flawless middle-class English accent to great effect, rarely telling anyone that she had grown up in an immigrant family in the East End of London, that her first language was Yiddish, and that her mother, a simple woman from the shtetl, had never learned to read or write.

While on the surface we were a fairly typical postwar nuclear family—complete with stay-at-home mom and breadwinner father—from a very early age I was acutely aware of the myriad ways in which the war was a

Figure 2.2:
Dawid, Rosa, and Helina Szliferstejn, the author's grandparents and aunt, in photographs taken in the Warsaw ghetto, probably in 1941.

continuing presence in my father's life (and in different ways, my mother's, too), setting him apart from most of those around him, including me. He was a quiet man with a haunted smile who spoke eight languages and had badly crooked teeth, was nearly forty when I was born, and was forever out of step with an American culture that prized novelty. Though my father never said much about where he had come from, I knew it had something to do with three fading photographs in a gilt frame that sat on a dresser near his bed. In those photos, a middle-aged man and woman and a younger woman stared into the camera, devoid of expression (Figure 2.2). They seemed curiously familiar, and yet foreign and strange, inhabitants of another world and yet also a part of the present. While I rarely paid much attention to the photographs, over time I learned that they were my father's parents and sister, and that they "died in the war." As a child, I did not have a framework in which to make sense of my father's early life. The photos near his bed were reminders of the ghosts in our midst, of a terrible secret that we shared and yet could not openly acknowledge. Our father's lost family was the proverbial elephant in the room, a hidden history that was off limits and yet shaped the daily lives of my younger brother and myself.

I could not help but think of my own parents' struggles to become normal as I read and analyzed transcripts of oral histories conducted with survivors in the 1990s, whose stories form the basis of this chapter, supplemented by recollections culled from descendants' memoirs and archived interviews. These survivor testimonies, in the collection of the United States Holocaust Memorial Museum, describe how in the 1950s and 1960s, in the early years of the Cold War, amid a world of uncertainties brought about by World War II and its aftermath, the home seemed to offer security and privacy, and was thought to be the arena in which survivors' "adaptation" would occur. They document the ways that survivors began to craft stories of restitution to share with their children, stories that normalized the past or emphasized moments of heroism. They reveal the different ways in which their children received those stories. And they tell of how experts began to take notice of the survivors and their problems.

As Holocaust survivors were busily making domesticity central to their search for normality, they were certainly not alone in doing so. Millions of returning soldiers also participated in the rush to family life. In the 1946 film *The Best Years of Our Lives*, the three main characters exchange thoughts about their years in the army and what life would be like after the war was over. "The thing that scares me most is that everyone is going to try to rehabilitate me," said Army sergeant Al Stephenson. "All I want's a good job, a mild future, a little house big enough for me and my wife. Give me that much and I'm rehabilitated [snaps his fingers] like that." Combat veterans of World War II "wanted to be treated like normal human beings who had had a number of unusual experiences," writes historian Hans Pols. They "distrusted the motives of psychiatrists, journalists and opinion-makers, [and] rejected any psychological approach to the problems and issues facing normal veterans on their return home."[2] Survivors of the Jewish genocide, as a whole, felt very much the same way.

While acknowledging the challenges facing survivors, resettlement agencies held out the hope of overcoming "behavior patterns" that might work against "adjustment," offering the hope that even survivors of the concentration camps, if given schooling, work, and a place to live, could integrate and carry on in the grand tradition of other immigrant groups. Social workers counseled survivors to leave the past behind and to create new lives in America.[3] "He is a survivor of an experience that deprived him of social relationships in any normal sense and of all earthly possessions," one report described the typical survivor. "His problems and personal characteristics are frequently neither understood nor accepted by the few friends or distant relatives he finds in America. The process of this adjustment is often complicated by behavior patterns, growing out of his experiences of persecution, which must be modified before he can be helped to take responsibility for himself." Counseling them to focus on the process of adjustment, they acknowledged that the survivor "may come to us with a feeling of distrust, both about himself and society, that makes his growth toward independence and responsible relationships a long difficult process." "For years, he has lived in an environment where the individual had no worth whatsoever. He needs to learn to become certain of his value, to make his own decisions, to trust us to help him before he can take any active part in rehabilitating himself or he may come with a feeling of martyrdom, bitterness or guilt... Even the best integrated personalities usually find the adjustment process a difficult one."[4]

Domesticity was a refuge, an affirmation of life over death, and an act of renewal.[5] Those who experienced war wanted to live "normal" lives, lives that would not be interrupted, that would have the family at their center, that would not stick out or appear different, and that would conform, as close as possible, to the "average" American family. The culture encouraged it, telling Americans to "look on the bright side" and not to dwell on the negative. (An ad man of the 1950s described television shows of the period as "happy shows for happy people with happy problems."[6])

While their American neighbors often chose to move away from extended kin, survivors had little choice but to do so, and they saw the families they were creating as sites of reparation—and normalization. Survivors rode the crest of the wave, creating quintessential mid-century households that closely resembled what Betty Friedan would later disparage as "comfortable concentration camps." Mirroring the powerful ideology of domesticity and gender that circulated during this era, in most families, the man was expected to be a satisfactory breadwinner, and the woman the "good mother."[7] In terms of the actual experience of family life, there was typically a great deal more variety than such stereotypes suggest, and many families embodied a much more fluid understanding of gender roles.[8]

What survivors' families shared was an intensity born of their relative isolation, cut off from extended family networks, and a focus on children. "It was just the four of us and nobody else," survivor Lucine Horn recalled. "None of us had anybody else. There were no grandmothers, aunts, or cousins. We had to be there for each other." Survivors' children were, as one psychologist put it, little "memorial candles," reminders of those who were left behind, and symbols of hope for the future. [9] Parents invested in them a sense of purpose, and a set of fantasies about themselves. But how would they talk about their pasts with their children?

Florence Eisen, a survivor from Poland who settled in New York after the war, recalled that for many years, she "didn't talk." She tried "to have good times" and "to forget," to "block out" the past so that she could go on with her life, and because she "didn't want to inflict pain" on her children. "I suffered so much," she said, "and when the kids were born, they were my whole life. I couldn't put this pain on them." She told her interviewer, "I wanted them to grow up not to know what mother went through." She wanted her children to "be happy," she said, "to grow up as American, normal children;

like all the other American next door children." Evoking language that was becoming pervasive in that "era of the expert," she said, "I didn't want to give [my children] a complex."

The postwar era was a period of an unprecedented psychologization of American life, when experts became psychic healers, assuming a much broader, more important role in directing the behavior, goals, and ideals of so-called "normal" people. A retrospective study of the attitudes and habits of over 4,000 Americans found that the reliance on psychological expertise was one of the most striking developments of the postwar years.[10] More and more people relied upon psychological expertise to make sense of their lives, and experts warned of the perils of "maladjustment" that hampered the potential for healthy and productive citizenship. In the classical psychoanalytic model dominant during the Cold War era, trauma was considered to be a temporary malady, after which one would return to "normal." Survivors could transcend their experiences and "adjust."

Seeking to construct new lives, and desperately searching for normality, survivors were wary of admitting their vulnerability and their psychic injuries to their children, and they feared being shamed and labeled as maladjusted, sick, or crazy. Because their stories of wartime chaos and victimization were anxiety producing, dangerous to tell, and terrifying to listen to, most avoided discussing their traumatic experiences explicitly. While each family had its own unique emotional economy—a set of rules that governed what could and couldn't be said, a dance of telling that changed over time—in speaking with their children, survivors tended to gloss over the most difficult memories. They managed the past, telling episodic fragments whose meaning remained purposely elusive, or transforming their stories into tales of triumph that kept the tragic nature of their experiences at bay.[11]

As most survivors saw it, they were not victims—the "real" victims were dead—but neither were they heroes, except for those few who were able to rise up against their oppressors. They did not embrace the category of "survivor." And yet, during these early postwar years, survival tales began to take shape within families. By describing the mundane aspects of everyday life, or extraordinary wartime moments, which typically entailed cheating death, they tried to reassert control over a story that otherwise seemed chaotic, and frequently beyond belief, distancing themselves from pain and insulating their children from knowing the worst. Nevertheless, deep memories frequently broke through, disrupting their efforts to become normal. Interviews with survivors and their children, along with published memoirs, suggest that while survivors tried to protect their children from knowing very much about their losses, the past remained acutely present just beneath the surface of everyday life, taking on a surreal quality. These interviews, which describe their lives in Cold War America, also speak of survivors' ambivalence toward psychiatrists and official agencies' efforts to label them.

THE DANCE OF TELLING

As her children were growing up, survivor Lisa Derman, whom we met in the last chapter, communicated with them "on their level," she said, constructing a fairy tale of her life. "Daddy and I were born in Europe, a far away place," she told them. She described having lived in a castle, taking vacations, having a loving family, embellishing the reality that she grew up in a shtetl under very modest circumstances. Derman reassured her daughter that she had "more comfort growing up than she had." She told her, "I had a grandma and an aunt, and a maid and a mother and a father that would shower us with everything. Of course I had no television, but I had toys." Little by little, said Derman, her daughter learned about her experiences. Over time, she and her husband filled in more and more of the details. "This is where your grandparents were born, true you have no grandparents. And there were very bad and mean people who didn't like them. Why didn't they like them? Because we were of a different religion, not because they were bad people. These were Germans, Nazis, bad people."

In my own family, the past was mainly discussed in relation to food: my parents shared anecdotes about the *flanken, kasha varnishkes*, and other hearty dishes their mothers had cooked. My mother was the daughter of highly observant Jews from a small town in the Warsaw region who had immigrated to London before the war; my father's family was from Warsaw, more educated and more secular. Their paths would never have crossed had they stayed in Poland, but the war scooped them up and created a strange meeting of distant cultures in America. Food seemed to be one of the few areas in which my parents, who came from vastly different Polish-Jewish backgrounds, bonded. If talk of Europe was all but banished from the kitchen table, food was a safe subject: a reminder of pleasant times and a source of comfort. It was a way for my parents to convey something of their pasts to each other, and to their children, and a normalization strategy designed to distance themselves from the emotions of telling and to protect their children from their suffering.

David Halbert, a descendant, similarly recalled that his father told stories about growing up, about playing in the woods, about making a pair of skis, and being self-sufficient. His stories were of "a very simple planned life, simple pleasures, you know life was really good then." Everything "back then," said Halbert, "just seems to be romanticized and just looked back on fondly." These stories helped his father, he said, "forget about the hardships and the problems he had." But many children were curious about things their parents did not volunteer: stories about why they didn't have grandparents, about what their parents did during the war, why they had strange marks on their arms, why they had accents, and why they seemed so sad at times.

Esther Adler emphasized her French rather than her Jewish background, downplaying her refugee status to avoid exposing her children to troubling information about her past. "I didn't speak about it," she recalled. "They knew I was foreign, yeah I was French," she recalled. But "when our kids were in school, there were several kids in classes that my daughter had, who had French parents, so that wasn't an oddity, that much of an oddity for her and I didn't feel I wanted to burden them." Nor did Irene Hizme, a child survivor, talk about her wartime experiences. But when her own daughter was about six or seven, she asked about the strange tattoo of numbers on her arm, and she was forced to reveal that she had been in a concentration camp. Her daughter never asked her about it again, and Irene never volunteered additional information. "I didn't want to lay this heavy burden. I wanted my kids to have a childhood," she recalled. "I wanted them to have everything that I didn't."

Survivors were often aware of deliberately telling piecemeal stories to children who asked about the past: stories that filled in some of the gaps of their knowledge while withholding a sense of narrative coherence. Barbara Farkas was born in the province of Arad in northern Transylvania, Romania. She went to school until the Hungarian army occupied the area in 1940. After the Germans occupied Hungary in 1944 and discrimination against Jews intensified, Farkas and her family were forced into the Oradea ghetto. She worked in the ghetto hospital until she was deported to Auschwitz. At Auschwitz, she worked in the kitchens to receive extra food, and was eventually deported to another camp, and forced on a death march. Toward the war's end, the Red Cross rescued Barbara, and she returned to Romania after the war, where she worked as a biochemist until she immigrated to the United States.

When her daughter was nine years old, Farkas told her that her "grandparents perished in Europe." She deliberately told this story in a passive way: "they perished there," rather than "they were killed by Nazis." When her daughter asked follow-up questions, she gave vague answers—"not exactly what she wants," she recalls. She was very conscious of bracketing out the past in order to live in the present, offering "no details, no sentiments about the past." Bella Tovey recalls similarly that she told her children that that both "her parents and Daddy's parents are not alive. Why aren't they alive? I said, 'Well, they died in the war.' 'How did they die?' 'Well, they didn't die: they died because of the war,'" she said, intentionally leaving out the details of their deaths.

Thomas Buergenthal, who was born in Czechoslovakia and was sent to Auschwitz with his mother and father, was also conscious of selectively sharing "different little snippets" of his past on particular family occasions, such as when his mother visited. For the most part, however, his children did not seem to be very interested, he said. He and other survivors were at times aware of sharing isolated events, fragments of stories that jumped back and forth between different time frames, lacking a coherent narrative. Sometimes children didn't want to listen because these stories were so disjointed that they were difficult to understand. But they knew not to probe more deeply.

While David Halbert said that his father spoke at length about his wartime experiences, his mother said little about them, or if she did, she spoke in generalities—"about being hungry, or frightened, but never about specific incidents." Halbert describes being afraid of inquiring further for fear that it would be too painful for her. "I found it hard to listen to my mother," he said. "It's not that I wasn't interested. It's that I felt that I had a pretty good idea of, of what the Holocaust was about and what happened through various movies, through various museums. And I just, I just couldn't listen to it from my mother." For Halbert, it was very difficult to see his mother express sadness, so he never asked her about her experiences. It bothered her that he rarely showed any interest. Yet if he had asked her, he imagined, she would not be able to share very much with him. "She would talk to me to a point" and then "start to back off anyway," even though, he says, his mother "wants to talk about it and she thinks it's important." If he had asked her, he thought his mother would have talked more—but he was too afraid to do so.

The fragmented nature of these stories led to considerable inconsistencies in the chronology of narrated events, forcing children to try to piece them together into coherent narratives. Lisa Kramer recalled that her father told stories about the war, but she was rarely able to fully understand them. "There are a lot of them, and I've heard bits and pieces retold by different members of the family who survived, and so it's very muddled," she recalled. "A lot of it was these crazy stories, you're running through the woods and then somebody left a note and it was in a blueberry patch, and you know, these crazy stories about running through the forest, and always some good coincidence happened. You know, somebody was found, or

somebody was saved. Or the opposite. Something went wrong and somebody died. A sibling died, or a cousin died or something. So those are the
ones I remember most."

Barbara Finkelstein, in a short memoir entitled "Return to Poland,"
described how "getting a coherent picture of the war from [her] father
[was] not easy" because he "will tell me about hiding with his father in
1942, jump to a story about a Nazi on a bus after the war, and continue
with an entirely different story about his father." In her father's mind, she
said, "all of the stories have one emotional point of intersection." That is,
they seem to have some coherence. But the absence of "a unifying story
line," as she put it, confused her. When she asked her father to tell her "a
chronologically neat story, a tale with a beginning, middle, and end," she
said, "he could not do it." She sat with him, stopping him, she said, at "every
sentence to demand a transitional phrase or clarification." With her own
lack of historical knowledge, when faced with her father's fragmented narrative, she became "irritated and my father [became] frustrated."[12]

In other families, there was quite a lot of talk about the war, and at
times an endless account of tribulation, sometimes obsessively so. From
a very early age, perhaps when she was as young as three years old, Esther
Dezube's father would tell her stories about Hitler, about children who
were killed during the war. "He would tell me that children's fat was made
into soap, that his nieces and nephews were killed when they were my age,"
she recalled. "The stories were always there."[13] While Esther said her father
told her "morbidly graphic stories," seemingly oblivious to how his stories
were received, her mother kept silent, to protect her daughter, and because
she could not figure out how to tell her story in a way that would not "scare
her," she said.[14]

Children were often conscious of parents' different narrative styles and
capacities. While Sandra Malkin's father "dealt with [the Holocaust] by not
talking about it," she said, her mother "talked about it a lot." She told her
daughter about *Kristallnacht* or other incidents, often crying in her presence. She talked about her father, or her cousin, or her grandmothers.
Malkin said she respected her mother for being able to tell her stories and
cry, for being "very, very vocal about her experiences." It was important,
she said, for her mother "to put it out for people to know about and remember." She saw her mother's storytelling as a therapeutic act, and even as a
political one, which confirmed her sense of her mother as "a very strong
person." She talked so much about the past, said Sandra, that she was "able
to get it all out" and rarely seemed depressed. However chaotic were her
wartime experiences, the narratives she shared with her daughter were
largely meaningful and coherent. While she says that her mother's stories

saddened her, Malkin says she understood that it was important for her to tell them, and to express her sadness.

Other descendants, however, were less sympathetic listeners, and even when parents spoke, they often didn't listen, or they refused to listen in ways that might allow them to fully understand what was conveyed—perhaps because the information wasn't conveyed in meaningful ways, or because it was too overwhelming. Author Lily Brett, in a memoir, recalled hearing her father's stories about Auschwitz in the 1960s. She was about eight. "It was a hot day and I didn't want to drink this orange juice he had bought for me. I thought it tasted funny. He said that when you are thirsty nothing tastes funny. He said, 'In Auschwitz I had to drink *pishy* from another man.'" Years after the fact, she noted the absurdity of her father's comment, its utter lack of intelligibility in the context of the present. "How weird it was that here we both were, [my friend] Rosa Cohen and I, comfortably off, sitting and talking in a very nice house about my father drinking another man's piss in Auschwitz."[15] Not all survivors had memories of engaging in such extreme behaviors, but all had experiences that seemed equally out of place in their postwar families. Living in a warm, comfortable apartment, without fear of persecution, how does one relate to a time in one's life when starvation and cold was all that one knew, when deprivation and fear were relentless, when one was forced to drink another man's urine in order to stay alive? The strange, irreconcilable juxtapositions of past and present, contrasting stories of postwar chaos with the mundanity of everyday life in the United States, became frequent subjects of descendants' visual art, fiction, and memoir.[16] They were too difficult to reconcile with one another in actual fact.

Descendants reported facing difficulties questioning their parents about their past because they didn't know what to ask them, or were afraid to do so. Janet Holland says that she never wanted to hear about her parents' experiences. Her father lost his first wife and children, a fact that she knew growing up, but she never broached the topic because she wanted to protect herself, as much as she wanted to protect her parents. Another daughter of survivors recalled, "Over the years my mother would sometimes make a reference to her parents, brothers or sister and I would never know how to respond. I wasn't sure if she was opening the door for me to ask a question and I was afraid I would say something that would upset her. I always felt that I was walking on egg shells."

They did not want to see their parents as powerless or witness their deeply painful emotions, and they feared re-exposing their parents to these memories. Storytelling, particularly storytelling that is resonant with so much strong emotion, requires a lot of work. It also does a lot of work. By telling a story about a traumatic past, parents engaged in emotion work, eliciting sympathy and also, at times, guilt. Little wonder, then, that descendants reported being averse to hearing these stories, and often avoided them. Viv, a daughter of survivors, writing on an electronic listserv, described her mother's "droning, monotone voice" and how she was subjected to "endlessly sad stories of the deaths and disappearances of her beloved family." As a little one, she said, she "always hoped the story would end differently, and that they would be saved." Still, she said, she never said a word. "I sat by Mom, like a loyal witness."[17] She felt compelled to listen to her mother's stories, even though she was clearly made uncomfortable by them. One wonders whether this is because of the way her mother told those stories: if they lacked coherence, or were told at inopportune times. Perhaps it was simply that Viv and her mother had a highly strained relationship, and that her mother used the stories to elicit guilt, and to wield power over her. This we cannot know, since we do not have access to the actual interaction, but merely to a daughter's recollection of it many years after the fact.

"The charged landscape of the past [my parents] inhabited as well as their endlessly repeated emotion filled me with shame," recalled Lisa Appignanesi in her memoir *Losing the Dead*. "I hated these stories. I couldn't bear them any more." She "longed to bury the past and its traces," she said, and "longed to be as ordinary as all my suburban friends. They had nice, bland, bridge-playing, club-going parents. Parents who could speak English in full, un-accented sentences. Parents who talked of mundane things, and not of concentration camps and ghettos and anti-Semitic laws and the dead and the missing."[18]

A child's receptivity to hearing a parent's story was determined by the story itself and how it was conveyed, but it was also shaped by the broader context of the parent-child relationship, and by the larger emotional economy of the family. Within each family there were often vast variations in the ways parents spoke about the past, and how their stories were received. Survivors often drew distinctions among children, sharing information with those whom they deemed more receptive, and keeping information from those who didn't want to know, saying only as much as they were willing to hear. Anna Kleinhaus shared a great deal with her two youngest children, but not with her older son, whom she described as "a closed person" who was not very communicative, and who was a rebellious kid who had little interest in Jewishness. Siblings in the same family often exhibited different degrees of curiosity, Sylvia Hennig described: "There were five of us at the kitchen table when I was a kid: my parents, my two brothers, and me. Sometimes my mother would begin talking about her experiences and my Dad and one brother would get up and leave the room—they couldn't take it. My baby brother and I would sit rooted there because we had the need to hear what she had the need to say." But other descendants talked about siblings who were just not interested in their parents' past at all, or if they were, they didn't show it.

At times, Thomas Buergenthal admits, his children seemed to lack interest, though he wonders in retrospect whether they "may have been afraid to ask," or didn't want to know for any "number of reasons." Still, he says, "in our family we always talked about these things," suggesting that he and his wife openly discussed difficult subjects with their children. Just as parents often distinguished among children who wanted to know and those who didn't, children were often conscious of differences between their parents: one parent was often more likely to talk than the other; one was more likely to share deep emotions than the other.

"No child wants to see their parents cry," said Stanley Glassberg. Because crying was a sign of vulnerability, and children wanted to see their parents as protectors rather than victims, children and parents did a dance around the stories. Parents told a little, children asked a little, children tried to gauge how much their parents wanted to tell, and asked accordingly. Sometimes a child didn't ask questions because she didn't want to upset her parents, or because she didn't know what questions to ask. If children didn't broach the subject, parents might misinterpret this as lack of interest, or even callousness on their part. When Renee Goldberg traveled to Israel with her children, they visited a Holocaust museum. Her oldest son, who was eight or nine at the time, who previously had little interest in his parents' stories, became, she says, "totally hysterical." Before that moment, she had "absolutely no idea that he had any feelings for this." So it came as a surprise to her that he felt so strongly about his mother's traumatic past. She said that she had not really talked with him much because "he's hard to talk to." Silence had led to mixed signals and missed opportunities for communication. I can recall similar experiences in my own family.

Years ago, I visited Israel with my parents and brother, and my father decided to take us to Beit Lohamei Haghetaot, the Ghetto Fighters Museum, which was established a few years after the end of the war by veterans of the Jewish underground and partisan units, to chronicle Jewish resistance efforts. It was 1980 and I had just graduated from college. I was desperately trying to break away from my parents and at the same time was intensely bonded with them. Visiting the museum offered a rare opportunity to learn more about my father's history in his presence, and yet I refused to enter the building that day. I knew virtually nothing about his immediate family, let alone his large extended family, and here was an opening to a past that my father had closely guarded—yet I refused to take it. So my father visited the museum with my younger brother, who was 13 at the time, while I waited alone in the rental car. When they returned, I learned that in an exhibit my father had seen a photograph of a schoolmate who was a leader of the ghetto uprising, and that he had broken down at the sight of it. I found myself unable to talk with him about it, or to console him.

The next year, when I was home visiting my father, I screwed up the courage to ask him about his parents, and whether so many years after the war, he still thought about them. He told me he rarely thought of them—he had erased them entirely from his mind. Then he paused, and said: "well, from time to time, at different occasions, I see them in my mind being led into the gas chambers"—end of conversation. I began to sob uncontrollably, and my father looked at me quizzically, as though he had no idea that I had even given his wartime losses a second thought, and was unaware that they had affected me at all. As my story suggests, just as survivors tried to protect themselves from the full weight of their stories, so did their children, at times, hold back deep emotions—which often sent mixed signals, at times straining relationships.

"I learned very little from my parents except the barest facts and dates and places, never what it was like or how they felt or feel now. What I learned the most was don't ask, spare the children any suffering and don't tell," said Joe, writing on an electronic discussion list. The dance of telling in which survivors and their children engaged was filled with tension and anxiety: of second-guessing about the other person, imagining his or her feelings and motivations, and often misunderstanding them, of strained relationships and unspoken tensions, of miscommunications and missed opportunities for intimacy. A descendant recounted a typical dialogue with her mother:

> Mother: There are things you'll never know about me.
> Daughter: I can't know them if you won't tell me. Tell me.
> Mother: I never will!
> Daughter: Then how am I supposed to understand everything?
> Mother: You're not. You're not supposed to understand everything.[19]

Israeli psychologist Dan Bar-On, who worked extensively with survivors and their children in the decades following the war, described a "double wall of silence" in which parents closed off the past, and children built their own walls. There were a few windows in both walls, he said, through which information could travel, but communication was highly constrained.[20] While children said that they "always knew" about their parents' wartime experiences, and that it was a part of their very being and their sensibility, few had a clear understanding of the formative wartime events in their parents' lives, or the worlds they had lost. One study suggested that they possessed no more factual knowledge about the Shoah than their American-Jewish peers.[21] "I knew bits and pieces but I could never make a picture out of it," was a common refrain. Children imagined the worst, developing fantasies about their parents and grandparents' experiences, or they blocked out the past, refusing to linger on painful memories. Holocaust stories were too transfixing, too overwhelming.[22] They could unsettle and upset, and incite guilt, shame, and despair—which is why many parents told stories that were designed to minimize their impact upon their children.

Julie Schwartzman recalled that most of the stories her parents told were "stories of survival, positive stories, positive things, positive things that people did." These stories told of hiding, deception, making do with little and doing all that was necessary, of forged identity papers, friendships and relationships of convenience struck with Gentiles, and of fighting for scraps of food within the ghetto walls. They offered heroic narratives whose endings, if not exactly happy in a conventional sense, embodied self-determination and willfulness. Mirroring the restitution stories that some survivors told neighbors and friends, they emphasized survival and overcoming, downplaying the tragic nature of what survivors had endured.

Theo Berg was born in Poland three years after the end of the war to mixed Jewish-Catholic parentage, and immigrated to the United States in the 1950s. His father told him a story that he will never forget, about Jewish retribution after the war, and a tacit agreement that permitted Jews to kill Germans. He and a friend cornered a German man in a dark alley and although the man had an axe, they overpowered him and killed him. Ted's father had the opportunity to fight back, and whenever he talked about the Holocaust, his stories always "featured him winning out against the Germans, against the oppressors."

As descendants recounted, fathers were more likely than mothers to tell stories in which they figured as heroes. After escaping from a slave labor camp, Stanley Glassberg's father joined the Czech army in exile, fighting with the Russian army against the Nazis. As Stanley recalls, his father told many war stories, and in every one of them he was the hero. He was proud of the fact that he was a decorated war hero and "had the opportunity to fight back." Glassberg's mother, on the other hand, was 15 when she was taken to Auschwitz with her family, and was the only one to return. She rarely spoke about her experiences with her children. William Simon's father volunteered for the Russian army on the front lines and then joined the partisans, and told his children tales of fighting the Germans. These stories emerged when the family took a long trip, when his father had a captive audience, or on Yom Kippur or Rosh Hashanah when they came home from synagogue and sat around together.

For most Americans growing up in the shadow of World War II, the war elicited positive associations—triumphant soldiers planting an American flag at Iwo Jima, young people joyously dancing in the street on VE Day. For American Jews, and particularly for survivors, the war conjured up a different set of images: bodies scattered, mangled, and torn, piles of clothing, shoes, and hair. This war, filled with loss and with shame, had little to recommend it. Perhaps knowing this, as a fourth grader, I tried to put a positive gloss on my father's war. I knew that at war's end, after being imprisoned in a Soviet labor camp, he was drafted into the Russian army— a fact that I embellished into an activity of such heroic proportions that my neighborhood friends bristled with envy. "Your father was a decorated soldier in the Russian army? Wow. That's so neat," my fourth grade classmate Michael Glantz registered approvingly. The fact of the matter was that I had no idea what my father was up to during that hazy period. I knew that the Russians were aligned with the United States, and that they fought a common enemy in the Nazis, but I knew little of the circumstances or details of that fight; nor did I know much about the circumstances through which my father came to this country. So I invented a usable, more socially acceptable past for my father, and shared it with others. Descendants told restitution stories, too, as my own experience suggests.

Writing of her parents' stories of survival in war-torn Poland, Lisa Appignanesi recounted that it was only in retrospect that she understood that they were tragic. "The emotion of their telling was something else," she wrote, "a matter-of-factness which lightly cloaked a bristling excitement, the excitement of triumph." The stories her parents told, said Lisa, were stories of heroism, "of Herculean feats or Odyssean wiliness, tales of escape, of happy-enough-endings, of amazing good fortune, sometimes of miracles. No one ever used the word 'survivor,' with its grim underpinnings of guilt and aura of everlasting misery."[23]

As she described, there was often a sense of disconnection between the information conveyed by their parents' storytelling and the affect with which it was told. Sometimes a story of death and destruction was told in a flat monotone, without a hint of sorrow, or the element of mystery and adventure was emphasized, to underplay the element of tragedy. By masking the emotions they felt while telling a story, survivors could distance themselves from the full weight of its significance. But if a story was told with facts devoid of feeling, or with feelings that seemed inappropriate to the content, it made understanding difficult.

By telling survival stories, survivors managed trauma and anxiety. If chaos stories were confusing and uncomfortable, heroic narratives that had happy endings and spoke of resolution were a familiar template of popular culture, and one their children could understand and relate to. Their parents' stories rarely had happy endings, except for the very fact of their survival, which most survivors did not revel in. Collectively, the story of European Jewry during World War II was the story of enormous loss—and defeat. The story of the establishment of the state of Israel, a collective survival story par excellence, was perhaps the sole exception.

Children of survivors frequently mentioned that their parents encouraged them to watch the movie *Exodus*, a 1960 Hollywood film starring Paul Newman, about the smuggling of hundreds of Jewish survivors into Palestine. Many survivors saw the establishment of the Jewish state as redemption for their losses. In the postwar era, commentators often described Israel as "the catastrophe's living memorial," and saw political work for Israel as tantamount to memorial building.[24] As this rhetoric became common across American Jewish communities and was incorporated into sermons, Passover seders, speeches, and Holocaust memorial programs, the militarized Jewish nation-state defined itself in terms of secular Jewish might, against the diaspora and its history of persecution.

Many survivors eagerly embraced this restitution narrative. New Yorkers took their children to the annual "Salute to Israel" parade on Fifth Avenue, waving giddily at schoolchildren marching with blue and white flags. If homes were filled with anxiety, and the past was a foreign country, for many survivors, Israel represented the redeemed future. Survival stories, whether they were stories of individual or collective survival (embodied in the Zionist dream), attempted to hold back "deep" memories of the past in favor of "common" memories designed to restore or establish coherence and closure.[25] They made the past more intelligible for survivors and children, warding off guilt and shame, and transforming tragic tales into progress narratives whose endings, if not altogether happy, at least offered a temporary sense of "closure."

To protect their children from their losses, and to protect themselves as well, survivors danced around their stories, telling them in fragments or emphasizing stories of heroism. But these losses permeated the everyday lives of the families they were creating. Children picked up information about their parents' pasts through untold stories, gestures, and mysterious envelopes. These traces of the past lived on in ways that are often not immediately knowable, shaping children's self-understandings.[26] Descendants often spoke of a palpable anxiety, a vague feeling that "all was not right with the world." Despite survivors' efforts to normalize the past, asserting control over something that seemed chaotic and unfathomable, traumatic pasts often resurfaced unexpectedly, disrupting everyday life.

NIGHTMARES FROM MY FATHER

Harry Alexander, who arrived in the United States after spending three years in a concentration camp in the North African desert, deliberately drove his memories inward, keeping them to himself. He buried himself in his work, keeping himself busy from "eight in the morning until one or two the next morning," until he was so tired he would fall into bed and go to sleep. "I had to be active like that, it was important . . . to make money, to make a living, to provide for my family," he said. Rarely did he even speak about his experiences with his wife. Still, "deep" memories of his past occasionally surfaced, often unpredictably, in everyday life.

"Once in a while," he said, "you think your past is going to come out and you don't let it out because you know that nobody understands it. And nobody wants to know. Once in a while I come out with it. I remember oh, that's good cold water. I remember I would have given ten years of my life for a glass of water like that." When he ate a particularly good sandwich, Harry remembered how when he was in prison in the desert when he and others were given bread they divided the crumbs among 20 men. "Every day a different guy was allowed to pick up what came off the bread as they were cutting it. I remember this, I used to pick up a crumb at a time. Sometimes this memory would slip out and my wife would say to me: Harry, are you picking up the crumbs again?"

Survivors described "triggers" or "flashes" that called up deep memories of the past—eruptions of emotionally charged moments, or fragments of "deep memory" that burst through into the present.[27] As I mentioned earlier, my father told me that he rarely thought about his parents, but every once in a while, an image of them being led into the gas chambers flashed into his mind. Traumatic memories such as these have the quality of deep memory, writes political theorist C. Fred Alford. "It is body based, raw, visual, expressed in images, emotion, and physical sensations."[28] But these messages from the past, memories of a different life, a different world, are typically pushed back, repressed, and silenced, in favor of ordinary or "common" memories, the ones that are less traumatic, the ones that are more easily shared, and over which one has more control. In these memory fragments, as sociologist Arthur Frank describes them, the past is remembered with "arresting lucidity because it is not experienced as past." They are unassimilated fragments of the past that "refuse to become past, haunting the present."[29] During the war, Willliam Loew passed as a Gentile with false papers, until he was sent to Auschwitz, where the rest of his family perished. After being liberated by the United States army, he worked in the American embassy in Germany; he immigrated to the United States in 1949. After the war, he said, "I never talked about my experiences." Still, every so often, he said, "I'll just flash through some event that I recalled," which he relayed to his wife and children. He was very self-conscious about not going very far: "They would be very much interested in that, but I would stop at that point. I just wouldn't elaborate on that." He recalled that there were many unpleasant memories that frequently "triggered me," though I would never relay that to my family." Thomas Buergenthal, who eventually became a prominent human rights lawyer, talked about seeing photographs of "people behind the barbed wire in Bosnia" that reminded him of his own past. "That brings it back, those types of things."

Bella Tovey was a young teenager when the Nazis invaded Sosnowiec, Poland. She was taken to a work camp, and then to a number of different ghettos, before she was sent to Bergen-Belsen concentration camp. Interviewed in 1992, when she was in her mid-sixties, Tovey similarly described her memories of the war as "the events that flashed through my lifetime." She was conscious of conveying story fragments to her children that lacked a coherent narrative frame. "Everything had its own point that they could actually combine it together, so they know it pretty much what I went through and they're curious and rightly so. If they ask questions about a specific event I could tell them, and I will tell them, and I told them, but I don't elaborate on that point. I'm not reluctant but I'm not enthusiastic. So, whatever they ask questions I do it. I'd rather live the present life rather than my past life. There's no glory in that, in the past."

Flashes of memory frequently entered homes as unwelcome guests, punctuating nighttime silences, and many descendants were conscious of hearing parents' screams in the middle of the night. Reversing the typical scene in which a parent responds to a child's nightmare, children sometime responded to parents' night terrors. When Irene Hizme had nightmares, her son sometimes woke her up, asking her if anything was wrong, to which she replied: "Nothing, just a little nightmare." When Erwin Baum's daughter heard him crying in the night she used to run, "Daddy, Daddy, what is it, what is it, what is it?" He woke up in a cold sweat and told her, "I just had this nightmare, this dream, of what was happening to me."

It was also a recurrent trope in second generation memoirs. In one, a boy hears a thump in the night, and goes to investigate and finds his father lying on the floor, his eyebrow bleeding. He had a bad dream about the camp.[30] In my own family, a complex subterranean world would emerge at night, when my father called out in his sleep, imagining being chased by German shepherds. "No, no, no!" he would shout out in his dreams some nights. My mother often woke up annoyed after a sleepless night, and told me matter-of-factly, "your father screamed again, and hit me in his sleep."

As Eva Hoffman writes, "Fragments of wartime experiences kept manifesting themselves with a frightening immediacy in that most private and potent of family languages—the language of the body. In my home, as in so many others, the past broke through in the sounds of nightmares, the idiom of sighs and illness, of tears and the acute aches that were the legacy of the damp attic and the conditions my parents endured in their hiding."[31] As her words suggest, despite survivors' efforts to normalize the past, deep memories often broke out, surfacing unannounced. "I do not know what form my parents' wartime stories took in conversation with their friends," writes Hoffman. "But in our small apartment, it was a chaos of emotion that emerged from their words rather than any coherent narration. Or rather, the emotion, direct and tormented, was enacted through the words, the form of their utterances. The memories—no, not memories but emanations—of wartime experiences kept erupting in flashes of imagery; in abrupt, fragmented phrases; in repetitious, broken refrains."[32]

Sometimes normally silent parents would blurt out something of significance, altering the perceptions of both parents and children. Isaac Rosen tearfully recalls that his father found a book in a library and began to look at it. "My father was looking through the book and I remember him crying, stopping, and then saying over and over again in Yiddish, *mein tatteh*, father, father." His father had seen a picture that startled him. He was in the Polish army when the war began. He never knew what happened to his parents. And then, decades later, he came across a picture of Jews being herded into a gas chamber and saw his father in the picture. "He pointed to him and I just saw a picture of this naked Jewish man marching to a building." That was how he found out what had happened to his father.

Isaac says that this moment was the first time he really felt an emotional connection to his lost relatives. He knew his grandparents had been killed in the war. "But to see my father there in tears, pale, very obviously emotionally shaken by this," was the first time "it started to be personalized, rather than something that was somehow more removed and far away." And it was the first time, Isaac said, that his father talked at length about his experiences. "I think that was one of the first times, probably the first time I could recall, him talking at all about those experiences." The past intruded uninvited, unsettling the sense of trust and continuity that survivors tried desperately to construct, and indicating to them, and to those around them, that the past could not easily be left behind. At times, these voices from the deep spoke of acute suffering and emotional disturbance.

Skeptical about whether psychiatric labels could ever do justice to their experiences, and fearful that they would be seen as "crazy," survivors were generally wary of consulting psychologists.[33] Yet painful memories registered in their bodies and in their minds, refusing to be buried. The past communicated with the present in wordless ways—reminders of a different life, of a life interrupted, that defied attempts to manage and control it, and often entered unannounced, trespassing on the present. One man described a mother who was fearful of showers and only took baths until she was nearly 70. Others described parents or grandparents with severe emotional problems. Jodi Kahn's father had what was then called a "nervous breakdown," and was hospitalized for the first time in 1972, when she was 18. When Andrew Shear's grandfather had a series of nervous breakdowns, eventually committing suicide, his parents told him that his grandfather had suffered a heart attack.

Alan Sadovnik's father spent the postwar years in and out of mental hospitals. suffering from what he also described as a "breakdown." When he was 14, he watched as his father was taken out of his apartment in a straitjacket. Four years later, he found him unconscious after he overdosed on medication. We can not attribute mental illness solely to the effects of Nazi persecution and experiences of grievous loss; individuals who endured similar experiences often reacted to them in different ways. But as Sadovnik suggests, it's impossible to separate his father's illness from his losses because "so much of [his life] was about the Holocaust. [His father] would say: I don't want to live, everyone else died, why am I here? Who are you to be happy?"

During the first decade and a half after the war, most psychiatrists believed that even survivors of concentration camps, if given schooling, work, and a place to live, could integrate and carry on in the grand tradition of other American immigrants, becoming part of the American tapestry.[34] A minority among them, psychologists believed, were profoundly troubled—crazy. Although social service agencies charged with the resettlement of survivors found a great deal of evidence that the newcomers were suffering from a wide variety of psychosomatic ailments, social workers and physicians, including psychiatrists, treated the survivors as they would any other immigrants, focusing upon locating housing and employment, which they saw as key to their reintegration.

They tended little to survivors' numerous somatic complaints, refusing to delve too deeply into the source of their clients' pain. In the classical psychoanalytic model dominant during that period, trauma was considered to be a temporary malady after which one would return to "normal."[35] Dwelling on past problems was considered counterproductive, and self-reliance was seen as the best medicine. There was not yet an understanding of "post-traumatic stress" that would pose ongoing problems for those who had undergone displacement and witnessed death firsthand, and survivors were typically counseled to live as if the past no longer existed. Self-revelation was discouraged.

In the early 1960s, the concept of "trauma," defined in relation to a tragic event and its traces, began to appear in psychiatric accounts of survivors, though the term was rarely evoked outside the insular circles of psychology and psychiatry.[36] Psychiatric journals began to run articles on survivors' ongoing problems, suggesting that trauma might be a permanent injury that could reshape personal identity, and that an individual's pre-war personality may play a lesser role than they had previously assumed. The term "survivor syndrome," coined by American psychoanalyst William Niederland in 1961, a refugee from Nazi Germany, to refer to a mental condition suffered by people who outlived the Nazi persecution, described the long-term effects of having been subjected to persecution.

Niederland suggested that surviving a concentration camp represented "traumatization of such magnitude, severity, and duration" as to produce a "recognizable clinical entity" that differed from other forms of psychopathology. Having clinically observed about 800 survivors of Nazi persecution, he described the syndrome as manifesting in the "persistence of multiple symptoms among which chronic depressive and anxiety reactions, insomnia, nightmares, personality changes, and far-reaching somatization prevail." He suggested that survivors' psychological profile included chronic and severe depressions, coupled with apathy, emotional withdrawal, and disturbances in memory and cognition; feelings of guilt (about their own survival while others died) marked by anxiety, fear, agitation, hallucinations, and sleep disturbances; and syndromes of pain, muscle tension, headaches, psychological disease, and occasional personality changes. But fearing that medicalization of their experiences simplified their experiences and objectified them, defining them by their victimhood, survivors refused to tell illness stories, or to allow others to narrate their experiences through that framework.

My father, typical in this regard, had little interest in consulting psychologists, and never did so, despite his distress, and the fact that he clearly suffered from depression and from frequent, jarring nightmares. I can recall a conversation in which I advised him to see a therapist, to which he responded, "That's for crazy people." He was not alone. Survivors had very low rates of seeking out therapeutic help.[37] Perhaps they took to heart social workers' earlier advice to live as if the past no longer existed, absorbing the dominant understanding of trauma as a temporary aberration. They certainly were fearful of being pathologized—labeled as "crazy"—and tended not to trust experts.

They knew intuitively that psychiatric diagnoses, focusing on individuals, could not grasp the experience of collective trauma, which was not only written in the mind and the body, but also constituted, in sociologist Kai Erikson's words, a "blow to the basic tissues of social life that damages the bonds attaching people together and impairs the prevailing sense of commonality." Collective trauma works its way slowly, insidiously into the awareness of those who suffer from it, so it does not have the quality of suddenness associated with trauma. But it is, Erikson writes, "a form of shock all the same, a gradual realization that the community no longer exists as an effective source of support and that an important part of the self has disappeared."[38]

Over time, more and more survivors came to use the language of psychiatry to seek recognition and compensation, making strategic use of psychiatric categories in order to make themselves intelligible to agencies offering financial restitution. In the mid-1950s, those who had been held in ghettos and camps began to receive some financial compensation for their losses.[39] The Federal Law for the Compensation of the Victims of National Socialist Persecution was established in 1956. Early restitution was restricted to property and did not take into account personal damage to victims of Nazi persecution, and at first mental disorders were seen as insufficient proof of damage. In line with older psychiatric theories, any traumatic experience, no matter how severe, could have only a temporary effect on the individual. All permanent disorders were genetic and therefore were unrelated to their persecution. In order to receive compensation, psychiatric examiners needed to be convinced that there was a firm causal connection between "the traumatic experience and the impaired state of health."[40]

In order to receive these monies, which were at times controversial among survivors, they were required to present medical and psychiatric documentation proving that they were suffering from enduring physical and emotional problems, and many survivors began to undergo psychiatric interviews as part of the application for reparation payments. In these interviews, the physician needed to specify "the mental condition of the claimant before and after his persecution experiences, the nature of these experiences, the present condition of the claimant, expressed in a diagnosis, and the causal connection of the findings with the persecution."[41]

Though money could not possibly compensate for their losses, many sought out compensation for the simple fact that they needed to support their families, or because they thought that Germany should be forced to pay. In the process of applying for compensation, many survivors interacted with the medical and psychiatric establishments in large numbers for the first time, and began to define themselves in their terms.

As restitution agencies became more likely to approve compensation for psychological reasons, my father obtained written statements from doctors who attested to having treated him in Poland for a variety of postwar ailments, physical and mental, including "general weakness, malnutrition, and chronic diarrhea," "anxiety, nervousness, sleeplessness, nightmares, and tendency to depression," along with "dizziness and palpatation [sic] of the heart." When my father was required to medicalize his problems, he did so, falsifying his history in order to fit into narrow conceptions of which victims were worthy of compensation. Survivors were eligible for compensation if they lived under Nazi occupation. But since my father had fled into Soviet territory during the war, and was not considered a victim, he fabricated a story that claimed that he had been in several ghettos and concentration camps in Poland: Krakow between 1941 and 1942, Plaszow from March 1942 to October 1944, Gross Rosen for two months, and Buennelitz from November 1944 to liberation in April 1945. He enlisted someone to write German authorities on his behalf, who testified that "Mr. Stein was wearing a David star [Star of David] in Krakow Ghetto." My father wrote:

I was born on January 3rd, 1920, in Warsaw, Poland. Before the war I was in perfect health. Now I suffer from a duodenal ulcer and chronic gastritis. Furthermore I suffer from an anxiety neurosis and depression. These illnesses are caused through persecution. Before the war I lived in Krakow with my parents. My father was a businessman; I myself studied pharmaceutics at Krakow University. My goal was to become a pharmacist. But the war ended my studies so I was only able to attend the university for one year. In October 1941 my parents and me were deported to the ghetto of Podgurz and then later on in March 1942 to the concentration camp Plaszow. My parents and my sister stayed there and are lost ever since.

The fact that I was separated from my family really upset me and I never recovered from that loss. In Plaszow where I worked in transportation I was once severely battered by one of the KZ guards. He claimed that I worked too slowly and he struck me several times over the head with a wooden club. I was bleeding all over, lost conscience [sic] and was brought to the camp hospital. There a Jewish doctor (Dr. Gross), prisoner himself, treated me. He told me that I had lost consciousness. After being beaten by the guard I very often suffered from headaches. For some time even my memory was diffused. After some days, however, I had to get back to transportation work. Later I worked in the tailoring of the camp, partly in heavy transportation and partly in cleaning. Via Groß-Rosen I then came in the fall of 1944 to the KZ Bruennlitz, which had an ordnance factory. There I also had to do very heavy work. I had to carry caissons and sometimes we were beaten.

After liberation I first went back to Poland. From there I came in November 1946 to Sweden where I stayed till June 1947. From Sweden I went to the United States where, however, I could only stay for a few month as I only had a transit visa. I thus went on to Cuba where I stayed for the next three years. Via Havana I then immigrated to the U.S.A. in April 1951. All the time after liberation I was plagued with anxiety neurosis. This had already started during the time in Bruennlitz. Although it became a little better after liberation it aggravated again later on. It was very bad during my time in Cuba where I needed medical attendance quite often. There I already had stomach trouble but no one diagnosed the ulcer. When I came to the United States in 1951 I went into medical treatment of Dr. Jaffe. He diagnosed the ulcer, gastritis and duodenitis as well as the anxiety neurosis and depression. I also suffer from a nervous heart. My doctor claims that the ulcer is a result of the anxiety neurosis. I often have nightmares from which my wife has to wake me up. I suffer from severe headaches, dizziness and from heavy nervousness. Dr. Jaffe prescribes tranquilizer (Equanil) and further remedies against the duodenitis (Pro Bantine). In addition I have to keep a strict diet. Due to these sufferings my ability to work is severely restricted. I also suffer from loss of memory.

I work in a factory mostly packing goods. I could have a much better job in the office of the magazine but due to the loss of memory it is impossible. Originally I had planned to continue my study of pharmaceutics but was unable to do so due to the fact that I'm almost unable to concentrate. I want to add that I can't remember the name of the physician who treated me in Cuba. In 1954 I married and my daughter Arlene was born in 1959.

In 1969, the checks began to arrive from Germany, which was fortuitous because my father's job as a manager at a small auto parts company, never all that secure, was on precarious footing. Initially, he received about $9,000 for medical expenses in connection with the "recognized illnesses." In the 1970s, partly as a consequence of this shifting definition of war injury, he began to receive a monthly "pension" from the German government, which amounted to approximately $500 per month at the time of his death in 1992. He did not relish getting those monthly checks. Once a month, a strange brown envelope came from Germany, and he quickly opened it, stuffing it into a desk drawer so that I would not see it. Sometimes he would ask my mother quietly, "Did the German letter arrive?" Reparations were a symbolic marker of his victimization, a much-needed source of cash, but they were also, as he saw it, blood money. His relationship to the medicalized categories in which he placed himself in order to receive that compensation was also fraught. He did fit into the clinical definitions, it seemed—he had a tendency to relive rather than recall the traumatic events—but he was not a "survivor" in the "official" sense, never having lived under Nazi occupation, in a ghetto or a concentration camp.

Germany imposed criteria based on geography and nationality that created distinctions among survivors: those living on the "other" side of the Iron Curtain, namely in Soviet-occupied Europe, or those who had changed citizenship, or who had spent less than a year in a concentration camp, received nothing in the early agreements. Survivors successfully lobbied for the extension of benefits to ghetto survivors, slave laborers, and hidden children. But my father, who had spent the war years in the Soviet Union, was not considered a "survivor." He had not suffered as much as those victim groups, it was true, if suffering is defined in terms of physical trauma, although he certainly suffered emotionally, having lost his whole family, his community, and his mooring. Like most members of his generation, he was wary of being pathologized by psychiatrists. And since he was never imprisoned in a concentration camp, he was torn about whether he was in fact a legitimate "survivor." His skepticism was reinforced by survivor organizations, which established unofficial hierarchies of suffering: those who survived Auschwitz, or other identifiable death camps, were placed at the top; those, such as many German Jews, who had fled right before the war, with most of their family members and possessions intact, were relegated to the bottom. In this macabre pecking order, people like Lawrence Stein, who had spent the war years in Russia, were situated above German refugees, but were excluded from the pantheon of "true" victims.

Nonetheless, my father used his status to attain financial restitution, which he considered to be small consolation for his tremendous losses. He enlisted sympathetic doctors to verify the fact that he suffered from health problems that were related to his wartime experiences. For him and for many other survivors, a psychiatric diagnosis was a double-edged sword: it medicalized the tremendous losses they had suffered, simplifying them and individualizing them, but at the same time, it validated their status as victims, and offered them the possibility of financial assistance, which many survivors sorely needed. The process of medicalization also pushed survivors to narrate their wartime histories to others in ways that few had done before, particularly to non-survivors.

So while they were ambivalent about illness narratives, as my father's experience shows, some survivors selectively made use of them in order to gain recognition and recompense. The "illness" label admitted something that survivors and their families had long known but were rarely able to articulate: that the experience of trauma was not easily integrated into a life, and had lasting consequences; normalization was not easily achievable. The process of medicalization helped to constitute the "survivors" as an entity that transcended national origins, acknowledging their ongoing suffering and beginning to conceptualize them as "victims" of Nazi oppression. By showing that the ongoing challenges facing survivors were observable, real, and written on the body, and that they should receive financial compensation on that basis, such labels began to lift the veil of shame, offering official recognition that they had suffered, and continued to suffer, in different ways.

But in a culture geared toward self-reliance, which placed faith in the individual's capacity to overcome hardship, victimhood was not yet an honorable category that one wished to be identified with. During the Cold War years, survivors had little choice but to conform, adjust to their surroundings, dedicate themselves to moving on, and try to minimize the ongoing effects of trauma. It would take their children, who came of age in a different milieu, to make identifying with victimhood more socially acceptable.

CHAPTER 3

The Children Wish to Remember
What the Parents Wish to Forget

The son wishes to remember what the father wishes to forget.
Yiddish proverb

As children of survivors moved into young adulthood in the 1970s, some of them fused feminism, ethnic politics, and humanistic psychology to develop a collective identity as the "second generation." Their quest to separate from their parents made them, paradoxically, more likely to listen to their stories, and more likely to coax their parents to share their stories with them. Armed with a new, more affirmative understanding of the status of victimhood, descendants urged their peers to "break the silence" about their familial legacies and to make storytelling a vehicle for self-transformation, collective identification, and social action.

By some accounts, this movement began in 1975, when five children of survivors, three women and two men, all in their twenties, sat around a table talking about their lives. They were graduate students and social workers, highly educated, and had been involved with feminism or the Jewish counterculture.[1] Some of them were born in Europe during the war, or in displaced persons camps immediately afterward. They published their conversation in *Response*, a small-circulation Jewish magazine.

"Thirty years after World War II, the memory of the Holocaust lingers with us," they declared. "For most survivors, it has a daily effect. It also influences the thinking of the children of Holocaust survivors." They assembled as a group, they said, "to discuss this part of our heritage." They wished to "examine the extent to which our 'Weltanschauung' is determined by the

World War II experiences of our parents and families," admitting, "much of this is guesswork." What they did find out is that "perspectives we thought were unique were in fact common to the whole group. More significantly, in our minds these perspectives were a result of the direct role the Holocaust played in our childhoods."[2] For families of Holocaust survivors living in the United States decades after the end of World War II, the war was far from over. As these children of survivors suggested, their parents' wartime experiences continued to exert a formative influence upon their lives. It was the first time the "second generation" declared its existence in print.

As the 1975 *Response* conversation suggested, World War II was often a taboo subject in the homes of children of survivors: their parents tended not to talk about it, and their children rarely if ever asked—they didn't want to cause them more pain. "When I was born," said Dina Rosenfeld, "my parents decided never to mention the Holocaust...They were going to forget all the pain, the past, and start anew, have faith again, I guess."[3] The participants in that early gathering spoke about their surprise when they realized that some children had grandparents, about the difficulty of having faith after the Holocaust, about their attitudes toward Zionism—some were fervent supporters of Israel and others less so—and about their ambivalence about the term "Holocaust" itself—the ways it seemed to transform the genocide into a definable, understandable "thing," when it did not seem understandable at all.

They discussed their involvements in campus politics, whether they felt responsible for making the world a better place, and the ways they were shaped by the student movements of the 1960s, even as they tended to stand apart from them. "I have always been extremely uncomfortable in the whole political arena because of the huge mob, say in front of Low Library at Columbia in '69," said Anita Norich. "That always scared the hell out of me. When people would chant, 'Stop the war now!' I was never able to respond."[4] Others agreed: they had a constitutional allergy to political rallies, which they likened to unruly, potentially fascist, mobs.

Finally, descendants discussed their relationships with their parents, expressing a great deal of love (when their discussion was reprinted in a book it was dedicated: "To Our Parents—who did so much more than survive") and resentment, too, for their expectation that they could or would redeem their losses. Foreshadowing what would become the movement's trademark blend of psychological introspection and identity politics, they spoke of the tension that children of survivors felt between fulfilling their own needs and meeting their parents' expectations, which they understood as a clash between American individualistic ideals and more traditional conceptions of familial obligation. "Reconciling the tension between being independent and finding fulfillment and meeting parents' expectations is something I haven't been able to do," Norich said. "Trying to make certain breaks while maintaining ties to home has been an impossible thing to achieve." But the reverse is also impossible, she declared: "I still can't figure out how we reconcile being children of survivors, and yet adults and professionals in America."[5]

As this early articulation of what would become known as the Holocaust "second generation" suggested, children of survivors were caught between two worlds: the world of their parents, which demanded loyalty and placed expectations on their children to redeem their losses, and a dominant individualism, accentuated by the generational rebellion of the time, in which baby boomers made a politics of asserting their autonomy and breaking away from their parents. Their survivor parents failed to understand the contradiction of urging their children to remain tied to them, yet also expecting them to be successful and ambitious. In addition to feeling misunderstood by their parents, they also felt misunderstood and unrecognized by their peers. Their friends often interpreted their loyalty to their parents as a failure to assert independence; most non-survivor Jews had little understanding of the war's impact upon their families, they felt. Many of these dynamics were common to other children of immigrants; what made the experiences of descendants different was the connection to trauma.

Meyer Goldstein suggested that being a survivor's son had "made [him] very private in certain Jewish activities, and in terms of political demonstrations and other events." Somehow, he said, "I see it as having made me closed-up about certain aspects of my Jewishness."[6] The only ones who seemed to fully understand them, he and others believed, were other children of survivors. "I think we instinctively know who we are; I can go into a room and immediately know who's one of us," said Goldstein.

Lucy Steinitz agreed: "I have a sense based on our discussion tonight that there's a separate sub-community of Jews, and we're all a part of it."[7] As she noted, as time created more distance from the terrible events, the more parents talked, and the more curious they, their children, were becoming. "The silence of many of our parents has instilled a public sense of taboo about discussing the Holocaust from which we are only now beginning to emerge," she declared. "We have only recently gained the emotional distance necessary to cope with many of the major influences the Holocaust has imprinted on our lives."[8]

Two years later, journalist Helen Epstein wrote about growing up as a child of survivors, of feeling marginal, harboring secrets, and having no one to discuss them with. Epstein had grown up in New York, the child of survivors from Prague. Her mother had been in Bergen-Belsen; her father, once an Olympic swimmer, worked a dress cutter in New York's garment district. While in Israel after the Six Day War, in 1967, she met an international group of Jews born after the war with whom she felt a much greater affinity than the Jews she had grown up with. We were "all possessed by histories [our] parents had lived," she recalled.[9] "My parents could not help me with this; they were part of it. Psychiatrists I distrusted," and clinical labels simply "disguised" her experience, she wrote. "There had to be," she wrote, "an invisible, silent family scattered around the world, who shared her experiences."[10] Her book, *Children of the Holocaust*, which interspersed her own story with the stories of other children of survivors, quickly became the bible of the second generation movement.

By telling personal stories about their lives and naming itself as the "second generation," these descendants helped to transform their personal experiences into a collective identity, much as other groups in the 1960s and 1970s had done before them. Epstein wanted "to give life and form to parts of [our] experience that weren't yet reflected in the culture."[11] As she wrote: "We watched group after group—blacks, women, homosexuals, ethnics, single parents, students, even block associations, organize, brainstorm and air vital issues. Some of us joined other groups, but we did not form our own."[12] Children of survivors comprised a "quiet, invisible community, a peer group without a sign."[13] Shortly after these words were written, nearly 2,000 children of survivors flocked to a conference in New York to share their experiences.

Like other postwar youth subcultures, children of survivors worked to "win cultural space" from the dominant culture, and the culture of their parents.[14] At Jewish summer camps in the northeast in 1969, the year of Woodstock, hippie culture encouraged middle-class suburban kids to don Native American beads and burn incense. One woman recalled that although most of her 12-year-old bunkmates were, like her, daughters of Holocaust survivors, "you couldn't tell." They wore tight, ripped jeans, smoked cigarettes and pot. The motto of the 1960s—don't trust anyone over 30—shaped their understanding of who they were, and the generational split was everywhere evident.[15] But as the writer Melvin Bukiet, a descendant of survivors, suggested, a full-blown generational revolt was impossible for members of this cohort. "You were born in the 50s so you smoked dope and screwed around like everyone else," he recalled. "But your rebellion was pretty halfhearted, because how could you rebel against these people who endured such loss? Compared to them, what did you have to complain about?"[16]

Recognizing the ambivalent position they were in, the "second generation" movement offered children of survivors the possibility of remaining linked to their families of origin, but in a fashion that would permit them to assert greater individual autonomy and agency. It fostered a "relational individualism" that situated them in relation to their parents—though without being merged with them.[17] It did so by naming itself as a group, beginning a conversation about what it held in common, and learning, with the help of professional therapists, to be translators, coaxers, and audiences for their parents' stories.

It would be a mistake to paint the second generation as monolithic, for like their parents, the descendants came from a variety of backgrounds and beliefs, including Zionism, socialism, socialist-Zionism, religious orthodoxy, secularism, and others, and were influenced by currents of the time: the civil rights movement, Jewish counterculture, ethnic separatism, feminism, and by therapeutic ideas.[18] Moreover, its members were not necessarily representative of the second generation cohort as a whole. Yet they came to speak on behalf of other descendants, often simply because they were more willing to be identified publicly, and because they saw the act of speaking openly about their experiences as a form of self-help that would pierce what they perceived as cultural silence around the Holocaust.

This chapter draws upon a diverse array of sources—including my own experiences in second generation groups (both face to face and virtual) and interviews with leaders of the second generation movement—to show how many descendants took strains of thought and action coursing through American culture at the time and used them to create new scripts for talking about their parents' traumatic histories. (To differentiate among these sources, and to protect the privacy of some respondents, I refer to interviewees and memoirists by both their first and second names, and to participants in second generation groups by their first names only).

NACHAS MACHINES NO MORE

As the 1975 conversation published in *Response* suggested, many descendants encountered difficulties managing the psychological boundaries that separated them from their parents. Their parents, for their part, were overprotective, expecting their children to redeem their losses and become, as Dina Rosenfeld had put it, "*nachas* machines," invoking the Yiddish word for the pride one gains from one's children or grandchildren—reflected glory. They complained that their parents were unable to see them as separate individuals, and often lived through them. Their children would have the "normal" lives they had been denied. The children wished to separate, but they felt protective of their parents, and guilty if they asserted their own needs, which led to resentment. And indeed, this became a primary theme of the support groups, as children of survivors came to ask: Who are we in relation to our parents? What do we owe them? Who are we to whine when our parents suffered so much? How can we separate from them, and lead our own lives, without hurting them?

Psychoanalysts suggest that in the ideal developmental scenario, early attachments resolve themselves through a gradual distancing from the parents and a more considered balance between criticism and sympathy, attachment and autonomy. But for many members of the second generation, the urge to protect their parents clashed head-on with the need to protect themselves, and conflicts often became acute. Children of survivors often felt overwhelmed by the weight of their responsibility, subjugating their own needs to their parents. Others, in an attempt to avoid excessive empathy, chose anger or cold detachment. "I suspect," writes Eva Hoffman, "that, in our progress to adulthood, most children of survivors were caught on their private see-saws, oscillating between the demands of autonomy and attachment, self-sacrifice and self-interest."[19] This was certainly the case in my own family, where I was on a very short tether. My parents enforced strict curfews, waited up for me at night, and offered clear restrictions on whom I was and wasn't allowed to associate with. Since there was little possibility of negotiation, when I was in my early twenties I fled 3,000 miles to California.

By the 1970s, the oldest children of survivors were reaching their thirties, and the vast majority, in their twenties, were moving into adulthood and forging personal identities in the wake of an ethnic revival that made a preoccupation with roots central, and a women's liberation movement that challenged norms of gender. The "second generation," which was highly influenced by these two social movements and, somewhat later, by the growth of therapeutic culture, came to believe that it was important to "break the silence" surrounding their parents' losses and, by extension, their own. Eva Fogelman and Bella Savran, psychotherapists and daughters of survivors, were convinced that there was a need to address the psychological health of the children of survivors. They came of age and received professional training at a time when psychology was becoming more sanguine about the possibility of individual change, and promoting a much more populist vision of the benefits that could accrue to those who were open to psychological insight. Humanistic psychology, founded by Carl Rogers and Abraham Maslow in the 1940s, offered an optimistic version of existentialism that saw personhood as a process of ongoing renewal, and psychology as offering individuals insight with which to grow and realize their full human potential—Maslow's "self-actualized" individuals. In the 1960s, humanistic psychology provided an alternative to conventional psychotherapy, melding the countercultural belief in the importance of achieving a "new consciousness" with a focus on individual change.[20] Fogelman and Savran were also influenced by feminist ideas coursing through the culture at that time.

At the time, many feminists believed in the potential inherent in human selves to change. They established consciousness-raising (CR) groups, encouraging introspection, emotional self-exposure, and the sharing of personal, experiential testimony. Fusing psychotherapy and politics, and viewing personal insight and public storytelling as vehicles for social transformation, these groups made the personal political.[21] Consciousness-raising considered personal experience and insight the purest form of truth; experience was seen as the origin of knowledge and the solution to social problems. By making experience visible—such as women's silent complicity in male violence—they believed that social movements effected change.

Informed by their psychological training and by the feminist self-help ethos, Fogelman and Savran came to believe that children of survivors could be guided to help themselves. But most Holocaust survivors refused to talk. Even many of their children who sought out psychotherapy often avoided speaking about their parents' experiences to their therapists, and if they did speak about them, they were often advised to break away from their parents—something that few could or would do. And yet most children of survivors had little capacity to prod their parents to share much about their wartime experiences, which operated as the proverbial elephant in the room in many survivor families, often with detrimental effects.[22]

Instead of encouraging them to make use of individual therapy with non-survivor therapists positioned as experts but who shared little of their experiences, they decided to organize support groups for children of survivors, and placed a notice in a Boston alternative weekly inviting children of Holocaust survivors to participate. Within a year, nearly 100 individuals in the Boston area alone responded. They formed short-term groups of eight sessions in which children of survivors talked about being different, about what it meant to be Jewish, and what it was like to grow up in survivor families.

Since their relationships with their parents were often highly fraught, or because they did not know what questions to ask them, many descendants began doing research on their own. Before the mid-1970s, descendants say they really had to dig in order to find information about the larger context of their parents' wartime experiences. They did not learn about it in school. They did not encounter it on television, or in movies. Stanley Glassberg grew up in Philadelphia surrounded by Holocaust survivors and "thought that every Jewish person was a Holocaust survivor." It wasn't until he was a teenager, he said, that he "realized that most people had no relationship to the Holocaust." His mother had numbers on her arm, as did some of his parent's friends. It took him a while, he said, to understand that "most Americans didn't really understand what had happened, and weren't all that aware of what the Holocaust was."

Although his father had shared stories of wartime heroism, often those stories were fragmented and difficult for Stanley to understand. He felt that he wanted to know more; he needed to make order out of what seemed like a series of haphazard events lacking a narrative. He went to the local library when he was in high school and began to do his own research, spending days in the library, hours and hours on end, searching microfilmed articles in newspapers about the genocide, assembling a book of clippings about the Holocaust, and constructing his own personal archive. He read every-thing he could get his hands on about Jews in Europe from 1933 to 1945, poring over newspapers, magazines, and periodical indexes. He had a vora-cious desire to know everything. Through this process, he said, his parents' past "became a story, it became a film, it became an experience that you're actually experiencing, that you know that the horror is going to happen. And you're reading it, and it's like reading a story. It's like seeing a film that you really love even though you knew the outcome, you're engrossed in it."

When Stanley became involved in a second generation (2G) group, he was finally able to ask his father more pointedly about his experiences. By doing his own research, he filled in the missing parts of these stories, con-textualizing them in a larger history of the genocide. These support groups facilitated collective memory work, and allowed descendants to share each other's stories. As Eva Fogelman recalled, descendants "would share all kinds of examples of how their parents were affected by the Holocaust to see whether it was the same in other households, and felt relieved that their household was not as crazy as they might have thought it was when they heard others' stories."[23] The taboo nature of the stories, she suggested, was linked to a sense of shame and descendants' fears that their families were crazy.

Parents weren't the only ones who required a great deal of coaxing to share their stories; children often needed coaxing, too, to break the ice and initiate such conversations with their parents. In the early groups, said Fogelman, "we had an initial interview where we would ask [children of survivors] a lot of questions so that by the time they got to the group they would already realize what gaps they had in terms of knowing what happened to their parents." Where were they during the war? What did they witness? Were they in camps, or in hiding? Between the first and second meetings, they were assigned to communicate with their parents, either in person or over the phone, in order to get more information about what had happened to them. After they had done that, "they reported back about the dialogue they had with their parents, what it was like to talk with their parents."[24]

By the mid-1970s, 2G groups were formed in New York and other cities as well.[25] At the time, the first courses on the Holocaust, inspired by feminism, ethnic studies, and a growing emphasis placed on speaking one's oppression, were beginning to appear on college campuses. Author Terrence Des Pres, writing in the *New York Times*, observed that his own classes on Holocaust literature at a small upstate New York college were filling up like never before, mirroring a national trend. "For Jewish students there comes a renewal of heritage and pride, and the gap between themselves and their relatives closes as their sense of family deepens." By learning about the Holocaust, Des Pres suggested, American Jews with little interest in their ancestors could reconnect with them, and survivors could be enlisted to connect them to the world of their ancestors. It had become a central aspect of American Jewish "civil religion," emphasizing the unity of the Jewish people, mutual responsibility among Jews, and the "imperative of Jewish survival in a threatening world."[26] But the movement that led to greater interest in the Holocaust, Des Pres suggested, was not limited to Jews. "A generation of young adults has arrived, Jewish and non-Jewish alike who are now prepared to face the worst."[27] Holocaust themes also began to figure in an increasing number of television programs and films.[28]

Small, therapeutically oriented 2G support groups spread quickly throughout the country, sign of a shifting generational consciousness. Most survivors saw therapy as a mark of mental abnormality and as the prelude to psychiatric hospitalization. At best, they saw psychological introspection as a luxury they could not afford. Their children were more favorably disposed to the psychological profession, which by the 1970s was in rapid flux. Humanistic psychology was calling into question the medical model of psychology and was encouraging many more people to consult psychologists in order to cope with a "normal" dose of emotional anguish.[29] Psychological consciousness was becoming seen as desirable, rather than something to be feared. As Malka, a descendant, suggested, "Our parents' generation survived by forgetting. Denial was a survival mechanism." In contrast, she said, "the second generation 'survives' by remembering."

"Our parents grew up in a generation and a culture where you didn't talk about 'unpleasant' things, you swept them under the carpet, you put on a brave face," said Malka. Emotions were something negative that you tried not to reveal. 'Don't be so emotional!'" In contrast, she suggested, children of survivors had come of age when "looking on the bright side" was no longer mandatory. Self-expression, even expression of negative emotions, was viewed positively. "I think we, their children, have had a lot of unlearning to do, and to accept that our feelings, good and bad, are valid and don't need to be suppressed or denied. And we're together on the same journey!"

Therapeutic discourse offered descendants, as well as other Americans, a way of managing various disruptions of biography, such as divorce, bereavement, and unemployment, and paved the way for an acknowledgment of the powerful impact of trauma.[30] By talking about their experiences, victims of trauma could work through the past and transform themselves into "survivors" possessing agency. Informed by emerging therapeutic ideas of self-actualization, the patient was revisioned as an active agent, in charge of his or her mental health, who was capable of recovery.[31] Rather than imagining that the doctor held the key to his or her cure, this emergent paradigm saw the sufferer as an active master of his or her fate. It appealed to an American individualist ethos that valued self-reliance and self-improvement. And it saw speaking as central to the process of recovery, self-examination as freeing, and urged individuals to make their private emotions public.[32]

COMING OUT

As a teenager and twenty-something young adult, I thought little of my family legacy of loss, and indeed of my Jewishness, which was indelibly associated with it. At some point I think I made a semi-conscious decision to place that part of myself, and a family history that seemed impossible to understand, let alone integrate into daily life, in a box while I went on the business of growing up. I did the things that "normal" female American teenagers and young adults, at least members of the aspiring middle class, are supposed to do: I concentrated on my studies, dated boys, and tried to figure out what I wanted to do with my life. Since the Holocaust legacy was a painful diversion that would not help me get on with the business of living, I set it aside.

Yet I couldn't completely separate myself from it. It haunted me, and saddened me, and entered my world at inopportune moments: as I brushed my teeth, embraced friends, rode on trains. I fantasized about waking up to learn that the terrible knowledge was simply a bad dream. I imagined sacrificing myself in order to undo that history, but I could not, and as I lived my life, it gnawed at me. I could not escape it, and I felt disloyal for even trying. I was reminded of it every time I looked at my father's face, or spoke with him on the phone. And yet there was so little space for discussing it in the "outside" world. Holocaust stories at that point were primarily personal and private, if they were told at all. Most of the time, I carried it around like a painful little secret—along with my same-sex desires. But it weighed on me.

In my mid-twenties, I decided to join a support group for children of survivors in the San Francisco Bay Area, where I was enrolled in a doctoral program. Although I was not Jewishly affiliated, I sought out the group, which was sponsored by a local Jewish organization. I knew that it was time to finally deal with this aspect of my life; I could no longer run away from it. But I was petrified, and uncertain what I would find. When I arrived at the Jewish center in town, I was ushered into a small room filled with folding chairs. There were about eight of us, ranging in age from 20 to 40, a majority of whom were women. We began by talking about where our parents came from, and what brought us to the group. I spoke haltingly, never before having talked about my family in public, never sharing my parents' stories even with my closest friends. They never asked; there was never really a place for it.

We went around the room, and one man revealed: "Both my parents are from Poland. My mother, after spending time in numerous camps was liberated at the age of 11 from Auschwitz. My grandmother survived, as did two aunts who had been placed with a Polish family." He went on: "My father's family was forced from their town in 1940 by the Germans in to the Soviet Union. They were together until the war ended. In 1946 my grandparents were killed by Poles, along with 11 others trying to cross the border in Czechoslovakia."[33] Many of us knew next to nothing about our parents' wartime pasts, which had often been off limits for discussion, and simply offered the names of the countries where they were born.

I shared the following: "My father was from Warsaw and spent the war years in Russia, in hiding, and in a Soviet labor camp. He returned to Poland after the war, and learned that his entire family had been killed. I don't know how or where. My mother was born in Poland but grew up in England. She was not a 'survivor' per se, though most of her extended family was killed as well." The experience of speaking those words was both powerful and jarring.

Through these introductions, which often began with our parents' experiences and moved toward the present, we were guided in locating ourselves within our family history. We talked about our feelings of guilt, anger, and rage toward our parents—which was what typically brought people to the group. For several of the men, it seemed that meeting suitable members of the opposite sex, women who could truly understand where they came from, was high on their agenda. There were vast differences among us. Some of us grew up with parents who talked incessantly of their wartime experiences and murdered relatives. Others were mainly silent. Some grew up in religious households, where one's commitment to Jewish identity was considered a pox on Hitler's plan. For others, the war created a breach with God. One woman in my group, whom I befriended for a while, discovered she was Jewish when she was nearly thirty, and carried the scars of a youth strangely out of kilter, which included an obsessive relationship with food. Another man described an abusive father who took his unhappiness out on his son by regularly hitting him with a shiny leather belt.

We were misfits, tortured souls, and often overachievers. But what held us together as a group? If a generation is defined by historical experience and attitudes or beliefs that follow from it, then the "second generation" is surely a very tenuous instance of it.[34] We often felt misunderstood by our parents as well as our peers, and seemed to share feelings of ambivalence toward our injured, typically overprotective parents. Even those of us who seemed successful on the surface had difficulty separating from our parents and claiming our own lives. Clearly, we were sufficiently conflicted by all these issues that we wanted to figure out who we were in relation to them.

During an early session of our group, I recall that one man described how each day, when he left home, he had to call his parents to tell them he had arrived safely. He signaled them by telephoning them, ringing twice. While his parents never picked up the phone, if he did this they were reassured that he was all right. Someone else chimed in immediately, and said, "me, too." And then another and another said the same. Another said that his family's signal was three rings: "One ring was always a risk. Or at least that's what my mom concluded. It might not have been heard, and then she would have been in limbo." It was a humorous give-and-take that mocked the free-floating anxiety that circulated within many survivor families, making parents cautious, fearful, and over-protective of their children. Mothers, in particular, seemed visibly worried at the drop of the hat, believing that their loved ones will suddenly disappear, snatched by some shadowy stranger. It all seemed very familiar to me; my mother did the same. It seemed normal growing up—until I went out into the world and found out that not all families were like that.

Meanwhile, on the other side of the country, in Philadelphia, Pam Neuborne attended a similar group. Pam's Polish-born mother survived Auschwitz and the death march at the war's end, and was liberated by Russian troops, losing her entire family except for one brother in the Holocaust. Pam's father was from a small town in Czechoslovakia, and grew up in a highly religious family. When Germany declared war, he fled to Russia and went into hiding; he was captured and spent the war in different labor camps. Her parents met in a displaced persons camp in Germany after the war. When her mother learned that she had an uncle in Philadelphia, he arranged for them to come to the United States. They were in their twenties when they arrived.

As a child, Pam remembers feeling "different," aware of not having grandparents when other children did, and of her father's intense anger and emotional outbursts, and her mother's sadness. Her father was mostly silent; her mother told her stories at various points about what she had endured during the war, leaving out the most traumatic episodes, and these stories were always accompanied by tears. Her parents socialized little with others. Pam speaks of having "low self-esteem," of always "feeling like an outsider," and being a "worrier." She says she did not consciously connect her familial dynamics—her father's criticisms, her mother's sadness, the silences and mystery surrounding her parents' pasts—with her family's Holocaust legacy until she was in her late thirties.

Then, Pam says, "I got in touch with...the beginnings of...what it might have been like for my parents. Up to that point, I don't think I wanted to think about it. I don't think it was real. I think going to Dachau actually made it real. And....when I came back, within a few months, I had fully identified myself with the children of survivors." She bought a copy of Helen Epstein's *Children of the Holocaust*, the first popular treatment of the lives of the "second generation," read it, and joined a support group for children of survivors that became, as she describes it, a surrogate family. This newly formed consciousness that she was a "child of survivors" was made possible by the emerging "second generation" movement that constructed new narratives of identification, through books and support groups. And then she attended a second generation group for the first time.

"Within five minutes, we were all incredibly comfortable sharing our deep-most thoughts with one another," she recalls. In the group, she said, "we [knew] that we would be really listened to and understood, because the feelings were shared by many of us. I would say that there was very, very little I didn't relate to that was shared that night. These are not friends. These are family of mine. And I think that's another thing that held us together too. We had no other family, and so this was an extended family for all of us. Absolutely it was." That shock of recognition is often how children of survivors describe their first encounters with other descendants. Finally, they say, *I found others like me. They understand.*

I did not share this experience of having had a *frisson* of recognition. I found as many reasons to feel alienated from the 2G group I joined in Berkeley as I did to feel a part of it. Even though I found the act of sharing my family story to be very powerful, identifying as a descendant was never high on my list. I was a young radical for whom class, gender, and (eventually) sexual solidarities had greater immediacy. I saw my identification with other descendants simply as a means to an end: to better understand my family legacy, and to integrate it into my life. And yet the experience reminded me of another support group I had attended just a couple of years earlier: a coming-out group.

When a group of lesbian strangers comes together, often they tell each other their coming-out stories—elaborate, often painstaking accounts of when they were first aware of their same-sex attractions, their first sexual experiences, when they first named themselves lesbians, and told others. Coming out is imagined as an experience of coming to see the light, or of traveling to a place of understanding, where the fog lifts and you realize that you are not the only one, that there is a name and an identity and a culture you can use to anchor your experiences. Stories are the currency of subculture: they help to bind its members together, and transform feelings of alienation into solidarity.

Second generation groups shared with lesbian/gay coming-out groups the belief that speech is preferable to silence, that disclosure can combat stigma, and that healing is possible. If before the gay liberation movement, gay and lesbian stories were private and personal, the coming out story emerged as a master narrative with which individuals construct a sense of individual and collective identity, demanding recognition by others.[35] Much as gays and lesbians could throw off their secret desires and come out, children of survivors could name their difference—the familial legacy of trauma and loss and come out as well. Mirroring the script fashioned by gays and lesbians, coming out as a child of survivors was a process that followed, more or less, a trajectory leading from shame and silence, to speech and an identification as a child of survivors, and the willingness to disclose that fact to others. It was also very similar to the script used by another therapeutically oriented social movement that emerged out of feminism: the movement against child sexual abuse.

A 1984 documentary about the second generation was called *Breaking the Silence*. In the film, Eva Fogelman speaks of her experience as a feminist, and how she came to believe that she needed to make a contribution in her own community by bringing to light the struggles of children of survivors. The film features the stories of half a dozen individuals, interviewed when they were in their twenties and thirties, and their parents, and includes a variety of expert psychotherapists. It begins with a discussion of survivors' descendants' recollections of their childhood, and the unspoken ways their parents transmitted their legacy of trauma to their children. One man speaks about how he always felt that he had to compensate his parents for what had happened to them. A woman describes her father's audible nightmares and their impact on her. Others describe parents who are unhappy people, and the ways they internalized their parents' fears and feelings of anger. A few tell of having rejected their parents and their Jewish backgrounds. They describe their inability to trust others, their feelings of alienation and loneliness, about the corrosive effect of secrets, and the struggle to open lines of communication with their parents, who are often resistant.

Because children of survivors are frequently misunderstood, they must form groups to forge an understanding of who they are, the film suggests. "Auschwitz, Dachau: I had never before heard my peers speak these words," one son of survivors recalls. But being around other 2Gs, he says, helps him understand that he is not alone. It opens up the possibility that he might be able to reveal his secrets. "I felt that I was living in a little concentration camp of the mind," one woman reveals. She wants to know about her mother's wartime experiences and tells her parents: "I need you to respect my search. If we don't know, what happens to the memory?" Her mother tells the camera: "I can't do it. I can't speak." In the film, psychiatrist Robert Lifton, who organized the first "rap groups" for Vietnam Veterans, describes the Holocaust second generation as a social movement that is "insisting on feeling, upon being true to their own history, confronting their own history." Indeed, the film was designed to further that movement, and to encourage other children of survivors to band together and begin to talk to their parents about the past. It was also designed to be shown to survivors, to get them to talk to their children. "When we break down the walls of silence," it declares, "we discover new strengths in ourselves and our families."[36]

Another documentary film—called *Breaking Silence*—appeared a few years after this film, and had a similar structure—though it dealt with the theme of child sexual abuse. The film tells the story of a woman who was repeatedly molested by her father, and the story of a man who was molested by an older boy, a close family friend. These incidents create a web of silent pain. The film reveals the private sphere to be a realm of secrets, lies, and violence, showing how incest destroys trust and diminishes the lives of its victims many years after the fact. Utilizing interviews with expert psychologists and sociologists, the film introduces the possibility that memories of past abuse may be repressed, creating pathologies such as sexual impairment and overeating. It celebrates survivors who find the courage to "break silence" and take back their lives, arguing, "You don't have to be a victim. You can break the power of the past by telling others." As one adult male victim tells the audience: "It's important to share these things, so people know that these things do happen."[37]

Both films call upon individuals who are confronted with a traumatic event that is, in the clinical definition, "outside the range of usual human experience," to master that trauma by speaking about it with others. They grapple with the legacy of family memories and how they are passed down generationally, depicting a struggle between parents and children, in which parents exert enormous power over their children. Both see the silencing of difficult family secrets as highly problematic, and urge individuals to throw off those secrets, and to assert clearer generational boundaries. And both films value the expression of emotions and see them as part of the recovery process, urging individuals to "get in touch with feelings" of shame and anger and express them openly.

In the sexual abuse movement, the process of breaking the silence is facilitated by a script, in which the suffering individual is guided in coming to terms with a difficult past, and becomes a witness on his or her own behalf. [38] Ellen Bass and Laura Davis's best-selling guide, *The Courage to Heal: A Guide for Women Survivors of Child Sexual Abuse*, took readers through a number of stages, codifying and circulating a "transformative traumatic memory script" designed to guide the individual through the process of recovery. First came the recognition that the past is a personal as well as a political problem; second is the injunction to overcome silence; and third comes the call for testimony—a public sharing of autobiographical information—as a means of transforming silence into speech. Through this script, individuals with disparate experiences could understand and narrate their experiences to others, overcoming their most injurious effects. It suggests that even those who had endured unimaginable horror could "heal" themselves through acts of storytelling.[39] Sociologist Ken Plummer, who studied the ways in which the women's movement, the lesbian and gay movement, and the recovery movement encouraged certain types of sexual storytelling, found that a common cultural trope uniting these movements is the modernist logic of the triumphant individual—one who has "suffered, survived, and surpassed."[40]

Yet one of the striking differences between these two films, and the movements they reflect, is the role played by the figure of the parent. In the sexual abuse movement, parents (and less frequently, older relatives or family friends) are implicated as perpetrators, and do not appear on screen—with the exception of one mother who speaks of becoming increasingly aware of the fact that her husband had abused their three daughters, and joins with them in condemning him. Sexual abuse victims are, as a rule, depicted in opposition to their parents. As Janice Haaken describes the movement against sexual abuse: "it signified an awareness of 'boundary violations,' particularly in female development." At the same time, it represented a "collective de-idealization of fathers in patriarchal families and a search for a morally sanctioned bridge out of binding familial obligations."[41]

For children of survivors, whose parents are the primary victims, things are somewhat more complicated; their parents play a somewhat ambivalent role in the quest for transformation. Parents hold the status of "real" victims and are seen as deserving of empathy, and yet their silence, which was designed to protect themselves and their children, is declared to be the immediate problem that demands redress. Who does silence really protect, asks the film *Breaking the Silence*? The answer, the film suggests, is no one. For their parents' generation, denial and silence may have been a route to normalization, but for their generation it blocks self-awareness and recovery. Consequently, the film is designed to get their parents to speak, for their parents' sake as well as for their own, and to initiate familial dialogues about the legacy of the Holocaust.

The comparison of these two films suggests that feminist and therapeutic discourse encouraged the children of Holocaust survivors to form distinctive subcultures in which individuals were encouraged to speak publicly about their families and to exercise greater agency over their lives. In the 1980s, a new "memory milieu" emerged to reverse the widely held notion that difficult memories should be held at bay. Instead, it saw victimhood as key to authenticity and a basis of political action. The second generation movement took root in this memory milieu and extended it, developing new cultural scripts for interrogating traumatic pasts and transforming them into public speech. With time, even more specialized groupings emerged.

Jewish Lesbian Daughters of Holocaust Survivors formed in 1985, and claimed 120 members in the United States and Canada, Israel, Nicaragua, and Australia a few years later (Figure 3.2). It was open to lesbians (but not bisexuals, transsexuals, or gay men) with one or more parent who survived the Holocaust. The founder of the group, Ruth Chevion, described being at a feminist legal conference in 1985, where she posted a small sign: "Are there any Daughters of Survivors here? I would like to connect." She marked the sign with a yellow star, a pink triangle (signifying Nazi persecution of homosexuals), and a blue woman symbol. A woman introduced herself and they talked, she said, for four hours. Then she met another woman. The search continued when she went home to her lesbian-feminist community in New Hampshire. An introductory letter welcomed those who fit this identity category for an "intensive weekend of discussion, networking and support," noting that they were "NOT a therapy group." In fact, they had little in the way of an agenda, other than to find one another and affirm their specific identity, and the ways their sexualities and status as children of survivors dovetailed with one another, and at times clashed.

In a 1987 film called *Separate Skin* by director Deirdre Fishel, which explored this theme, Emily, the protagonist, is a woman who cannot escape the recurrent image of her parents' tattooed arms.[42] Their sad, well-meaning invocations to marry, settle down, and build a "normal life" haunt her daily as she attempts to make a rocky relationship with a man work. She wants nothing more than to please them, to live up to their expectations, but when it fails to happen, she is left unsatisfied and confused. Soon a young woman rents a room in her flat, and enters her life quickly and unexpectedly. The woman is everything Emily is not: independent, bubbly, and fancy-free. After some initial conflicts, they strike up a friendship, and eventually a romance. The young woman shows her simple pleasures that she never imagined before. They spend hours walking on the beach, making love, laughing at silly things. Yet all the while, images of her melancholy parents continue to intrude upon even the happiest of moments, dampening her joy, enlisting her guilt. Eventually, with great ambivalence, Emily allows herself to assert her own desires and claim her love for the woman. It is a happy, though bittersweet ending.

The metaphor of separate skin that gave the film its title drew parallels between the difficulties that children of survivors face in trying to separate from their parents and become their own persons, and lesbians' struggles to come out, which also typically involve separating from one's family of origin. It spoke of the ways in which therapeutic culture, feminism, and identity politics overlapped, moving children of survivors toward ever more specific forms of identity. The trajectory of identity-based movements, the second generation movement among them, is inevitably toward ever greater specificity. Even after we acknowledge "certain categories of difference," wrote theorist Shane Phelan, "there will always be more to us than those categories. We are specific individuals as well as members of multiple groups."[43]

This turn to specificity was, in many respects, the logical end of identity politics and the idea of liberation that inspired it. This political script saw authenticity—being true to oneself—as the antithesis of repression. Informed by humanistic psychologies of personal growth and creativity that defined so much of American life and thought after the 1950s, it inquired: "How do we locate the authentic person, the genuine self, beneath the layers of conventional behavior that family and society imposed on the individual?"[44] The goal was to throw off outmoded social rules, family expectations, sexual repression, and silence—and reclaim the self within.

DON'T MOURN—ORGANIZE

Some second generation activists were wary of the movement's overly psychological emphasis, and they were skeptical of efforts to generalize about the psychological dispositions of survivors. Worrying that clinical diagnoses simplified survivors' experiences and at times pathologized them, Helen Epstein (who wrote *Children of the Holocaust*, the 1979 book that helped encourage descendants' growing self-consciousness) wondered whether survivors had a great deal in common with others who had been traumatized by war, including non-Jewish prisoners who had survived Hitler's concentration camps, or Japanese internment, or Soviet labor camps, the survivors of Hiroshima and Nagasaki, Roma, and Armenians, as well as Asians and Africans who "had escaped wholesale slaughter, had been forced to emigrate, and who had rebuilt their lives elsewhere." Epstein and others also feared that psychological studies of survivors, and the second generation movement, "ignored the strengths [we] had observed in our parents."[45] The sheer fact of having survived and created families suggested that the survivors possessed a great deal of resilience, she and other argued. Indeed, Terrence Des Pres's influential book *The Survivor* emphasized the survivors' "faith in life."[46]

Some second generation activists agreed: "Their faith is their strength—and our heritage. What greater expression of this exists than the desire by survivors to marry and have children, despite years of personal confrontation with death and destruction? Our birth was a miracle. Who in the death camps would have guessed it?"[47] And as Epstein noted in an even more nuanced formulation: "We had all grown up in situations of great complexity, acutely aware of how our parents were driven by an impetus toward life as well as death."[48] In all the "talk of trauma and neurosis," said Menachem Rosensaft, who helped to found the International Network of Children of Holocaust Survivors, "I did not recognize either myself or most of my friends."

Jeanette Friedman attended the first gathering for children of survivors in New York in 1979, recalling that it focused on "the most disturbed children of survivors and lacked an activist slant," which she defined in relation to public, institutional change rather than individual, personal transformation. Friedman was incensed that there was little popular consciousness about the Holocaust either among American Jews—who "knew nothing about the Holocaust," she said—or among non-Jews like those she met at Brooklyn College, where she was a student. Amid clashes between blacks and Jews at Brooklyn College in 1969, Friedman recalled, one woman told her that "she had the right to bomb student center bathrooms because my father enslaved her grandfather down South." Friedman retorted that her father was not a slaveholder but was himself enslaved by Nazis, to which the other woman replied, incredulously, "Your father was a *what*?" At this point, Friedman "began to understand that nobody knew about the Holocaust." Even her survivor parents, she said, were guilty of erasing its memory, refusing to speak of the Holocaust and preferring to "emphasize the observance of Judaism in the good, old-fashioned, European-orthodox style."

When she heard about an anti-Semitic incident in Fort Lee, New Jersey, and the emergence of Holocaust deniers, Friedman was motivated to act. "For the first time in my life," she said, "I was seeing swastikas." Although she shared a desire for greater public recognition of the Holocaust, Friedman was not particularly sympathetic to the psychological emphasis of the existing second generation movement and what she called "psycho-social bullshit." Rather, she said, "I was interested in social action." She formed a second generation group that was more activist in emphasis, calling itself a "project for Holocaust education." The group convinced local synagogues in New Jersey, which resisted at first, to integrate Holocaust commemoration into their annual activities, and they responded to acts of anti-Semitism and racism when they occurred in the area. "We didn't just sit around talking about ourselves," she recalls.

Friedman echoed leftist critiques of identity politics: that it made a politics of melancholy and furthered a political sentimentality in which brooding over one's losses prevents one from seizing possibilities for radical change in the present.[49] Sigmund Freud famously suggested that melancholy, defined as endless mourning, led to an unhealthy fixation on lost objects or ideals.[50] Some activists agreed. As a popular leftist political button proclaimed at the time: "Don't Mourn—Organize!"

When second generation groups in different US cities engaged in activism, they did so typically around Jewish issues such as the plight of Soviet Jewry, Holocaust education, and combating anti-Semitism.[51] At a conference in Los Angeles in 1987 (Figure 3.1), a broader agenda was proposed, one that was "committed to solidarity with the State of Israel, to world peace, and to the fundamental principles of universal freedom, justice, democracy and equality." Its central goals were "to represent the shared views and interests of children of Holocaust survivors, to perpetuate the authentic memory of the Holocaust and prevent its recurrence, to

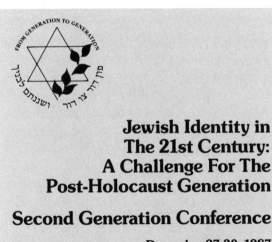

Figure 3.1:
The International Network of Children of Jewish Holocaust Survivors, founded in 1981, linked second generation groups and individual children of survivors throughout the world.

strengthen and preserve our spiritual, ideological and cultural heritage, to fight all manifestations of anti-Semitism and other forms of racial, ethnic or religious hatred, and to raise our collective voice on behalf of all human beings, Jews and non-Jews alike, who suffer from discrimination, persecution, and oppression anywhere in the world."[52] Gesturing toward the belief that the Holocaust was an instance of persecution with similarities to other ongoing forms of persecution, descendants' groups nonetheless tended to affirm the uniqueness and specificity of the Holocaust.

Those further on the Left, such as a group calling itself "The Generation After" in late 1980s New York City, had a more universalizing agenda, dedicating itself to "insuring that the Holocaust not be forgotten, repeated or inflicted on any people." It mobilized to protest neo-Nazi activities and organized memorial events, drawing links between anti-Semitism and racism. This universalistic politics of memory echoed a rhetoric common among Jewish student radicals in the 1960s. When questioned about their

Figure 3.2:
Jewish Lesbian Daughters of Holocaust Survivors, an outgrowth of the lesbian feminist and second generation movements, sponsored annual gatherings in the 1980s.

motivations for engaging in antiwar activism, a majority of Jewish members of the Students for Democratic Society (SDS) mentioned that the Holocaust was fundamental both to their sense of Jewish identity and to the development of their political values. A leader of the student Left of the 1960s recalled that he believed that "American bombs were the closest thing to an immoral equivalent of Auschwitz in our lifetimes."[53] In one survey, a quarter of SDS activists said they had relatives who were oppressed by the Nazis.[54]

Jewish New Leftists universalized the Holocaust, associating it with American racism at home and abroad. "I've always remembered linking in my own mind what happened to blacks to what had happened to Jews," said Norm Daniels, an SDS member who lost many relatives in the concentration camps.[55] SDS leader Mark Rudd, famous for his role in the Columbia University student strike and his eventual founding of the radical Weather Underground, attributed his radicalism to his refusal to be a "Good German." The "great mass of Germans," wrote Rudd, "in their ignorance, in their denial, and especially in their silence, allowed the Nazis to do their work."[56] They did not dare to challenge their leaders and their state, allowing their country to be swept up in a fascist fervor.[57] While children of survivors were probably less likely to be engaged in radical movements of the 1960s than many others of their generation, they were, however, touched by the ethnic revival and the rise of identity politics during the following decade.

In the 1960s, after striving to conform to the Anglo-Saxon standard, descendants of many European immigrants followed suit, and as Matthew Frye Jacobson argues, they "quit the melting pot."[58] Suddenly, having Italian, Jewish, Greek, or Irish lineage became something that was desirable. The ethnic revival spawned Greek dance groups, a resurgence of interest in learning Polish and eating Polish food, the publications of books such as *The Joys of Yiddish*, and a growing interest in family genealogies. As ethnicity became an important part of the quest for identity among many descendants of European immigrants, many Jews who had enthusiastically embraced American identifications, aspiring to WASP status, began to proudly claim their Jewishness. As Jacobson tellingly observes, this shift in identifications "relocated normative whiteness" from Plymouth Rock to Ellis Island, creating a national myth of origins in which immigration was key. If earlier in the century the "hyphenated American" was seen as un-American, in the 1960s claiming immigrant status and ethnic lineage became key to national belonging.

In the late 1960s, out of the breakdown of the New Left, an emergent politics of identity encouraged individuals to claim stigmatized aspects of identity (such as lesbianism, blackness, disability) rather than more universalizing ones. This politics of identity would come to influence how many young American Jews thought about the Holocaust. A group of black feminists articulated this ethos in an oft-cited 1977 statement that declared: "We believe that the most profound and potentially most radical politics come directly out of our own identity, as opposed to working to end someone else's oppression."[59] Increasingly, rather than fight battles for universal values such as fascism versus socialism, the recognition of a group's cultural distinctiveness, including the injuries it had sustained, emerged as a central demand of social movements on the left.[60] Politics, it declared, begins at home.

Growing pride in ethnic roots, coupled with a resurgent Zionism forged in the aftermath of the Six Day War, helped to create a receptive audience for Holocaust stories. But even many of those who saw commonalities between the Holocaust and other forms of oppression at times bristled at attempts to draw equivalence between the genocide of European Jewry and other atrocities. For example, a second generation group in Los Angeles staged a protest at an art exhibit in the lobby of the Jewish Community Building in Los Angeles, which depicted a parallel between human rights violations in El Salvador and the Holocaust. "As Children of Holocaust Survivors," they suggested, "we are committed to fighting oppression worldwide and we support all efforts to enhance human rights in El Salvador. It is also our duty to preserve the unique and authentic history of the Holocaust. We must be scrupulously careful never to allow its significance to be diluted."[61]

Others were critical of the second generation's fusion of psychology and politics, wondering whether a collective identity founded upon victimhood subsumed individual differences. Though sharing the experience of tremendous loss, survivors coped with that loss in different ways: some exhibited extreme post-traumatic stress; others showed extraordinary resilience. Jack Jacobs, a son of survivors, grew up among Yiddish speakers who were members of the Bund, the pre-war Jewish socialist movement. When I asked him about whether he identified with the "second generation" movement, he told me: "I think that I was not so traumatized and that it was a warm and loving household. The difficulties, such as they were, are often explicable by factors that have nothing to do with the Holocaust, per se, or which may have to do with the Holocaust, but which are over-determined and thus can just as easily be explained by class factors and the particular psychological dynamic of my family and other stuff."

While acknowledging the persistence of the past in the everyday lives of survivors and descendants, some descendants nonetheless resisted the tendency to make a politics of Holocaust victimhood. "My father was never a victim," Anita Norich declared when I interviewed her many years after she first participated in the early discussions that helped spawn the movement of descendants. "There was more to survivors than surviving." Similarly, she suggested, there was more to children of survivors than being children of survivors. Although Norich was born in a displaced persons camp and came to think of herself as having many things in common with other children of survivors by virtue of her parents' experiences, she never saw herself as having ongoing psychological problems that were rooted unambiguously in the Holocaust legacy. Partially in response to that legacy, she chose to become involved in Jewish communal projects such as studying and teaching Yiddish. Still others became fervent Zionists, on both sides of the political spectrum.

THE VIRTUAL EMOTIONAL DIASPORA

More than a decade after my initial participation in a second generation support group in Berkeley, California, in the late 1990s, I joined a "virtual" support group, an Internet listserv for children of survivors. Many of the dynamics I observed in my first support group were still evident, though in somewhat altered form. By this time, the second generation was solidly in middle age, and many of our parents were now dead, or at the end of their lives, and yet descendants' struggles to separate from their parents, and the challenges they faced in doing so, were still salient. David, a descendant, talked about the fact that as a child he "just wanted to be like all the other kids." He declared that he didn't want to deal with " all the incomprehensible misery that was just below the surface in my parents. Of course I realize that 'my plight' as a child of survivors pales in the extreme compared to their experiences. Nevertheless, I now accept these feelings of resentment as being inevitable and unhealthy to deny."

A number of individuals spoke of over-identifying with their parents, fantasizing about their parents' pre-war and wartime experiences, sometimes to the point of obsession. Shoshana described a friend who imagined that she had been at Auschwitz, like her mother. For eight years she obsessively read books on the Holocaust and couldn't stop. "Every time she thinks she's had enough and can't bear to read one more word on the subject she finds another book and starts reading again. It sounds to me like she's got a problem." Michael acknowledged similar problems: "Somehow I've taken on a survivor's identity, and feel so much like it all happened to me, that I must feel the sorrow, take it away from my parents. I feel that my life is an assignment, a mission to make up for my parents' losses and give meaning to their survival. This motivates my extensive community work. It is also a burden. I have so strongly identified with this that I've taken on much of my father's identity, his mannerisms, his humor, his sorry and depression, his emotional inaccessibility."

Deborah shared the fact that she had seen the movie *Fiddler on the Roof* four times, often crying uncontrollably. At one point she learned that her parents had lived lives similar to Tevye and his family, in a shtetl in Eastern Europe. Yet the movie, she admitted, "upset me even before I knew I was a peasant." This American-born child of survivors was clearly never a peasant, yet she had internalized her parent's stories, and their experiences, so completely. Often these identifications were carried in bodies and unconscious thoughts. A number of individuals revealed that they carried their parents' distress on their bodies, in the form of rashes or nervous tics, and many had recurrent dreams about the Holocaust. For most of their families, emotional intensity was the general rule, pulling family members ever inward, and they resented their parents' accents, their difference. As children they wanted to be like other kids.

While the task of separating seemed particularly pressing as descendants of survivors moved into the teenage years, it continued in middle age, as their parents became old, and often frail and even more needy. As Sharon revealed: "I definitely do need to put distance between my parents and myself, not so much because I hate them (I've moved well beyond that point, though it was the context in which I defined my relationship with them for much of my early life) but because I still have a hard time knowing how and where to establish the appropriate boundaries that keep me from feeling like I'm being swallowed up by their incredible emotional neediness." She explained how she and her sister put as many miles between themselves and their parents as possible. "I wanted to stake a boundary line with people who had no concept of boundaries—for my father, we were property, for my mother, salvation, guardians...I felt totally negated and impotent, as if my hands were being chained, my voice muzzled. Whatever my experience—not the physical and emotional violence I experienced in my home, the paranoia, the overprotection, the irrational rage—it could never measure up to their survival, so the basic message went, it had no validity and deserved no sympathy."

It had never occurred to her that there could be two different perspectives—her parents' and her own—coexisting in the world and that hers might be perfectly legitimate. "I had no inkling of the possibility of, let alone, necessity for psychological boundaries, places beyond which others couldn't enter without invitation, and so naturally it had never dawned on me that I might be entitled to them," Anne Karpf, an English descendant of survivors wrote in a memoir. "To me, private had always been equivalent to secret: my parents were coterminous with me—we were unicellular, an atom. Now fission was being proposed."[62]

As adults, some descendants came to rebel against being "*nachas* machines," recognizing that no matter how well they did, and how much they wished to make their parents proud of them, it was never enough, and they could never redeem their parents' pain. They tried to separate from their parents by refusing to listen to their stories—or by refusing to listen to them sympathetically; others made physical breaks to construct their own lives. They faced difficulties in expressing anger toward their parents, seeing them as vulnerable and feeling responsible for them. Even those who seemed relatively unscathed by the severest of separation-attachment problems experienced their relationship with their parents as a difficult balancing act: "We have to balance our mental health—which has an impact on our spouses and children—and our need to nurture ourselves, against the need to support the parents [whose] mental (and physical) health is poor," wrote Irene. "We cannot sacrifice this generation and the next on the altar of being good to the survivor generation."

And yet most descendants had little interest in giving up on their parents. "I don't resent [my parents] for who they are," said Rachel. "Maybe when I was younger a little bit. I understand that they went through hell, and I'm just going to have to be accepting. I'm not going to be able to change them. So you either respect them or you distance yourself, or you don't have anything to do with them. When you don't have a family, it's not an option. They're the only family I have." For most children of survivors, leaving one's family was not an option. Accordingly, second generation groups attempted to help individuals find a balance between separation and attachment, encouraging children of survivors to partially separate from their parents, and to see themselves in relation to them, but in a less "merged" fashion. For many "2Gs," this separation would emerge relatively effortlessly, as they got older. "When I was younger [I] blamed my parents for everything," said William Simon, "but as you get older and the more you understand your parents and the more you understand just the way life is, I understand that they did the best job they could and you couldn't really fault them for that."[63]

Empathy requires one to put another person "in yourself," but it also requires one to draw a boundary between that person and oneself—and to realize that they are not the same. In other words, empathy entails closeness as well as distance—"being able to say 'it could have been me' but at the same time asserting that 'it was not me.'"[64] By enabling them to develop greater empathy for what their parents had endured, the second generation movement aided descendants in separating from their parents. Through that movement, many descendants learned new ways of talking about their familial experiences; by participating in support groups, they developed the tools to speak to their parents and others close to them about a subject that had largely been off limits: the impact of the genocide on their own families. In the process, they developed greater empathy for their parents, and a greater capacity to see themselves as both connected to and distant from their parents' wartime trauma.

So while the psychological emphasis of the movement at times simplified the experiences of survivors, it helped to transform the meaning of victimhood and survival in important ways.[65] Survivors, it argued, were in fact victims, too: they may not have perished, but they experienced trauma, which had lasting effects. Moreover, victimhood should not be a source of shame: it could in fact be a potential source of personal strength. By asserting control over their narratives and finding their own voices, victims could draw on the experiences of coping with the catastrophe and could achieve sovereignty over their own experiences.[66] While survivors did not generally share their children's introspective orientation, it was through their encouragement, example, and coaxing that survivors eventually came to speak more openly about the past. By the following decade, survivors gained the moral authority to bear witness, commanding an increasingly important presence in Jewish communities and beyond.

CHAPTER 4

Claiming Victimhood, Becoming Survivors

All sorrows can be borne if you tell a story about them.
Isaak Dinesen

In the 1980s, audiences for Holocaust stories expanded beyond Jewish communities as more and more Americans seemed interested in hearing the stories of the Holocaust from those who had experienced them first-hand; survivors were increasingly called upon to act as public witnesses. In oral histories, survivors often regarded this period as a watershed moment in the rise of Holocaust consciousness: they could finally speak, and they could find others who were interested in listening. "All of a sudden [the Holocaust] became public knowledge," said survivor Erwin Baum, speaking with amazement of the ways once private stories moved into the public sphere, bringing their losses out of the shadows. "We were holding it very, very suppressed," he said. But in the late 1980s, he finally began to talk. It was too painful before, and his experiences, he said, "haunted him every day, and all night."[1]

He and other survivors described how, at roughly that moment, Holocaust stories began to move out of the realm of the family, the terrain of "thick memory," and were communicated to ever more dispersed audiences.[2] Irene Hizme, a child survivor, said that she didn't talk about her experiences until 1985. While her husband and children "knew," she never shared all that much about her past with them. But beginning in the 1980s, she said, "[i]t was becoming a little bit more okay to be a Holocaust survivor. People were finally interested." Holocaust stories, first told within the worlds of survivors and their families, began to circulate far beyond them, in a culture where painful memories were increasingly discussed in public. Many survivors gained the moral authority to bear witness, commanding an increasingly important presence in Jewish communities and beyond.

"It was only really in the 1980s," said Dorianne Kurz, that the Holocaust became "a subject for general conversation." Life cycle changes, coupled with the growing cultural visibility of the Holocaust, spurred a different kind of storytelling—in which survivors attempted to come to terms with or master intensely disturbing experiences, and to gain recognition from others.[3] Rather than transcend the past and "get on with their lives," as they were advised to do when they first arrived in the United States, with the passage of time, they were able to develop greater insight into their interrupted lives, and ways of narrating them that would convey a sense of the extent of their losses. And once they began to tell their stories to dispersed publics, and others began to recognize their experiences them, their identification as survivors deepened.

As I have suggested, for at least two decades after the end of World War II, there was little in the way of a unified understanding of who the Jewish survivors of Nazism were or what they had endured, or even of a "Holocaust," imagined as a singular entity spanning years and locations, encompassing different nations and forms of expulsion, displacement, and extermination. Those who settled in the United States after the war were known as "refugees," "displaced persons," "greenhorns," individuals who hailed from a particular town or nation, or survivors of Buchenwald, Dachau, and other concentration camps. Few spoke openly about their experiences to their families, much less in public, having been convinced, sometimes for very good reasons, that others did not want to hear. The vast majority of survivors limited their public revelations to those whom they believed understood them best: other survivors. They faced difficulties integrating their traumatic pasts into their everyday lives, and did not, for the most part, see their personal distress as something others would be interested in. And while they joined together with others like themselves for social and commemorative activities, they rarely saw themselves as a collective identity transcending national origins, or having a political purpose.

"Immediately after the war, we were 'liberated prisoners'; in subsequent years, we were included in the term 'DPs', or 'displaced persons.' Eventually, we became 'emigrants' or 'immigrants,' as well as 'refugees'; in the US we were sometimes generously called 'new Americans.'" So wrote Werner Weinberg, who was imprisoned in Bergen-Belsen. Weinberg noted that "for a long time the fact of liberation and migration were not reflected in a name assigned to us, and there was a good chance that we, as a group, might go nameless." But one day, he said, "I noticed that I had been reclassified as a 'survivor.'"[4]

The figure of the Holocaust survivor, uniting individuals across different nationalities and wartime experiences, began to coalesce in the 1960s. Author Elie Wiesel became the survivor spokesman *par excellence*. A devout Hasidic youth, Wiesel was born in 1928 in the Transylvanian town of Sighet. In his first book, *Night*, based on this own wartime experiences, which appeared in the United States in 1960, he narrated the inner world of the victims and their experience of collective trauma. Wiesel suggested that by telling one's story one could, in one critic's words, "regain one's soul" and a "sense of life-affirming meaning in a death-ridden universe."[5] By narrating his traumatic experiences in order to integrate them into his life story, Wiesel emerged as the public face of survivor-witnesses. While he emphasized the exclusive nature of Holocaust survivors' experiences and their incommunicability to the uninitiated, Wiesel's role as a moral spokesperson helped to popularize the notion of a Holocaust, and placed survivors at the center.

In a generic sense, the term "survivor" refers to those who have suffered yet survived damage knowingly inflicted on people, or resulting from disease or addiction. Over time, the term became associated with a sense of agency, even heroism. The words of Rosalyn, a descendant, encapsulated this understanding: "My parents, now deceased, were actively engaged in staying alive, were determined, and persevered throughout the war years. Later, they moved well beyond angst to carve out successful lives, both materially and spiritually. They may have been victimized, but they were not victims, and more closely relate to the archetype of the Hero."[6]

The image of the survivor as hero was immortalized by Terrence Des Pres, who celebrated, in his 1976 book *The Survivor*, what he considered to be survivors' extraordinary talent for life and moral endurance. As I suggested earlier, many descendants, who were concerned that their parents were being pathologized by the psychiatric profession, and who distrusted clinical interventions that positioned their parents as damaged, permanent victims, welcomed the hero frame. Humanistic psychologists were also concerned that some popular views of the survivors minimized the ways that even the most traumatized of populations, including survivors of genocide, can manifest resiliency and move on afterward.

But some found this emphasis upon survivors' agency troubling. The psychologist Bruno Bettelheim charged Des Pres and others with distorting the experiences of survivors by "depicting them as active agents responsible for their survival," when it was often passivity and lack of agency that enabled survival.[7] Two decades later, author Lawrence Langer also criticized such talk for "consoling rather than confronting." When we speak of "the survivor instead of the victim and of martyrdom instead of murder," he wrote, "we draw on an arsenal of words that urges us to build fences between the atrocities of the camps and ghettos and what we are mentally willing—or able to face."[8] Others wondered whether all the focus on individuals' resiliency actually did more harm than good, minimizing the ongoing emotional and economic challenges facing survivors.

American culture's "feel-good" ethos was certainly adept at transforming tragedy into pathos, anointing survivors as heroes and thereby keeping them at a safe distance. But at the same time, interviews with survivors and archival evidence suggests that the rubric of the "survivor," defined as witnesses capable of offering testimony, empowered many individuals to speak more openly about their lives, and to see themselves as a collective entity transcending national origins and wartime experiences. I have suggested that survivor discourse resonated with a number of cultural currents, including psychotherapeutic ideas of overcoming through speaking, feminist beliefs that speaking about previously private matters was a political act, and the penetration of self-help ideas into discourses of health and illness, which heralded the rise of the cancer survivor.[9]

Among the factors that had kept Jewish survivors of the genocide from identifying as survivors was a pervasive sense of guilt ("Why did I survive and not they?"), which led many individuals to identify with their murdered loved ones. Many survivors hesitated to speak for fear of speaking for the perished, or refused to lay claim to victimhood, suggesting that the true victims were all dead. Shame also impeded speech: many survivors described experiencing the feeling that those around them were averting their eyes, turning away from them. In order to identify as survivors, they first had to acknowledge that they, too, were victims, even if they had survived. Psychiatrist Robert Lifton, who worked extensively with survivors of the Holocaust as well as Hiroshima, suggested that by acknowledging one's feelings of guilt and establishing a bond between the living and the dead, in part by assuming the role of witness, "death-haunted" survivors could begin to recovery their humanity and "creative energy."[10]

When they finally spoke more openly, survivors had varied reasons for doing so: to convey their stories to children and grandchildren and record them for posterity; to bear witness on behalf of family members who were murdered; to counter those who would deny the Holocaust ever happened, who were increasing in visibility in the 1980s; and to reflect upon their own lives and gain some control over their past.

Many described how life cycle changes facilitated their growing willingness to speak. Earlier, they were too busy forging ahead—making a living and raising a family—to spend a lot of time narrating their painful pasts; plus, few had the tools to do so. As they grew older, many were spurred by a heightened sense of mortality, and a growing urgency to tell their stories. Many spoke simply because, finally, they could. Distance afforded reflection and greater ability to order their experiences. They told their stories, too, to create empathic bonds between themselves and others, particularly their children and grandchildren.

WHY DIDN'T YOU TELL ME BEFORE?

"In the beginning, we didn't think too much about the past," said Erwin Baum, referring to the first two decades after the war. Survivors were preoccupied with remaking their lives, and didn't have much time to dwell on "the war" until the business of making a livelihood and raising children diminished in focus, he said. With the passage of time, new openings emerged. As their prior emphasis on working and raising children receded, many survivors attributed their capacity to speak more openly to the fact that they had more opportunities for reflection.[11] Lily Margules: "When we became a little older, we had a little time to share our experiences, to talk about it. Because we became more mature and became better educated and had a little more time to give, and were not so busy with little children and the diapers and the problems."

Collectively, as they advanced in years and had greater access to contextualizing information, they were also better able to understand their own experiences in relation to broader historical events. Thomas Blatt: "Now that [we're] retired, [we] have time, and [we] go back to it, and start to tell, and to write." The boom in survivor memoirs was a sign of the times. As they neared the end of their lives, many survivors wrote memoirs, often self-publishing them, or publishing them with small presses. In the 1950s and 1960s, survivors published one or two memoirs a year, according to one account; during 2008 alone, at least 240 were published.[12] Older people frequently undertake a kind of interior journey in which they review their lives, delving into aspects of their lives they had previously glossed over or denied. Their children were more receptive to listening, and some even hungered for this knowledge.

"Children are not interested in the past," said Dorianne Kurz. "When people talk about the First World War, I glaze over. You know how things are before you were born? They're ancient history, they have no relevance." But over time, the past can become less distant. In the early 1980s, as most descendants moved into their twenties and thirties, they began asking their parents more pointed questions. When Jodi Kahn was in her late twenties, she said, she was "on a mission to find out." Stories she had never before heard now began to come out: stories that didn't have happy endings or redemptory messages. She learned about aunts, uncles, and cousins she never previously heard about, about the fact that her parents had children before she and her siblings were born, who had been killed. She heard her parents cry, and she had a deeper sense of the extent of their losses. "Something had changed," she recalled. "I felt capable of asking them about things that were taboo before. And they were more willing to speak."

Silence and stilted speech had created a chasm between many survivors and their children. But as they became adults, the descendants grew more interested in their parents' stories, and possessed a better context for understanding them. When most descendants were of elementary school age in the 1950s and 1960s, the Holocaust was not yet part of history curricula, or it was conflated with the events of World War II. In the last chapter, we saw how some descendants formed a collective identity, articulating a sense of themselves as connected to but also separate from others of their generation, and also from their parents. As they moved into their twenties and thirties, they developed a new interest in and capacity to listen to their parents' stories. Some of the most psychologically attuned members of this cohort saw survivorhood as a mark of distinction rather than stigma. Developing a collective identity as the "second generation," they coaxed their parents to tell their stories, to varying degrees of success.

But even those who never embraced a second generation identity, or who were not particularly introspective, underwent life cycle changes that made them more receptive to learning about their parents' wartime experiences. "When my son became a father himself he understood it more," said Lucine Horn. "My daughter as well. It evolved by them going into our shoes." When they had children of their own, she said, they understood for the first time what it must have been like for their parents to lose their parents, and they came to appreciate that their own children had grandparents, even if they did not. They were also more able to conceptualize the Holocaust "on a global level as well as a personal level," said Horn. "They understand about the gas chambers, and they relate to our experiences, and what we went through, and that's very important."

Descendants developed greater empathy for their parents, became more capable of listening to their stories, and as we saw in the last chapter, more willing to prod their parents to share their stories. Thomas Buergenthal recalled that when his children were small "they had no interest at all" in his wartime experiences. "They sort of knew." As they got older, they showed more interest, encouraging their father to write his memoir. After his heart bypass operation, he decided to finally begin writing. Once he did so, he found that many things began to "come back that had long been forgotten." "They now say, 'write it down,' or 'why didn't you tell me that before?' referring to this story, or that story." But when they were younger, says Buergenthal, "they had no interest whatsoever," or "at least none that I could perceive." Now, in contrast, he says, "they really are very interested and they want to know this and that." Acknowledging the gradual unfolding of their children's interest, many parents began to speak more openly.

Descendant Isaac Rosen, a journalist, decided to bring a tape recorder along one day when he was visiting his parents in Philadelphia with his infant daughter. He set up a microphone and started interviewing his parents. He "decided [he] was going to get this stuff down." That was first time he "heard a lot of their stories," he said. It took them sitting down together "in a structured way." Before, he said, "it was just like a scattered thing and the recollections were too vague . . . I had gotten snatches [of] them over the years." It was not until he was "well into adulthood," he acknowledged, that he was able to probe further. Acknowledging his parents' mortality, Rosen said, "he needed to get their stories down." Reflecting on why he was finally able to question them, he said: "Maybe it was because of distance, and more discussion, or maybe as an adult I was better able to feel with them." His last statement is an interesting one, suggesting that it wasn't simply the stories that were difficult to listen to; it was difficult to witness parents' feelings of sadness, grief, or terror.

But coaxing a parent out of silence was frequently very difficult. As a teenager, Susan Stern recalled, "I wanted to know about my parents' wartime experiences very badly, yet dreaded the moment of having to raise the issue." But the older her parents got, "the more they recollected." They didn't sit around and talk about it because, she said, "I didn't want to hear it from them." Nonetheless, "almost everything will spark off a memory of the way it used to be."[13] Although she and others were fearful of communicating with their parents, anticipating that they would go crazy, or cry uncontrollably, or have nightmares that night if they dredged up the past, when they actually did so, many found that it was not as difficult as they had anticipated. When children showed interest, parents often responded accordingly. They were often touched by their children's interest, and over time came to talk more and more.

As colleges came to offer courses in Holocaust history, they offered descendants opportunities to probe the contexts of their own family histories. Sandi Goodman grew up hearing German while living in New York's Washington Heights neighborhood, which was in the 1950s and 1960s a largely German Jewish refugee enclave. In the 1970s, when she was in college in New York, she took a course about the Holocaust. She began to wonder about her mother's experiences, and how they connected to the history she was learning. So she began to ask her mother questions, occasionally at first, about once every month or so, and then more frequently. "Once I had opened the door," recalled Sandi, "my mother talked." In the dance of telling, parents often looked to their children to give them cues about whether or not they were interested and ready to know. "Once I started to talk about it with her, it was a more present topic of conversation. By initiating it, I gave her permission to delve into it further," and having initiated the conversation, said Sandi, "this changed my relationship to my mother." After the ice was broken, they forged a new intimacy, and stories she had never before heard now began to come out—stories that didn't have happy endings or redemptory messages.

The proliferation of books, television shows, and movies about the Holocaust helped to frame survivors' experiences, providing a context for parents and children to tell family stories. In 1978, the television mini-series *Holocaust* was viewed by 120 million people. It was, in many respects, a Jewish version of the popular book and miniseries *Roots*, which traced one African-American family's history back to an African man captured by slave traders in 1767. Like *Roots* before it, *Holocaust* challenged the traditional role of historians as experts and producers of meanings, and promoted an emotional identification with history's victims, making the search for one's lost ancestors a key element of ethnic identity. It brought the tragedy into millions of Americans' homes, creating new affective bonds between survivors and unknown publics—though survivors were not always pleased with their depiction. This and other television programs helped to create a mass audience for Holocaust stories, encouraging survivors to tell their stories, and offered cultural scripts that gave children of survivors newfound license to prod their parents to tell their stories, and a deeper understanding of what kinds of questions to ask them.

Erwin Baum's daughter watched a movie called *The Final Solution*, a documentary released in 1983 that featured Nazi hunter Simon Wiesenthal, interspersed with clips of the Warsaw ghetto, the gas chambers, and other Nazi atrocities, and propaganda speeches by Hitler and his henchmen. Prior to that experience, "she would never want to hear about the Holocaust. It didn't ring the bell." But after she saw the film, Baum recalled, "certain things in it start to come together and she said to me: why don't you write your experiences down?" It was the first time she had ever shown any interest in her father's story, said Erwin. Why then? It was now safer to inquire. She was a young adult, and the Holocaust was a recognizable "thing," a historical episode that was widely recognized and discussed. Still, it was not easy. Taking note of his daughter's newfound curiosity, Erwin asked her: "What do you think about your father?" He recalled that she responded by "scribbling her feelings about me on a little piece of paper.... So that's how she did it."

Ann Bander accompanied her parents to Claude Lanzmann's mammoth nine-and-a-half-hour documentary, *Shoah*, released in 1985. "That was really difficult," she recalled. Afterward, her parents "were shaken up." But it was "important to them that I saw it," she said. "I saw what their country looked like, what those peasants were like." Watching movies together often provided a basis for discussion, and even if there was little discussion, suggested to parents that their children wanted to know about their lives. Lily Margules said that though her son knew about the genocide of European Jewry, through history classes in school, in college it became a subject of growing interest, and he read voraciously about it. But he never talked with her about it. "He couldn't place his mother in this situation," she said. It was safer to keep these "deep memories" separate. But, increasingly, the private and public spheres blurred. Clearly, the culture had changed, said Dorianne Kurz. In the 1940s and 1950s, she said, "one tried to shield children from hearing bad things." Today, in contrast, she said, "violence is an everyday thing on the television," and "bad things" are part of everyday life.

This growing public discussion also afforded many survivors a broader contextual understanding of what they had endured. Thomas Blatt spoke of the fact that over time he accumulated knowledge and gained a better grasp of the chronology of wartime events. Because survivors generally did not possess a larger narrative of the war, or concepts with which to describe their experiences, it made narrating their stories difficult. This was particularly challenging for those who had been children during the war years, for whom memories of the events were fragmented, at best. After putting aside her losses in an attempt to move on, Bella Tovey, a child survivor, began to read about genocide shortly before she retired. "It kind of came together. I needed to understand a little bit." She read history, novels, anything she could get her hands on. It helped her to order what was before a tangle of disconnected events that lacked a chronology or connective tissue. She spoke of the importance of being able to narrativize her experiences, and the pivotal role that gaining historical knowledge played in that process. "These are not problems that a therapist, or a psychologist or psychiatrist can help with," she said.

In communities across the nation, survivors were also increasingly called upon to speak about their lives at synagogues, churches, and community groups, and they became prized additions to high school classrooms, sharing their stories with schoolchildren as part of Holocaust-focused curricula or more general lessons in "tolerance."

SPEAKING TO STRANGERS

Eva Edmands, a child survivor, moved to the Midwest after the war, where she met her husband. They joined a Unitarian church, made some friends, and she slowly began to reveal her background to them. "I was initially afraid of rejection and discrimination," she said, but she "found that people were very interested, because in New York, Holocaust survivors are a dime a dozen, but here, they don't have this access." This encouraged her to speak at a Sunday fellowship meeting. It was the first time she had spoken publicly about her experiences. Despite her fears, it was a great success, and she began to speak more and more, to crowds of 50, 100, even 500. Little by little, Edmands said, she developed a reputation as a Holocaust speaker, regularly visiting secondary schools in Lawrence, Kansas, where she lived. She also wrote a book about her experiences, which she donated to every secondary school in Lawrence so that children can access it in their libraries. As she described these activities, her growing self-confidence and pride was palpable. "I said I have to do it, and I made up my mind [I] wasn't going to be afraid, and then I wasn't." Edmands saw these acts of public storytelling as connected to a higher purpose: to bear witness.

There had been public witnesses to the genocide throughout the postwar era—most notably at the trial of Adolph Eichmann in 1961, when survivors became, as Annette Wieviorka put it, "an embodiment of memory."[14] At various moments, survivors spoke to other survivors, to government officials entrusted with achieving justice, or to experts who might offer the medicalized accounts they needed to attain financial restitution from Germany. But with time, more and more survivors, often coaxed by speakers bureaus in local communities, began to tell their stories to strangers, achieving some mastery over their experiences, while sharing their experiences with others.

"I just don't go out to speak so that they will learn the horrors of the Holocaust," Nesse Golden said. "I go out so they would understand how precious life is, how you can help each other, how you don't join a gang, or a group that you will be sorry about." She feels that her testimony is important, "to remember the dead but most of all to teach the living what hatred and indifference can do." In telling their stories, many believed they were transforming their felt sense of loss and meaningless death into a positive message for future generations.

Telling the story of wartime atrocities, for Dorianne Kurz, was a way for her to honor her parents. "My mother's memory is a very important thing to me." By telling her story, she believes she keeps her memory alive. Irene Hizme began to speak publicly in the 1980s, coaxed by a therapist who specialized in treating survivors. She began to speak, she said, because she felt an "obligation to my parents, if not to anybody else, to speak of this." Suddenly, she said, she "found herself" speaking at schools, synagogues, appearing on TV, and in books. She says that speaking and writing poetry "[have] helped [her] greatly." She speaks publicly about twice or three times a year, she says, and "it [doesn't] get easier as you keep doing it." Nonetheless, she feels that she has a duty to continue speaking. "I'm trying to do something for humanity with it."

Sociologist Kai Erikson has observed that for some survivors of natural disasters, "a sense of difference can become a kind of calling, a status, where people are drawn to others similarly marked."[15] Speaking in public helped to alleviate the shame that many Holocaust survivors experienced when they first arrived in the United States, when few wished to know what they had endured. Shame is a social emotion, an indictment of the self by those around you. Unlike guilt, which can fester quietly inside you, writes Jacqueline Rose, "shame requires an audience."[16] If shame is a social construct, moving beyond shame requires the repair of social bonds, and the rebuilding of what some have called "the interpersonal bridge."[17] Indeed, by speaking publicly, in schools, community groups, and to unknown interviewers, many survivors found their voices, as well as a sense of purpose.

Some of the survivors interviewed by the United States Holocaust Memorial Museum even became celebrity-witnesses in their own right. Nesse Godin's Wikipedia page informs readers: "for the past 40-plus years, Nesse has been a busy individual, speaking about the Holocaust to domestic and international audiences. She has appeared before a variety of audiences including the United States Naval Academy, United States Military Academy, the Department of Defense, the Department of Energy, the United Nations General Assembly, numerous schools...universities, churches, synagogues, civic groups and teacher's conferences."[18] Other survivors who had given testimony to the museum, and to other archival projects, appeared in documentary films, and were invited to luncheons with high-ranking government officials and Jewish elites.

The story of Irene Hizme and Rene Slotkin, twins who were experimented on in Auschwitz by Nazi physician Josef Mengele, were featured in articles in the *New York Times*, and became the subject of at least one documentary film. For many years, Irene had experienced resistance from survivors whose experiences were more typical. "I mentioned to someone casually that I am a Holocaust survivor, and they just kind of looked at me and said 'you're too young, it couldn't be.'" As a child survivor, she felt invisible in the larger world of Holocaust survivors. "They negated my whole thing," she said, wondering, "what could you possibly remember, you were so little?'" For lack of knowledge about her own history, let alone the larger history of the war, she could not make sense of her experiences to either herself, or to others.

In the late 1970s, when Hizme attended some lectures by Elie Wiesel, she felt, she said, that she "needed to find out more." So she started "looking and asking questions, and I guess doing research on what really happened." It was then that she began to read books about Auschwitz, and she found out about the experiments that had been done to her. Those on the edges of the "Holocaust survivor" category frequently felt marginalized because of their age, their mixed heritage, or because they had wartime experiences that were somewhat unusual. But as survivors mobilized politically, and became a more visible category, many of those who had once been on the periphery, such as child survivors, were able to find their voices.

Hizme said she speaks out of an obligation to her parents' memory, and because she believes her story can teach others about the human consequence of hate. She wants to "do something for humanity," she says. After she began to speak in community groups and schools about her wartime experiences, she "found [herself] speaking suddenly to schools, synagogues, appearing on television, and in books" and was in demand as a survivor spokesperson. She was "out" as a survivor for the first time in her life. "I had friends who had known me many, many years who are totally astounded, shocked," she said. "They could not believe that I was a Holocaust survivor. They said, 'you're so American.' I took that as a compliment of sorts." Being a survivor, and talking to others about it, gave her cachet, and a sense of purpose.

Survivors of the Holocaust, Eva Hoffman writes, "rarely thought of themselves as 'survivors' until the term became routine, and at times even an honorific."[19] Today, when survivors speak, particularly in small towns, says Ellen Blalock, director of Survivor Affairs at the United States Holocaust Memorial Museum, "[t]hey're treated like rock stars. Their audiences cry, they're emotionally overwhelmed. They're empowered," she says. Many Americans who have no connection to the Holocaust, she told me, "have trouble fixating on that period in history. They've heard about Adolph Hitler but they don't really know much about what happened." Survivors tell them: "don't hate." They're trying to do whatever they can to inform and make a difference. They are trying to honor their families." As she sees it, talking makes their lives meaningful.

Many survivors came to see themselves as having a special mission, at times defined in political terms, to counter those who would deny that the Holocaust ever happened. They feared their stories would be distorted by Holocaust deniers, who began to speak out with some regularity beginning in the mid-1970s. While some deniers went so far as to claim that the Holocaust never happened, most focused on questions of German intentionality, arguing that there was never a plan to annihilate the Jewish people—it simply occurred in the course of World War II. Others drew a moral equivalence between Hitler, Stalin, and Eisenhower, arguing that it is wrong to single out the Germans for doing what had been done by other nations.[20] Holocaust deniers, embraced by neo-fascist organizations in Western Europe and England, as well as the United States, tried to mainstream themselves, passing themselves off as legitimate scholars and questioning the veracity of survivor testimony.[21]

Few survivors saw themselves as political people. They tended to associate the realm of politics with the actions of genocidal states or totalitarian social movements. But when they heard of public acts of Holocaust denial, it often spurred them to take more visible roles. Lily Margules began to hear that some people "wanted to rewrite history" and came to believe "this is our time for us to speak up." They were doing it to preserve the memory of their dead families, she said. "By silence, [we are] committing a very big injustice to those who cannot speak."[22] Holocaust deniers acted, in effect, as inadvertent coaxers, pushing survivors to tell their stories in public. Bella Tovey agreed to be interviewed by the United States Holocaust Memorial Museum when she heard about a 1976 book by Arthur Butz, an engineering professor at Northwestern University, called *The Hoax of the Twentieth Century*, which argues that the Holocaust had been deliberately contrived in order to justify the creation of the state of Israel. The book is one of the most widely distributed texts of Holocaust denial. The fact that it purported to be a scholarly work, and "not just some of these skinheads denying the Holocaust," she said, made her act. When Erwin Baum learned about the phenomenon of Holocaust denial, it prompted him to volunteer to speak publicly. "I said, well you come talk to me. Here it is, my picture [pointing to a picture of himself during the war]. I was there." But most were not interested in "airing their dirty laundry," and they became public witnesses only when they were prompted by their children, or by Holocaust deniers.

With time, out of the generalized identity of "Holocaust survivor," subsidiary identities vying for recognition and speech, such as child survivors, emerged. "My whole life is trying to find where I belong...I didn't even feel welcome with other Holocaust survivors because they belittled my experience," said Irene Hizme. As noted above, she was part of a unique sub-set of child survivors: twins who had been experimented on in Auschwitz. Irene said she found her voice in 1985, when an organization of twins who survived Auschwitz gathered in Israel. "I thought Rene and I were the only ones," she said. But then she learned that there were over one hundred sur-vivors all over the world who shared many of her experiences.

But it's never easy to talk, she said. Every time she speaks publicly about the war years, and about her time in Auschwitz, she "gets pushed back into that time" and it takes her weeks to recover. She says she is always con-scious of holding back, and not speaking of the worst. "There are certain things that I don't want to try to put into words because I can't," she says. "I can't and I don't want to." She and other survivors said they were often conscious of keeping some details private, and not narrativizing all of their experiences, for fear of overwhelming their audiences, or dredging up deep memories they wished to hold at bay. Even those who willingly spoke in public often expressed ambivalence about becoming objects of curiosity. They were members of a generation that had typically erected high walls between their public and private selves—they were not baby boomers, for whom biographical self-revelation was part of a generational sensibility.

In addition to speakers bureaus, archival projects began to collect survi-vors' stories, institutionalizing ongoing small-scale efforts that had been initiated in many Jewish communities.[23] Some of these projects, such as the Fortunoff Archive at Yale, co-founded by Dori Laub, a psychoanalyst and survivor, were informed by therapeutic ideals. Laub, who saw the ther-apeutic nature of the project as its core, compared the relationship between interviewer and interviewee to what analysts call transference, describing how "the listener to trauma comes to be a participant and co-owner of the traumatic event: through his very listening he comes to partially experience trauma in himself."[24] Led by a team of psychotherapists, the Yale archive collected 4,000 interviews, primarily with Holocaust survivors living in the United States.[25] Each interview, which ranged in length from 30 minutes to several hours, averaging between one and two hours, tried to recapture the interviewees' thoughts and feelings about their experiences—rather than simply a historical record of the experiences themselves. The collection of testimonies, which took the form of life histories, allowed survivors, in the words of Geoffrey Hartman, one of the founders of the Yale project, to give "order, mastery, and relief to the unmastered past."[26]

In the testimonial form we see elements of the therapeutic paradigm at work, with its emphasis upon intimacy, directness, the validation of personal experience, and the importance of active listening.[27] Testimony requires an individual speaking from experience, and one or more willing listeners, who act as witnesses. In the testimonial form, truth is not the primary criterion of value, but rather it is the degree of affective connection between speakers and listeners. Literary critic Shoshana Felman describes testimony as "composed of bits and pieces of a memory that has been overwhelmed by occurrences that have not settled into understanding of remembrance, acts that cannot be constructed as knowledge nor assimilated into full cognition, events in excess of our frames of reference."[28] What testimony offers those who speak is the possibility of achieving some mastery of what Arthur Frank, in his book *The Wounded Storyteller*, calls the "narrative wreckage" of the past.

The social, relational character of the testimonial process was thus even more crucial than its goal of producing knowledge about Nazi oppression. Though these stories described "a universe of death," Hartman suggested, the very fact that they were communicated by a living person who "answers, recalls, thinks, cries, carries on" transformed them into something quite different. Each oral history, he said, is animated by a "quest to recover or reconstruct a recipient, an 'affective community' and [thus] the renewal of compassionate feelings."[29] It was informed by an emergent understanding of the importance of storytelling in "recovering" from trauma. As psychologist Judith Herman suggested, this work of reconstruction "transforms the traumatic memory, so that it can be integrated into the survivor's life story" by insisting that the "goal of recounting the trauma story is integration, not exorcism."[30] If an earlier notion of "survivor syndrome" cast the survivor as deeply wounded, and lacking the capacity to speak, an emergent notion of trauma, and what was coming to be called "post-traumatic stress," suggested that the positive regeneration of the self is contingent upon the ability to articulate and integrate the harm done to it. While acknowledging the difficulty of fully narrating the traumatized self, it emphasized the importance of attempting to do so.

Few survivors who agreed to offer testimony saw it those terms, of course. Many agreed to be interviewed to honor those who perished—family members, friends, and communities. For them, testimony was a form of memory work, particularly in the absence of tombstones, funerals, and the conventional rituals of mourning. Through this memory work, they addressed family members, often for the first time. Many hoped their own children and grandchildren would have access to their stories, and would keep them for posterity. By constructing a role for the interviewer as empathetic listener/audience member, the formal structure of oral testimonies often afforded survivors a safer environment for telling their stories.[31]

While Willliam Loew was conscious of relaying to his family fragments of his wartime experiences when they emerged, and was very self-conscious about holding back the rest of the story, when the United States Holocaust Memorial Museum approached him for an interview, he said yes. "I made that information available to the [museum], and if they are interested in it, they could view it, they could read it and know it." Having told only fragments of his story to his family, he used his interview as a way of telling the "whole" story, and offered it to the museum so that his family could access it if they wished.

Thomas Buergenthal admitted that anyone viewing his video interview would "know more than my children know" about his experiences. He was very aware of telling them snippets of his experiences in the past, "flashing through some event that I recalled." He might tell them about the event, but always "stop at that point without elaborating." There was no reason for them to know more, he said. Now, if they want to know more, they can watch his video. While he was uncertain whether they would actually do so, he felt grateful that they could watch if they wished.[32] Many survivors were concerned that after they were gone, their stories would die with them. The most common reason they gave for speaking was to share their stories with loved ones.

While oral history projects and museums offered the promise of attentive audiences, or at least active coaxers, survivors frequently saw their children and grandchildren as the primary audiences, hoping they would watch the tapes, and perhaps come to a deeper understanding of their experiences. Dorianne Kurz agreed to give her history to the Holocaust Museum in Washington, DC, in 1990 not so much for "historical reasons," she said, but because she wanted her brother's children to have a copy of the tape. Her nieces were born well after the war. "What they do know of World War I, World War II, the Crimean war—it's the same to people who were not living [at] that time," she lamented. Since she had no children of her own, they were her only living links to the future, she said. "I want [my nieces] to know the story and I was anxious for them to have a copy of [my tape]. That made me think of other children who maybe didn't have an aunt, or a father who were survivors, who should have an opportunity, in even 200 years" to listen.

The notion of history "from below" that inspired these archival projects valorized the authority of "experience" over historical documentation. In archival projects there is a tension between eyewitness testimony and bearing witness, between historical facts and experiential, or emotional truths. In 2006, Annette Wieviorka chastised her fellow historians for relegating reflection on the Holocaust "to the various 'psys'—psychiatrists, psychologists, psychoanalysts," lamenting that the outpouring of survivor testimonies had become a kind of "social therapy" in which emotions are put on public display.

Wieviorka contrasted this new focus on emotions with the historian's critical stance. The latter, she writes, holds "emotions, likes, and dislikes at arm's length. Historians sift through various possible ways of representing the past.... When called on to pronounce on issues of public concern, [they say] what is true and just. Testimony [on the other hand] appeals to the heart and not the mind. It elicits compassion, pity, indignation, even rebellion." She went so far as to compare the emotional displays of the present to that of Nazism, which derided reason "by playing on feelings such as hate or emotions." Holding events at a distance, she wrote, "does not preclude feelings of empathy with the victims or horror at the complex system that produced mass death," she wrote. Quite the contrary, "it restores the dignity of the thinking person."[33]

If the Holocaust was becoming "Americanized," transformed into a significant aspect of American public culture, what really seemed to upset some critics was a "feminization" of memory that privileged emotions over reason, and experiential over expert knowledge. Raul Hilberg, a historian who was himself a survivor, similarly lamented that "any survivor, no matter how inarticulate, was often considered superior to the greatest Holocaust historian who did not share in the experience."[34] He was critical of the growing move toward seeing experience as a higher, more authentic truth based on uncontestable evidence; the fact that the survivor had become the ultimate authority on the Holocaust, he said, pointed to memory's distortions.

These commentators were united in their distaste for survivor testimony on the grounds that it was too emotional, and relied too heavily on personal experience as a source of knowledge. In the conceptual split between "history" and "memory," in which history is understood as a chronicle of events that requires critical detachment, and memory as that which involves deep immediacy, and which is always in process, they sided with history. Collectively, they were critical of the exponential growth of survivor testimony, which challenged the traditional role of historians as producers of knowledge and meaning about the Holocaust. Many of the critiques lodged against survivor testimony and the growing importance of memory (versus history) had previously been lodged against women: that they are too emotional, volatile, and unreasonable to be entrusted with power and authority.

But others were more concerned with accurately representing survivors' emotional truths. Rather than being concerned about how testimonies sacrifice facts in favor of emotions, the great challenge confronting the testimonial process, they believed, is figuring out how to elicit stories of chaotic experience, stories that defy linear, rational narratives, without steering the storyteller away from her feelings, or emphasizing restitution and progress instead of loss and meaninglessness.[35] Some critics were concerned that by their very structure, archival projects tended to smooth over difficult emotional truths. Although the Fortunoff project at Yale employed trained volunteers who were attuned to interactional dynamics, using a somewhat open-ended interview structure, critic Lawrence Langer observed that interviewers tended to undercut the stories that surviving witnesses were telling by subtly directing them to narratives that emphasized "the resiliency of the human spirit." Or they urged them to speak about the moment of liberation, as if that moment ushered them into freedom. Survivors, he argued, did not think of liberation as any great dividing line ordering their experience. Nonetheless, unhappy endings were often erased, and happy ones were affirmed in the interest of encouraging a redemptive narrative— what Langer called the "comforts of common memory."[36]

The tendency to emphasize redemptory narratives, some suggest, is even more pronounced in interviews conducted by Steven Spielberg's massive Survivors of the Shoah Foundation Visual History Archive, which has come to dwarf all other efforts in scale.[37] The project followed, to a great extent, the cultural penchant for restitution stories; though the interviews spoke of tremendous loss, they were structured as a trajectory of continuity. These narratives followed the form of a life history, in which individuals began their stories in the prewar period, continued through wartime, and ended with their postwar lives. At the conclusion of the interview, survivors were encouraged to introduce their children or grandchildren to the audience, conveying the implicit (and sometimes explicit) message: "we beat Hitler"—"who wanted to kill us all."

A few years ago, when I asked my undergraduates to listen to and analyze histories archived by the Shoah Foundation, they were struck by the fact that they seemed "much more factual than emotional," as one female student put it. "The interviewees recounted, in chronological order, everything that happened to them during that time period and the ordeal they went through," she wrote. "I expected tears and emotion and hardship, but for the most part the interviewees simply spoke. They answered the questions the interviewer posed to the best of their ability and then they moved on to the next question." One might argue that the Spielberg testimonies embody the therapeutic ideal that no matter what happens to an individual, healing and "closure" are always possible.

Analyzing the testimony of one survivor, and comparing it to her own oral history of the same subject, sociologist Diane Wolf concluded that the Shoah Foundation version understated her subject's exploitation by his own family members, and minimized the fact that though the war ended in 1945, "its effects bore down on him for years after." By focusing on the war years, the interview created a "clearer division between right and wrong, between victims and perpetrators, and offers a more linear view: from obliteration to regeneration, from destruction to redemption, and from destitution to success." The testimonies gathered by Spielberg's Shoah Foundation, Wolf cautioned, "will create post-memories focused on romanticized notions of Jewish prewar life, followed by Jewish persecution and death, and then redemption," simplifying a complex history.[38] In reality, survivors' post-Holocaust lives were a mix of achievement and loss, ambivalence and conflict, marginality and success, resilience and devastation.

Still, one can imagine why these projects sought to organize survivor narratives in a relatively straightforward, chronological fashion. Linear narratives conform to our understanding of how stories "should" be told. Trauma stories, which speak of chaos and interruption, in contrast, are impossible to fully tell, and are too uncomfortable for audiences to hear. They are painful, anguished, and deal with death. They question the modernist narrative of progress, which underlies so many of our cultural expectations, particularly in the United States. Therefore, one has to find other ways of telling the story, even if it compromises truth. For testimony projects, which involve interactions between the traumatized and strangers, very few of whom were trained as therapists, and were designed, in large part, to be listened to by other strangers, this was a very difficult, if not impossible task—and there were prohibitions against going off script.

Moreover, survivors and their families often appreciated the formulaic nature of the testimony structure: it afforded survivors a safer environment for telling their stories, and a safer environment for others to listen to them. David Halbert, a child of survivors, talked about the fact that while he had "a pretty good understanding" about what his parents had endured during the war, they never shared detailed stories with him about it, and he admitted that it "was very hard for him to listen to them." Eventually, he anticipated, that if his parents taped their histories for him, "maybe someday I'll be able to listen to more detailed stories—when I'm ready." That would allow him to selectively learn about the experiences, and possibly even talk to his parents about them. But at that point, he said, he would "choose how in depth" he would "want the conversation to be." He welcomed the fact that he could listen to his parents' stories without their presence.

Testimony projects encouraged a much more linear form of storytelling than the kinds of fragmented, episodic stories that survivors typically shared with family members. Melody, a child of survivors, reported that her father's sister and many of her relatives' friends were contacted and interviewed by the Shoah Foundation project. "I had no idea about the past before the War until I saw the video," she said. "I learned so much about my grandparents and great-grandparents through this visual story." And while she had thought that her mother could never tell her story to an interviewer, she was pleased to see that "she did it with dignity and pride."

When Jennifer Hollander listened to her mother's interview at an exhibit about Auschwitz at the U.S. Holocaust Memorial Museum, she "fell apart." She describes emotions "breaking through the barrier" that she had erected. Since then, she has been to the museum several times, twice with her mother, and says that she "keeps waiting for that feeling again," but she's not "nearly as emotional as the first time." Viewing her mother's testimony, in other words, despite the structured nature of the endeavor, was cathartic, and with repetition came a capacity to achieve some mastery over painful feelings, rather than distancing oneself from them. If they were first hesitant, as they moved toward the end of their lives, survivors flocked to tell their stories to interviewers, often on their children's urging. The Shoah Foundation (now called the Institute for Visual History and Education, a branch of the University of Southern California's Shoah Foundation) had by 2012 collected 52,000 testimonies.

All storytelling is filled with gaps, of course. When people talk about their lives, they actively frame their experience to suit their present needs, filtering their descriptions of actual events and behaviors. Jonathan Keller described how an interviewer from the Shoah Foundation taped his parents in a one-day marathon session that, he said, "must have lasted close to twelve hours." His parents, he said, considered the finished tapes part of their legacy to their grandchildren. "My sister and I had grown up hearing those stories," he said, but "my children hadn't." His parents wanted to make the tapes available to their grandchildren when they became old enough to understand. Jon said that when he sat down to watch the tapes himself, he was struck both by "what was omitted," as well as "what was included." So, he said, while his parents told stories he had never heard before, he was also surprised that his parents spoke a lot about the siblings they had lost, but "had never before mentioned their names."

As they told their stories to strangers, at the behest of video archives, speakers bureaus, and school groups, survivors commemorated the dead, stood up to Holocaust denial, engaged in autobiographical work, and most important to them, provided a record of their lives and those they had lost, for their children and grandchildren. Over time, and through the sharing of their stories, many descendants came to know their parents better, which often resulted in greater intimacy. But speaking required the translation of deep, thick memories—memories of sounds, smells, and wayward emotions—into stories that could be conveyed to others safely, in terms that they could understand and learn from. As much as they wanted to tell their stories, survivors often experienced the process of translation as a kind of betrayal, as a smoothing over of difficult, traumatic knowledge, which disrupted the authenticity of their experiences, in favor of easier, common memory.

When Nesse Godin began to speak to schools, she "unloaded what [she] had in her memory, in [her] feelings." She tried to get her husband to "give testimony," too, she says. But "he just cannot do it." He told her that his "blood pressure goes up too high." Still, she says, she feels that testimony is "very important, to remember the dead and to teach the living what hatred and indifference can do." Her husband disagrees. "God bless him, he's lovely, he's great, I love him," she said. "But he wouldn't talk to anyone. Not even me. I wanted to go with a tape recorder, take his story, but he doesn't want to." But as time passes, she wonders, "maybe it's time to leave it to rest."

OPRAH GOES TO AUSCHWITZ

Isaak Dinesen's words in the epigraph at the start of this chapter suggest that by telling our stories, we try to gain some control over our lives, organizing the past so that it makes sense—a task that seems particularly crucial for those who have endured traumatic experiences.[39] For many survivors, achieving a sense of coherence meant identifying with their prewar and wartime pasts, which they had distanced themselves from in order to create postwar lives. Through this process of identification, the diverse, fragmented group of individuals who had endured Nazi persecution, who were variously defined in relation to their liberation from the camps, their displacement, and their status as new immigrants, had, by the late 1970s and early 1980s, congealed into the collective identity of "survivor."

Erwin Baum said that once the Holocaust was widely discussed in the 1980s, people would hear his accent and ask him where he was from, to which he would reply: "Warsaw, Poland." In the past, he said, that would be the end of the conversation. But now questions would follow, such as "Where were you during the war? Were you in a concentration camp?" Baum was uncomfortable with all the newfound attention. "No matter where I go, I go to my doctor, I sit on a bus, a subway, have a conversation with a stranger about politics, people say, 'I see you are a European. Where are you from?' And then it starts, and the children are around and they hear it, they listen." As Dorianne Kurz said, after she started sharing her story, "people find you interesting, or an oddball, or noteworthy."

By the 1990s, survivors came to be seen as bearers of truths that were out of the reach of "ordinary" individuals.[40] In a stunning reversal of the reception of survivors during the first decades after the war, more Americans saw survivors as having access to special, privileged knowledge. Because they have been close to death, some believed, they possessed increased consciousness about life. This became evident to me several years ago, when my son, who was then 11, received a note from his Hebrew school inviting him to visit the Museum of Jewish Heritage in New York for Yom Ha Shoah, Holocaust Remembrance Day. In the note, parents were advised: "survivors will be in the galleries meeting and speaking with the visitors. Docents will be guiding the students through the galleries and especially to the survivors. This is an amazing opportunity for our children to interact on a very personal level with these remarkable individuals." Were survivors really remarkable individuals? Well, some were. But most were rather ordinary individuals who were forced to endure remarkable circumstances, who somehow survived to tell their tales.

The growing public visibility of the triumphant survivor accelerated during the 1990s, when Steven Spielberg's *Schindler's List* made the Holocaust a trauma drama of wide cultural resonance, and the newly erected U.S. Holocaust Memorial Museum in Washington, DC, thrust the survivor onto center stage as the authentic voice of Holocaust memory. The Holocaust was no longer simply a Jewish tragedy; it had become a universal one. The foregrounding of the Holocaust in popular consciousness, symbolized by memorials, museums, films, and the proliferation of survivor testimonies, could be seen as part of a broader preoccupation, especially in America, with traumatic memories and catastrophic histories. "Coming to terms with the past," wrote Barbara Mizstal, "has emerged as the grand narrative of recent times."[41] The period of forgetting would be no more, replaced, as media scholar Barbie Zelizer put it, with "a period of remembering to remember."[42]

Perhaps it should come as little surprise, then, that Oprah Winfrey would invite the survivor-witness *extraordinaire* Elie Wiesel to appear on her show during two special commercial-free broadcasts aired in May 2006. An ad for the program announced: "Oprah accompanies Elie Wiesel on his last trip to Auschwitz. See the Holocaust through the eyes of a man who lived it." On the first broadcast, Winfrey and Wiesel travel to Auschwitz, and visit the death camp and its museum. "I have no answers," says Winfrey. "All these years later, you have no answers," she tells Wiesel. And still, she says, "In spite of everything, you still must believe." The two "survivors"—one

Figure 4.1:
In 2006, Oprah Winfrey traveled to the site of the Auschwitz death camp, where she interviewed Elie Wiesel for her television program. In retrospect, she called it one of her "top five show moments." Copyright © Harpo Inc./George Burns.
Reprinted with permission from Oprah.

a survivor of sexual abuse, substance abuse, and racism, who has battled weight problems, the other, the survivor of the twentieth century's unparalleled mass murder—walk hand in hand (see Figure 4.1).

The *Oprah* broadcast exemplified the therapeutic paradigm of Holocaust storytelling, with its emphasis on intimacy, directness, and "real experience" in a confessional mode. While attesting to the Holocaust's singularity as an event testing the limits of human experience and understanding, by placing Oprah and Wiesel together, the show drew an implicit equivalence between very different traumatic experiences, paralleling the move made 20 years earlier by feminist psychologists who broadened the category of "post-traumatic stress" to include victims of abuse in the family, mainly women, alongside veterans of Vietnam and other wars.

For Israeli sociologist Eva Illouz, the *Oprah* telecasts showed how an Americanized therapeutic culture had transformed the Holocaust into a narrative in which the victims became the bearers of a story of "self-overcoming, improvement, and triumph," and how as misery is recycled into a narrative, the self becomes "a double hero: because of what it has suffered from a hostile world and because it can claim ultimate victory over that world and its own self, by overcoming itself."[43] Lee Siegel, writing in *The New Republic*, similarly observed that Oprah has an extraordinary ability to transform all manner of personal problems and historical tragedy into an "immensely reassuring and inspiring message." Watching *Oprah*, he says, "does fill you with hope. It also plunges you into despair. She has become something like America itself."[44]

As the mass media made survivor discourse into a commodity, the relentlessly optimistic, therapeutic tendencies in American culture were working to transform the survivor from a tragic figure to an individual possessing a considerable degree of agency who exemplified authenticity and the realness of suffering, struggling, and coping. At times it all seemed excessive, particularly when it converged with what cultural theorist Marita Sturken calls our "comfort culture," which smooths over loss, transforming it into kitsch, consumerism, and public acquiescence. The remaining "Schindler Jews," who had worked in Oskar Schindler's factory and were immortalized by Steven Spielberg's film, became celebrity-survivors who were in such high demand that they were often booked for speaking engagements over a year in advance.[45]

Critic Alvin Rosenfeld decried this sentimentalizing of the survivor, whom he wrote, enjoys a "greatly heightened public profile and carries about him [sic] an aura that solicits honor, respect, fascination, and no small degree of awe." My own encounter with a young woman who worked in the oral history division of the United States Holocaust Memorial Museum in Washington, DC, who had no familial connection to the Holocaust, seemed to substantiate this claim. When I asked her what the most surprising part of her job was, she responded: "getting to know survivors and seeing that they're just 'ordinary people.'" Ellen Blalock, the museum's head of Survivor Affairs, qualified this somewhat: "They're amazing people, and very human. They have quirks and are cranky too. But they also have a nobility because they've seen and endured things." In other words, the simple fact that they had encountered death, narrowly escaping it, she believed, made them worthy of attention.

The survivor honorific emerged at a time when traumatic experience had come to be invested with moral value and authority, and when trauma became an "envied wound."[46] Echoing earlier critiques by Bettelheim and Langer, some commentators suggested that by helping to transform victims into "survivors," social workers, archivists, museum workers, and other cultural entrepreneurs were succeeding in transforming feelings of despair, disappointment, and passivity into sovereignty and omnipotence, linked to an emergent ethos of neoliberalism. This regime, according to communications scholar Shani Orgad, "recasts everyday experience as a series of manageable problems which are understood and resolved by the autonomous self aspiring to self-possession and happiness."[47] Others saw the survivor as the embodiment of the Christian belief in dignity through suffering. In the late 1990s, when I interviewed Christian conservative activists in Oregon, who had mobilized against gay and lesbian civil rights, if I identified myself as Jewish, they were curious and often even more receptive to talking with me. Their philo-semitism was rooted in the belief that Jewish people were closer to God because, as one evangelical Protestant woman told me, "they had suffered so much."[48]

Of course, survivors did not ask to be anointed as either religious or secular saints, and they were often uncomfortable with being seen as such. And yet these shifts in social understanding enhanced their growing recognition, facilitated their storytelling, and enabled many of them, finally, to find their voices. Those who shared their stories with others often found that by doing so they could more fully integrate their past into their lives, rather than distance themselves from it. They moved out of a "universe of death" and were able, finally, to assert the "continuity of life," as psychiatrist Robert Lifton put it.[49]

As I have suggested, therapeutic ideas were becoming pervasive in American culture, and the "victim" was coming to be valorized as a figure who deserved respect and empathy, rather than shame. Feminists made "testimony" central to the process of sense making, community building, and political action, influencing the ways that many middle-class Americans, particularly baby boomers, talked about themselves. Children of survivors, who were among those who were influenced by this emergent victim discourse, coaxed their parents, finally, to share their stories; as survivors learned to tell their stories, they often became the stories they told. But to see survivors as figures of "distinction"—as the repository of special, authentic knowledge, purely on the basis of having survived—is questionable, many survivors themselves believed. The "distinction figure" may help the listener more than the victim, and may figure largely as a defense mechanism that listeners apply when confronted with stories of suffering.

Just as those who told their stories had many reasons for doing so, those who remained silent, or were ambivalent about claiming the mantle of survivor, also had multiple, complex reasons for feeling that way. Sometimes individuals do not speak because they are cognizant of the limits of memory's ability to re-create the past, and of the essential unshareability of the experience of atrocity.[50] The decision not to speak, which the therapeutic model sees as evidence of repression, may actually be a conscious, empowered choice. Some feared that talking would make them relive the events; others believed that they could not do justice to the memories of their loved ones, or that they lacked the linguistic or conceptual tools to describe the events as fully as they wished. Some feared expressing exposing their deep emotions in public; others wondered what the point of all the talking really was.

"I really don't like much dwelling on the past because there is nothing I can do about that," Edwarda Rorat, a child survivor, told her interviewer, "but I just hope this interview will help somebody." The further they moved from the events, and as their ranks were receding, they often bristled at those who would see them as distinction figures or heroes simply for the fact that they survived. Being a survivor "is nothing to be proud of," said Erwin Baum. Survivors weren't heroes, he believed. They were complex individuals, and were never simply heroes or villains, wounded or healthy, victims or martyrs.

Several years ago, at a community Passover seder in New Jersey, I shared a table with a man who was then in his eighties. When I asked him what brought him to the event, he responded that he was active with the local Jewish community council, and was invited because, he said, somewhat sheepishly, "they call me a Holocaust survivor." As he spoke, I thought back to a book I had read in a college anthropology course many years before, about Ishi, the last remaining member of the Yahi, the last surviving group of the Yana people of California. Ishi was believed to be the last Native American in Northern California to have lived most of his life completely outside of European American culture. He emerged from the wild near Oroville, California, leaving his ancestral homeland in the foothills near Lassen Peak, and after being discovered by a Berkeley anthropologist, was deposited at the university's museum, where a parade of visitors came to gawk at the member of a lost tribe.[51] Were survivors similarly the remaining members of a lost tribe of Jews who inhabited prewar Europe, who could recall a world before the destruction? Some felt a little a bit like Ishi—placed on display, objectified, fetishized.

The gentleman I met at the seder, originally from Berlin, had been caught in the *Anschluss*, forced to flee, losing his home and a number of family members. But was he a "Holocaust survivor," if that term signified a collective identity, a sense of fellowship with the hundreds of thousands of others, from varied countries, who had multiple, complex relationships to their Jewishness? Of this he was not altogether certain. The public image of the "survivor" had long been that of a Jew who had survived the concentration camps—an image reinforced by survivor organizations. But this reluctant survivor did not fit that category.

Even those who were born into Jewish families, but whose Jewish identifications were not central, often wondered whether they were "really" survivors: for example, a woman born into a Berlin Jewish family, who fled

Germany and settled in the United States or Australia or Canada, marrying a non-Jewish man, who does not identify as a "Holocaust survivor," preferring a more "universalistic" definition of herself as activist; those who were persecuted by the Germans for their Jewishness and their homosexuality, but whose complex identifications preclude association with one identity grouping; or people like my father, who spent the war years in Russia, and who never lived under Nazi occupation, though he lost his entire family, and who was therefore excluded from many definitions of who constituted the "survivor."

Every identity excludes as well as includes, privileges certain types of storytellers, and simplifies experience.[52] Some have argued that identifying as a survivor psychically connects victims of the genocide to the perpetrators, defining them in relation to those who tried to murder them.[53] Others have suggested that because the survivor identity requires individuals to take part in self-disclosure, and sees secrets and the preservation of a zone of privacy as anathema to the project of recognition, those who preferred to convey meaning through implicit rather than explicit forms of communication were marginalized by the growing cultural expectation of public storytelling. It is an identity framework that is predicated upon transcending feelings of despair, disappointment, and passivity, and becoming a self-responsible agent that revolves, according to Shani Orgad, "almost entirely around the excision of suffering and pain, thus accentuating the liberal (particularly post-1960s) worldview of individual's entitlement to life without suffering."[54]

Indeed, in listening to the stories of survivors that have been archived, one hears talk of a great deal of suffering, but typically it is suffering that has been relegated to the past. Rarely does one find evidence of continuing shame, anger, and blame. Perhaps individuals felt that it was socially unacceptable to express such sentiments; perhaps the unspoken assumptions of the interview context enforced rules that excluded such expressions. Still, it seemed to me that survivors had rarely been able to make peace with the past. This became clearly evident to me in 1993 on my trip to Warsaw, to commemorate the fiftieth anniversary of the Warsaw Ghetto Uprising, that heroic but ultimately failed attempt on the part of a small band of Jewish resisters to defend the ghetto.

As part of the commemorative activities, a group of survivors and their children took part in a memorial ceremony at Treblinka, the site of the former death camp, where the majority of Warsaw's Jews had been systematically murdered. It was a rainy, cold day, and at the end of the mournful ritual, in which a number of dignitaries and survivor spokesmen politely commemorated the dead, an old man commandeered the microphone, and introduced himself as a survivor from Canada. We expected him to make an announcement instructing members of his delegation where to meet their buses. But instead he began to shout angrily, "On this site, countless numbers of our men, our women, and our children were taken to their deaths!" His voice grew progressively louder and louder. "How could the world have let this happen?" he boomed, as people began to file out of the vast, barren site of the former camp, his voice echoing against the somber fields surrounding it. "Millions of our people! How could this have happened?" The incident disturbed the sense of closure carefully orchestrated by the memorial committee and revealed, for all to see, that traumatic histories live on many years after the fact.

If the survivor identity was predicated on transcending despair, one can imagine why many survivors refused to take on this role. While narratives of victimhood and survival helped some individuals to organize their sense of self and integrate their painful memories more effectively into their lives, for many, the rubric of the "survivor" remained out of reach, perhaps because of lingering feelings of shame, or because of their incapacity or unwillingness to transcend feelings of despair. While telling one's story offered the possibility of integrating one's past into the present, it also required individuals to separate from the dead, which they may not have been capable of, or willing, to do.[55]

In 1972 Larry Stein, my father, wrote of his wartime past in a letter to his cousin Irena in Poland: "I never mention anything about any of what happened to Pearl and the kids," he told her. "Why should I? What is there to be proud of?" I believe he was deeply ambivalent about his own status as survivor, and indeed about the label in general. He believed that having survived was not a special status that should be embraced—it was a matter of dumb luck, or accident. Never having been imprisoned in a concentration camp, he tended to downplay his suffering: "others suffered much more than I did," he often said. Labeling himself a survivor would also have required him to psychically separate himself from his parents, his sister, and the rest of his murdered family, which he may not have been willing to do.

My father did not live long enough to see the U.S. Holocaust Memorial Museum in Washington, DC, which was dedicated the year after his death, or even *Schindler's List*. Had I twisted his arm, perhaps he would have shared his story with those who were beginning to collect survivors' accounts. But for various reasons I never did: I lived on the other side of the country, his traumatic experiences were a taboo subject, and it remained, until his death, something that our relationship could not breach. Had he lived to see the growing institutionalization of Holocaust memorial culture, I wonder whether he would have changed his tune, and claimed the identity of "survivor." I imagine that he would have been deeply ambivalent about according his experience an honored status, an envied wound. Rather than embrace the emergent culture of triumphant suffering, he would have greeted it with a great deal of skepticism, not at all convinced that talking would help. Perhaps, with my coaxing, I could have convinced him to talk, but I never did. Therefore, his story, along with the stories of other ambivalent witnesses, will not be part of the archival record.

It wasn't until after my father's death in 1992 that I began to try to piece together his history, to get to know him and the world he had lost. At around the same moment, unbeknownst to me, descendants throughout the world were doing much the same, extending our parents' stories further in the past, and producing new stories of our own.

CHAPTER 5

Ghosts into Ancestors

Ghosts long to be released from their ghost life and led to rest as ancestors. As ancestors they live forth in the present generation, while as ghosts they are compelled to haunt the present generation with their shadow life.

Hans Loewald

To love someone is to put yourself in their place, we say, which is to put yourself in their story, or figure out how to tell yourself their story.

Rebecca Solnit

As they became mindful of the fact that they were becoming the primary bearers of living memory and generational continuity, descendants' desire to know more about their shadow ancestors often intensified. By the new millennium, more and more survivors' children engaged in genealogical practices, excavating family stories, photographs, and letters, traveling to parents' places of origin, and telling stories about their memory projects. As the survivor generation declined and the "second generation" entered middle age, they redoubled their efforts to excavate, piece together, and re-fashion their fractured legacies. If, in an earlier moment, this work had focused on eliciting stories of their parents' wartime experiences, as the descendants moved into mid-life, their knowledge quests deepened, often extending further backward, into the prewar years. They sought out stories that would situate their parents' and grandparents' lives and conjure a picture of the world they lived in before the destruction.

Wishing to touch and smell the worlds their parents had left behind, and to know more about the grandparents they never knew, they traveled alone or in groups to their parents' places of origin; they conducted oral histories with surviving relatives; they produced films and memoirs that narrated their parents' biographies, and they searched for documentary objects such as letters and photographs. Like detectives and archaeologists, these post-Holocaust memory workers began with fragments of evidence and worked backward, searching for clues, deciphering signs and traces, and making deductions.

Helen Fremont, the daughter of Polish Jews, vividly described in a memoir how she gradually pieced together the story of her family, gathering bits of information from her mother ("anecdotes stripped of context, shrouded in mystery"), from libraries, museums, and other survivors. She and her sister spent days and nights on the phone, examining their lives from every angle, finding clues and hints "scattered across our childhood and adolescence." They "plunged into history books and met with survivors, historians, and rabbis," calling each other every day "bubbling with ideas and leads." With time, a story began to take shape of "overlapping layers of history and family, fact and omission."[1]

Eve, who grew up in a community of Jewish refugee poultry farmers in southern New Jersey, drew a division between "Americans," including Jews and Gentiles, and survivor families like her own: "The Americans had a history," she said. "They could trace their history. They had grandparents. They had uncles and aunts, and most of us didn't." In addition to having few relatives, children of survivors rarely had access to physical representations of their extended families—photographs, heirlooms, or mundane, ephemeral objects—traces of the past. "You know, people have pictures," said Eve. "My husband has pictures from like the 1800s or something. I didn't even know what my grandfather looked like."

At times, even if photographs of murdered family members existed, parents hid them from view. Sam's father was married before the war and had two children, both of whom were killed. His father immigrated to the United States, remarried, and had two children, Sam among them. His father had photographs of his first family, from the early 1930s, that he had hidden from his children all of those years, but he finally showed them to them when Sam was in his early twenties, when he broke his silence about his first family. But after that initial conversation, they never again spoke about them, and Sam never again saw the photographs. He was acutely aware of their absence.

"I have a very heightened sensitivity to films, to photographs," said Shelley. "Because I don't have any scrapbooks of family pictures, every face could be a face of a relative. Even though the number of my mother's family is finite, when I see pictures of hundreds, they all become related to me in a sense because any one of them could be a true family member." She spoke eloquently about this absence, and the ways she sometimes found herself scouring historical photographs of prewar European Jewry for images that seem familiar. "I'll never know which ones were. On rare occasions my mother has found books, from before the war, of people who were in her family, of very formal stylized portraits, and I look at them kind of like I look at a picture of Queen Victoria—it's such a far relation." Acknowledging the difficulty of the task, she said: "It's such an abrupt halt in any kind of family continuity because there are no letters or photographs or visual sightings or meetings. It's trying to relate something personal to a stranger."

Susan similarly suggested that children of survivors and adoptees shared a sense of incompleteness. "True we know who our parents are," she said. "But so much has been robbed from those of us who lost grandparents, aunts, uncles, and potential cousins," said Susan. "I always felt 'incomplete,' or at least not like my friends with American born parents because I never knew my mother's immediate family." This sense of absence motivated her to search for evidence of her familial history. "I became very interested in finding out my parents' and my families' histories so that I could understand who I was and why I was here, and how I became who I was."

Encouraged by her involvement in the second generation movement, Susan took some tentative steps toward filling in the gaps of her knowledge when she was in her early twenties. Her genealogical work intensified when she reached middle age and her parents neared the end of their lives. "I was uncomfortable with not having a family pedigree, even among other Jews who presumably would understand what was missing from my own life." Susan expressed discomfort with not having a "pedigree," a story of origins. This absent story became salient and troubling to her as her parents aged, and as she had children of her own.

Nathalie, who was born in France to Polish parents, named her first son after her father and realized that "[she] had no knowledge of [her] family history before the Shoah." Her roots journey began, she says, with a single question: "I was naming my son after my father—but after whom was my father named?" She talked to an aunt in Paris who, she said, "started to babble about the family and giving me names of dozens of people." It then "hit" her: "my family existed before the Shoah. I know it may sound stupid but I had never internalized there was something before the Shoah. In America maybe or in Asia there was life before the Shoah. But not where I come from." What is remarkable about this comment is the claim that she had never understood that her family existed before the Holocaust, which suggests that events of the war so dominated her and other children of survivors' imaginations that they had little idea that there was ever a "before."

"Now that I am alone, and my parents are fading away mentally," Malka, another daughter of survivors revealed, "something has happened to me." She registered a powerful desire "to go back," and to "share [her] process with [her] grown daughters. "The feelings have opened up again. I feel compelled to search for missing relatives," she said. And drawing upon therapeutic language, she said, "I need closure. I need not to be left alone with this pain, before they are gone from me. I am no longer numb, as I was for many years."

As a participant-observer in an electronic mailing list for children of survivors ("2G"), I was struck by how many individuals were involved in genealogical projects of some sort, and I became interested in finding out more about what motivated such memory work. I also conducted a series of open-ended interviews with children of survivors living in the New York area, and read a dozen published memoirs by children of survivors, looking for evidence of genealogical activities. (Interviewees are identified by first and last names; participants in the listserv by first names only.)

On a second generation discussion list, there were lively exchanges in which individuals shared information on tracing lost relatives, compared notes about their respective successes and failures in tracking down concentration camp records, and described visits to their parents' places of origin. Their motivations for undertaking this research varied: some wished to search for surviving relatives and make contact with them; others simply wanted to find some kind of tangible proof of their parents' and grandparents' lives; some wanted to be able to develop a clearer understanding of their family backgrounds and the chronology of wartime events; while others wanted an opportunity to mourn their losses. What they shared was a desire for origin narratives that offered greater clarity and coherence.

As they discussed their parents' places of birth, they helped each other make sense of their findings and supported those who wished to undertake such memory work. For some searchers, the prospect of finding living relatives was a prime motivation. "I've been researching family and relatives for over 30 years," writes Annette. "Recently, I had a breakthrough and found family in Israel. I feel my search has come to an end. In other words, one of them knows how most of the family perished in the Holocaust. Both my parents are deceased and these people seem to be replacing them. Does this make sense?"

Elaine wrote: "Just a couple of months ago I received a fax with the name of a relative that I never knew existed! I cannot even begin to describe how excited I was when I received a letter from him. Can you imagine receiving a letter with a name that you thought was wiped out from the face of the earth?" Responding to this post, Cecile wrote that she was "so moved" by the account of the search that she was motivated to do the same. "I am inspired by your persistence and bravery in searching into the painful past, of the fate of your relatives," she said, observing how commonplace it was at that moment. "It seems an interesting phenomenon, some 2nd-gens are undergoing at this time, the need to know and educate themselves about the sketchy past, so someone will know, before it is too late to find out."

She, too, was considering undertaking her own memory work. "I know little about the fate of any of my mother's family, who all perished," Cecile admitted. "Many were young teenagers. My father had many relatives who were murdered as well....Would you please give me the details of the agencies you contacted and the addresses? I would like to follow up on this." She was conscious of the fact that time was running out. "It will only be me and my daughters who will know," she said, "as my parents are not very cognizant of the present these days." This genealogical work afforded descendants the chance to come to know their parents better, to mourn them if they are dead, and to pass this information to their children.

A GENERATION IN SEARCH OF STORIES

Sociologist Anthony Giddens has written that the "reflexivity of modernity" leads to doubt rather than certainty, as identities are constantly called into question. We try to address this growing doubt through forms of identity work: planning, journal keeping, and consulting therapists. We reflexively construct our self-identities by preparing for the future, as well as by "reworking past events." We work hard at constructing an "integrated sense of self" that maintains a semblance of continuity through time, connecting past, present future.[2] In many respects, the second generation exemplified this trend, and had a great deal in common with other Americans. Since the "roots" movement of the 1960s and 1970s, genealogy has become one of the most popular hobbies in the United States. In an anthropological sense, genealogies are products of imagined kinship relations that connect people over time and across space. Genealogists hunt for a line of descent or pedigree in order to locate themselves in temporal schema and narrative history. The further one journeys back, the more one has in common with others—common ancestors, common points of origin. The contemporary expansion of genealogy represents a search for identity and origins in an uncertain world.

But while genealogists seek to establish a line of family continuity that comforts them with pleasurable memories of endurance, second generation memory workers begin with knowledge of trauma—a "dramatic loss of identity and meaning, a tear in the social fabric affecting a group of people who have achieved some degree of cohesion."[3] While hobbyists reach far back into history to reconstruct lines of biological succession over several generations or more, post-Holocaust genealogists, operating in the context of families in which the traumatic past was typically off limits, and having grown up with little knowledge of their ancestral heritage, are content to reach back only one or two generations—to their parents and grandparents. They are not merely hobbyists seeking a vicarious connection to unknown ancestors: they are individuals for whom war and genocide severed a connection to their familial roots, who wish to construct a sense of continuity. In this sense, one can see genealogical projects undertaken by many children of survivors as a continuation of their quest to "break the silence" about the Holocaust—a silence imposed by the survivors and others, and in which many children of survivors were complicit—and as a reckoning with ghosts.

Their motivations were not altogether different from those of adoptees who are denied knowledge of their genealogy, who develop an intense desire to know about their biological parentage—a British psychologist calls this "genealogical bewilderment"—and Betty Jean Lifton, an activist for adoptees' rights, compares the experience of adoptees to that of "survivors of a holocaust of one kind or another."[4] The psychological impact of "being saved from the perils of war or famine" and of being adopted, she writes, is similar: both lead to a severing of familial roots. "Lacking full knowledge of that clan, he or she feels an alien, an outsider, an orphan, a foundling, or a changeling—outside of the natural realm of being," says Lifton. She or he therefore hungers for answers that "the mystery of their heritage has denied them. Who am I? The adopted adolescent asks. Who do I look like and act like? What religion and nationality am I?"[5]

For some adoptees, being denied information about one's biological parentage leads to a sense of inauthenticity, of having a "false" self, and not feeling connected to anyone. Such arguments imply the existence of an essential "core" self beneath a "false," socially imposed self. A psychologist who has written extensively about the Holocaust second generation suggests that the descendant child grows up sensing that he or she never actually knows the parent's "true" self.[6] Positing a primal need for origins and equating biological origins with authentic identity, they suggest that genealogical knowledge can uncover the "real" self within. But rather than see the desire for origins as somehow essential, one might interpret it in terms of the widely held cultural expectation that individuals should know about their beginnings. Late modern societies require individuals to sustain coherent biographical narratives, or "self-stories," that can be shared with others.[7]

This memory work is often highly gendered; the vast majority of those who describe their excavation projects on second generation listservs and write about them in memoirs are women. Some might explain women's over-representation as post-Holocaust memory workers (at least among those who report on such practices publicly) as evidence of their traditional roles as ritual keepers: women are more likely to do "kin work" to maintain ritual observances and emotional ties among family members. Anthropologist Micaela di Leonardo suggests that women do the emotional labor that builds and maintains familial bonds: sending holiday cards, organizing family gatherings, and so forth.[8] Female memory workers, particularly those who have been influenced by feminism, often embraced therapeutic ideas of self-discovery and revelation, which have provided a major impetus for such projects. Indeed, women have disproportionately been active in the "second generation" movement, and seem to be more heavily invested in genealogical projects.[9]

Descendants initiated memory work at two different moments of heightened sensitivity to the past: after having children, and after losing a parent. These were moments when, according to Erik Erikson, people become concerned with generativity, with establishing and guiding the next generation, and when they are more aware of their own mortality.[10] This is not to say that all children of survivors, or even all women of this cohort, are equally invested in such practices, and indeed some individuals are much more likely to take this role on than others. A number of descendants remarked that they played the role of genealogist—tracking down lost relatives, constructing family trees, organizing excursions to their ancestral homes. Their siblings, and even their parents, did not always share their interest, and were sometimes amused or even downright hostile toward it. Nonetheless, they persisted in their efforts.

Often their parents conveyed little more than fragments of past experience—images of fleeing across borders, of having little to eat, of hiding—a random string of events that was difficult for them to perceive as a story. They may have described an incident without explaining what caused it, or what it might in turn cause, offering fragments of a story lacking order.[11] Consequently, descendants faced challenges in understanding the temporal and cause and effect relationships linking various events in their parents' lives. What were their parents' and grandparents' lives like before the coming of Nazi destruction? What was the sequence of wartime events that displaced them from their homes? What was the temporal duration of different events? What locales did the events take place in? These are some of the lingering questions they are left asking.

They are acutely aware of the passage of time. As the last links to living memory of the Holocaust, they see themselves as a bridge between their parents' generation and that of their children. While a parent's death closes off the possibility of knowing certain things, it may also free individuals to undertake memory work that was off limits when parents were living. Rena began to read about the Shoah when she was in her early and mid-thirties, and then stopped, she says. She didn't start excavating any further until two years after her mother died, when she found letters written by family members who had perished, when she was in her late fifties. Over about a year, she said, she found several batches of letters in different places, written to her parents, and to a sister of her father in England. There was a postcard from her mother's mother from Thereisenstadt to someone in her home village. They were letters written from Belgium, Holland, internment camps in France, and other places. For a while, she said, "I felt that I was a roller coaster of emotions as these relatives who had only been names began to show personalities to me through their writing."

For those seeking information about dead relatives, the recovery of lost objects, such as letters, photographs, or even names listed in a concentration camp documents, can make them feel closer to the dead; the objects act as talismans that carry the affective weight of the past. Parents hesitated to speak about their dead, frequently because they wished to shield their children from their losses. Since their parents rarely if ever talked about their dead relatives, children of survivors knew little about them. For Rena, who knew names and ages, but little else about these relatives, finding their letters gave her, for the first time, some sense of who they were as people. Others, like Helena, were content to find physical proof of her mother's family story in a calendar of events from the Auschwitz concentration camp. That piece of evidence "is the only page commemorating those whom, during my trip to Poland with my mother, I forced myself for the first time to call grandparents and aunts and uncles," she wrote.[12] Having tangible, physical proof of the existence of these individuals who had before occupied a ghostly existence, led her, for the first time, to call them her relatives.

In the absence of human remains, by finding such artifacts, or locating their ancestors' lives in a specific place, descendants report feeling a kind of corporeal presence that mediates the absence of the dead, and offers newfound connections to them. "Zawiercie is about 20 miles away from Auschwitz, and even an overloaded freight or livestock train doesn't take long to get there," Helena noted. Finding physical traces of these lives becomes, for these memory workers, a way to claim these dead relatives as their own, and to transform their "ghosts into ancestors," as psychoanalyst Hans Loewald described.[13] Simcha, whose grandparents and aunt were deported from France to Auschwitz contacted Yad Vashem, Israel's Holocaust museum, and found the date and history of the transport they were on to Auschwitz. She excitedly reported on her discovery to other participants on the discussion list: "Today I got a reply from Yad Vashem, only two weeks after I sent in my request," she wrote. "My heart was in my stomach when I opened the envelope and sure enough, enclosed were photocopies of records on both of my grandparents. The information is heartbreaking. I feel like I am in mourning today."

Indeed, one could see this memory work as a kind of mourning "by proxy," as psychoanalyst Anna Fodorova put it. Describing the second generation, she wrote: "Everything about 'their dead' remained blank: their names, their age, their life stories; where, when, and how they met their end." In effect, they "disappeared without a trace." There were no photographs, no items of clothing they wore, no utensils they used—"nothing that could help construct an image of who they were." The first generation, their parents, often shielded their children from loss by referring to the dead as their parents, sisters, and brothers, rather than as their children's grandparents, uncles, and aunts. The next generation therefore "missed out both on meeting these relatives and also, by being denied the experience of formulating words such as 'my grandmother' or 'my aunt,' the opportunity to identify with them as concepts." The absence of naming, writes Fodorova, created a vacuum in which "the dead could only be internalized in the form of a painful, secret absence."[14]

As children of survivors entered middle age and had children of their own, many began to enthusiastically excavate the past—facilitated by the rise of genealogical sites on the Internet, and listservs for second generation members, and by the growing cultural interest in "roots," histories of victimhood, and by the influence of therapeutic discourse. Some individuals were in search of living relatives in far-flung places; others simply wanted verification of relatives' deaths, or physical evidence of their existence. The electronic lists constituted an interpretive community that inspired them to undertake searches, helped to make sense of their findings, and supported the work of mourning. Some individuals concluded their efforts, satisfied that they recovered the information they had sought, or had recovered as much as they possibly could, given the limitations of their resources. For others, however, a name on the Internet or even a photographic image was little substitute for the immediacy and materiality of "being there." They wanted to smell the smells, hear the languages, and walk in the footsteps of their ancestors. Therefore they sought more direct encounters with their parents' lost worlds.

THERE'S NO PLACE LIKE HOME

Holocaust survivors and their descendants constitute a significant proportion of Jewish "heritage" tourists to Central and Eastern Europe. Some travel in search of those who hid their families during the war; others come to pay homage at the death camps, or simply to see where their ancestors once lived. Bringing communities of memory into closer contact with their collective past, these journeys share some commonalities with those that devout Muslims make to Mecca on the *hajj* or that orthodox Jews make to the Western Wall.[15] At the same time, for Jewish survivors of genocide and their descendants, these are not simply "roots" journeys: for them, Europe is a "traumascape," a "distinct category of place transformed physically and psychically by suffering" that forecloses the possibility of easy identification.[16]

The relationship between Jewish immigrants living in the United States and their European kin, which was once marked by continuous, if sporadic, back and forth travel and communication, evolved, after World War II, into one in which a shared past is the only common denominator. For most of the postwar period, the Cold War made much of Europe virtually off limits to those in the West. Travel became easier after the fall of the Soviet Union in 1989, and has continued to develop as Poland, Hungary, and other former communist nations have come to recognize and value Jewish tourism and Western tourist dollars, renovating historically significant buildings and erecting markers and monuments at various sites. Noting the rise in Jewish tourism to Eastern Europe during the 1980s and 1990s, one observer wryly suggested: "No visitor to the area can look through a camera viewfinder and be assured that another American or Israeli will not suddenly appear to mar the 'pristine' view."[17]

Some have attributed the rise in roots tourism to the fact that "humans remain sensual beings, and they are ill at ease with information that can be perceived only as a representation of itself." In other words, the search for authenticity and "realness" may become more important precisely because so little of the past remains.[18] While many members of diasporic groups travel to their ancestral homeland hoping for closer contact with an authentic "Irishness" or "Chineseness" or "Jewishness," today an unmediated identification or easy return to an ancestral homeland is, of course, impossible. When young Chinese-Americans travel to their ancestral villages, for example, rather than discover homelands stuck in time, their mythical conceptions of Chineseness are frequently challenged, and they develop new understandings of themselves.[19] In other words, "home" is not simply recovered—it is built through the work of the imagination and emotions and is grasped through reconstruction.

Much as Jews are drawn to Jerusalem's Western Wall, second generation memory workers touch the last remaining wall of the Warsaw ghetto—a reminder that "home" is forever out of reach. These sites conjure memories of close extended families, security, and warmth, but they are also sites of dispossession, where nostalgic attachments and visions of wholeness are tempered by the reality that Jews faced anti-Semitic pogroms in many European nations, and never felt themselves to be full citizens, despite having lived there for generations or more.

Immediately after World War II, many survivors traveled to back to their hometowns in search of remaining relatives. These were painful journeys that often took place amid fears of anti-Semitic attacks, which were quite common, particularly in postwar Poland. Recounted in *yizkor* books, which memorialized their lost communities, returnees' first impressions inevitably include the striking absence of Jews. They found towns in ruins, with cats, dogs, and chickens roaming freely, and bustling places where little seemingly has changed. But for the survivors, the absence of Jews often means that life is absent, and they feel alien and out of place.[20] These journeys forced survivors to confront the enormity of their losses, and many vowed never again to return.

While survivors had memories of the worlds they had lost, their children did not. They had story fragments, and scattered objects upon which descendants had projected their fantasies—what literary critic Marianne Hirsch terms "postmemories." Their relationship to their parents' places of origin were shaped by these imagined reckonings. That they would take these journeys at the close of the twentieth century was influenced by their stage in the life course, and by political events, including the fact that after the collapse of the Soviet Union, former Eastern bloc countries were opened again to Western travelers.

Their trips often entailed a great degree of emotional labor, and travelers often reported that they were on edge, and did not fully enjoy the food, or the landscapes, or the sheer pleasure of traveling. Anita traveled to her mother's town in Poland in the early 1990s after the Polish government erected a memorial plaque at the first synagogue burned down by the Nazis. "I can tell you this," she reported on a second generation listserv: "they are as anti-semetic [*sic*] now as ever and hate the Jews with a vengeance—I saw it first hand. I feel very, very little pity for them." Jeanette concurred with Anita's negative assessment: "I have no love of Europe," she declared, and "though as a kid I thought it was quaint, my last couple of trips proved to me that the blood soaked soil of that continent reeks like hell itself and there is Zero socially redeeming value there, as far as I am concerned." Mincing no words, she pronounced it "a depressing place," noting "the sizes of the chimneys in Germany are astounding."

After arriving home, Ginni offered the following cautionary advice for others planning similar trips to their ancestral homes: "Poland is a VERY difficult place to visit—as you can well imagine, so I'd recommend preparing as well as you can, physically (bring toilet paper, especially if you're a woman who might get her period), emotionally (How to prepare to walk on soil where so many people died such cruel deaths, as people now, go about their daily activities, is no an easy task)." If Jeanette saw Germany as a depressing place filled with monstrous chimneys, Ginni saw Poland as a vast cemetery filled with damaged, backward people. "The people there seemed as damaged as you'd imagine people who survived seeing their city torn to shreds and their family and neighbors die," she wrote. "They are also very new to democracy and poverty is great."

Here we see children of survivors expressing antagonism toward the nations that, in effect, expelled their parents. Theirs is an anti-nostalgia founded, at least in part, on American exceptionalism. Why, then, do members of the second generation undertake such voyages? For varied reasons. Some trips are initiated by parents who wish to show their children where they grew up, or who want to introduce them to the individuals who aided their survival. While descendants sometimes initiate these trips, enlisting their parents to accompany them as tour guides, many travel without parents, if their parents do not wish to go, because making the trip would be too difficult emotionally, or because their parents are dead.

In 1975, when she was a sophomore in college, Esther Dezube traveled to Poland with her mother, who wanted to visit the man who had saved her life. Since there were no Jewish groups organizing trips at the time, they went with a Roman Catholic group, led by a priest whom they never told they were Jewish. They spent a week with the family who saved her mother and father in Warsaw, and then went to see Esther's father's house. The trip allowed Esther to initiate a dialogue with her mother and gave her greater empathy for her experiences. Esther and her mother, who had had a very tempestuous relationship, became "quite close" on that trip," she says. "She would hold my hand and I didn't want to hold her hand because I thought that was not the right thing to do," she recalled. "But she would never hug and cuddle and kiss me. I was not a huggy person either. But we did hold hands then. It was almost like the world against us."[21]

They search for beginnings and endings, a continuous narrative of their parents' and grandparents' lives, a chain of events in a cause-effect relationship occurring in time and space, and for a coherent origin story of their own.[22] These memory workers are not simply recovering memories: they are creating genealogical narratives that "express the profound feelings they have in the present."[23] Undertaking this memory work with their parents at their side seems to intensify the feeling that they are "back there" in the past. Travelers say they have a better sense of "what made their parents who they are."[24] Jack always wanted to visit Poland with his father, but his father refused to go because, he said, "the loss was overwhelming for him." It would have been "devastatingly hard to go to a place that you had lived your entire childhood and adolescence and there is nothing there; there's not a person, not a school building, not the apartment you lived in, not the place where you had your first job and there is no one there, not a one, not a single person that he knew in all of Warsaw," he said. "I think that that was way more than he was willing to handle."

The structure of the journey is by now familiar: the voyager travels to an unknown landscape with a family member, or with a translator. They rent a car and travel to an ancestral home, to find a ruin of a destroyed building. All around them, curious townspeople congregate and a translator asks: How long have you lived here? Did you know the Levinksi family? They lived here before the war. The townspeople respond: no, but point to another section of town and suggest: "they would know." They soldier on, sometimes enlisting public officials or local experts to guide their search. The searcher wonders how his grandfather must have felt walking down those streets. He walks in their footsteps and tries to imagine their feelings and responses to their changing environment, and tells himself: "that would've been what they would've seen."

One grows up with grandparents or parents who are old, who seem so different from one self. By placing oneself in the land of their birth and reenacting journeys, real and imagined, that their relatives may have taken, descendants are able to picture them as their age and therefore bring them symbolically closer. Their parents had little doubt about reality; they saw that world in color; for their descendants, the images are in black and white. These trips offer them the possibility of developing a more multidimensional sense of place.

At first, a second generation memoirist writes of her own compulsion to seek the actual site of her familial roots, the motivation was nostalgic. She wanted to know, she says, the look of the land, the smell of the air, the sounds of the street. She wanted images that could support "a sense of the world" that had shaped her father and mother. She wanted "mental pictures for a kind of internal family album, material details that would help me imagine the past of each of my parents and, by implication, the past of theirs."[25] Indeed, accounts of children of survivors' pilgrimages to the birthplaces of their parents are rife with sensual descriptions, as evident in this memoir by Lisa Appignanesi:

> A woman has spread her wares on the pavement—huge panniers of raspberries and dill. I sniff at them and again realize that the outdoor smells of rural Poland are familiar to me. Something about the odor of weeds in moist earth, of hidden blueberries, or fern, or plum and apple boughs heavy with fruit beckons to me. I had always assumed these were smells of the Canadian countryside, but they are here, now, on this street.[26]

These travelogues feature thick descriptions of the sights and the smells of food, and of the streets—and the looming presence of absent ancestors. On a website documenting her travels to Lodz and Krakow, Poland, one woman wrote the following: "Driving through the city in torrential rains (and on the now elegant street where they once lived) I feel my mother's presence." Where the former ghetto was liquidated, "standing on a hill beside a huge statue of Moses, overlooking a vast park, I feel the melancholy in the air." Later, as she walks through a cemetery, past centuries-old tombstones "shrouded by nettles and shifted with time, I feel haunted by whimpering spirits of the dead."[27]

Individuals undertake these trips as way of knowing their parents' places of origin in a more complex way, of understanding who their ancestors were as people rather than simply as casualties, and coming to know these places with greater clarity, and to know their parents better. As these heartfelt travelogues suggest, they also seek to engage with these places emotionally. Who were their parents, they ask, "before" the traumatic events that changed their lives forever? How did they live? How did they survive? The ability to see and touch these places gives them an emotional resonance that makes them "real."

During the last year of the war, memoirist Barbara Finkelstein said, her father told her that he hid in the woods with a woman and her six-year-old son. But Finkelstein finds herself unable to "conjure up what this means exactly." Even though she traveled to the Polish woods, she says, "I cannot picture my father as a sixteen-year-old boy, lighting a match to roast potatoes, sleeping without a blanket in the forest, talking to a woman and her child." She imagines herself in his place. "My fear of bugs, rats, and mice, let alone killers, would have unhinged my mind in several places." In the end, she says, she laments the "deficiencies of her imagination." Despite her best efforts to understand what her father endured, her father's story about "hiding in the woods," she says, "has always been a mystery that my mind could never negotiate."[28]

These encounters with the "real," with places once imagined as "past" but which live on in the present, often require a great deal of imaginative work. The descendants move through the streets declaring, "this may have been where my grandfather lived," but the original buildings are likely to be gone, the storytellers, for the most part, are absent, and their parents' wartime experiences are too terrible, or too far from their reality, to fully grasp.

For years, Alan Sadovnik tried to convince his parents to visit Germany. He had always wanted to see where they had grown up, and felt that it was important for them to return. His father refused to travel to Europe, claiming he had nothing but bad memories; his mother had little desire to visit either. But in 1995, Alan successfully persuaded his mother to join him on a trip to Berlin. On a tour sponsored by the city for Jewish returnees, they visited his mother's old house, the ruins of the old central synagogue, and the cemetery where his grandparents were buried. Initially she was afraid to speak German again. But once she tried, "She would go to anyone who would listen," Alan recalls: "We'd go to the bakery in the morning, and she'd say: 'I was born in Berlin. We left here in '39 on the *kindertransport*. I'm back, and here's my son.' And basically what she was saying was: you didn't kill us all. And it many ways it was a triumph for her."[29]

They toured Berlin and met family who he never knew existed, including a cousin who had married a Catholic and survived the war. For Alan, "[i]t was a very emotional trip," he said. "We both cried a lot." Despite the fact that his mother was reluctant to go, it proved to be "an amazing experience...now she's so grateful she did go. I think it provided some closure." Alan said the trip gave him "a sense of roots, and reinforced the horrors." A daughter of survivors who visited Poland with her father similarly recounted that the visit "helped me to more fully understand what life was like for them prewar and during the war. When my Dad was looking around his town, he was seeing it as it appeared in 1939 and was able to impart that to us. Otherwise, since no Jewish building is left there, I would have had no way to knowing what I was really looking at."

As they grew older, many descendants developed a curiosity about whether the mythic images, cobbled together from parents' stories, or from movies and novels, were in fact accurate representations. A common refrain one hears among those who travel to their parents' places of origin is "I only ever saw the names of these places in books. Here they were in reality." Some describe an almost mystical familiarity with homelands they have never before visited. Sandi Goodman was born to German-Jewish parents who were connected to a larger community of refugees in the Washington Heights neighborhood of Manhattan. Her mother often spoke lovingly of the town where she grew up, south of Stuttgart, in the Black Forest, where her family had lived since the 1600s. After the war, her mother, like many German-Jewish refugees, remained proud of her German roots, and viewed Nazism as an aberration rather than an expression of true Germanness. She continued to buy German products. In 1989, when she was 32, Sandi decided to travel to Germany with her partner. While she had never before visited, she said she had a sense "in her body" that she had "been there before." She rented a car and drove around the countryside, and "knew my way around instinctively," she said.

Sandi remembers being behind the wheel of the car and feeling instantly familiar with the landscape. When she visited her mother's hometown, where a German dialect was spoken, she recalls, "I understand everything they said." They visited a family who knew her grandparents. When she knocked on the door, an old woman opened it, and took one look at Sandi and called her by her mother's name. "I don't even think that I particularly looked like my mother," she recalled in amazement.

Places of origin that had been so dramatically severed from their parents' lives live on as shadows in the imagination, and the psyches, of many children of survivors. They travel to these places in the hope of collapsing space and time, and making them, for the first time, "real." Such journeys often begin with what literary historian Svetlanta Boym calls "restorative nostalgia," an attempt to draw connection to an imagined, often idealized, community of origin. But they frequently result in a more complex relationship to that place or family of origin—a "reflective nostalgia" that acknowledges that one can never go home, that sees the quest for origins as inconclusive, and acknowledges that the past can never again be.[30] Many individuals who take these trips find them to be so moving, or unsettling, that they write about them, or make films that document them. A growing spate of written and filmed memoirs features children of survivors who travel to the place where a family member lived, or was either murdered or rescued during World War II, who narrates the family member's life history, and reflects upon her own relationship to the past.

QUEST MEMOIRS

In 1979, when she was 30, Helen Epstein, a journalist, wrote the first popular book about the experiences of children of survivors, which helped lay the foundation for members of the second generation to develop a collective identity. Twenty years later, and solidly in middle age, Epstein decided to learn more about her mother's past, and subsequently published an account of her mother's early life in Prague. Like many children of survivors, this excavation project began shortly after her mother's death. The research took her to far-flung parts of the United States, Czechoslovakia, Austria, and Israel, to archives, and family friends and acquaintances, and took eight years to complete. In the book Epstein intersperses the story of her mother's life with an account of Czechoslovak Jewry, chronicling three generations of women in her family.[31]

Hundreds of similar memoirs—part travelogue, part elegy—followed suit, including such titles: "Coming Full Circle," "Return to Poland," "The Journey to Poland," *Ashes and Miracles: A Polish Journey; Journey to Vaja, Konin: A Quest; Hiding Places: A Father and His Sons Retrace Their Family's Escape from the Holocaust*; "Return to Poland: In Search of my Parents' Memories"; *One Family: Before and During the Holocaust*.[32] As these titles suggest, the narratives are often organized as quests that reveal hidden secrets about a family member, and describe the author's own coming to terms with his or her parents' past.

In one such book, Lev Raphael, the son of survivors from Germany, describes growing up in the United States, haunted by his parents' past, and loathing everything German. Those feelings shaped his Jewish and gay identity, his life, and his career. He was certain that Germany was one place in the world he would never visit. But after his mother dies, he decides to journey to that "poisoned land." Much to his surprise, he finds a distant relative living in the very city where his mother had been a slave laborer. In the process, we learn, the author discovers "a new self: someone unafraid to face the past and transcend it." The memoir blends travelogue and trauma memoir, describing in great deal the therapeutic effects of coming to terms with his mother's traumatic past. Journeying to a place that once held so many family secrets, and that was the focus of so much traumatic energy, became the route through which "the barriers of a lifetime began to come down."[33]

For Raphael, finding a distant relative still living in the place of so much death becomes a link to the past. Many descendant memoirs are organized similarly around the emergence of information that challenges the author's conceptions about the past. Raphael believed that all of his relatives had been killed, and is proven wrong. Mimi Schwartz, in another memoir, grows up believing that all Germans were murderers, only to find that was not the case in her father's small town. Schwartz compares her own experience as an American teenager brought up "on milkshakes and hamburgers," with her father's boyhood stories, growing up in a village in Germany where, according to her father, "before Hitler, everyone got along." She "rarely took the stories seriously," she said, suspecting that her father embellished them to hide the bitter truth from her. But then, many years later, she heard "a remarkable story" of Christians from that village who rescued a Torah on the night of *Kristallnacht*. That propelled her on "a twelve-year quest that covered three continents" to find out more.[34] Her book describes that quest, and her own simultaneous story of awakening.

Other memoirs are more concerned with documenting family histories. For example, Andrew Kolin's *One Family: Before and During the Holocaust* uses testimony, archival and secondary sources, providing a detailed account of the family's pre-Holocaust period. He describes their occupations, emigration, political activities, military service, and the role they placed in the meat business in Warsaw prior to World War II, as well as their participation in the struggle for Polish independence. The author then shifts the narrative to the chain of unfolding events that determined the fate of the family during the Holocaust, including their decisions to flee and resist. He concludes with a discussion of the role of history and memory in the family.[35]

In this emerging literary genre, children of survivors narrate a parent's history, placing it in the context of the history of Jews of a particular place, recalling extended family networks now vanished. Mixing travelogue, memoir, and history, these are homages to their parents' lives, situating them in time and space, supplementing textual accounts with family photographs and sometimes even lovingly reconstructed maps of lost landscapes. They document descendants' quests for knowledge, understanding, and connection to barely known pasts. *The Fiftieth Gate, A Journey Through Memory* by Mark Raphael Baker, an Australian son of survivors, includes a detailed map (Figure 5.1) of his parents' wartime journeys from their small Polish villages, to concentration camps, to displaced persons camps in Germany, through Switzerland, and finally to Australia, where they settled, and where the author was born.

A subgenre of descendant memoirs features books that are co-narrated by children and their parents, which explore the parents' wartime experiences, children's excavation projects, and the bonds that are forged through the process of jointly telling a family history.[36] With the rise of electronic publishing, such collaborative memoirs are multiplying in number, as descendants are able to publish their own books. In one such book, *No Goodbyes: A Father-Daughter Memoir of Love, War and Resurrection*, descendant Naava Piatka interviews her father, who shares with her tales of "family drama, political upheaval, sexual seduction, divorce, mass murder, and betrayal." Through his tales, she says, she was "thrust into an epic

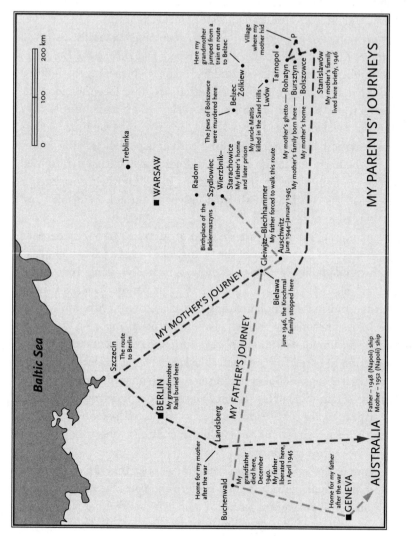

Figure 5.1:
Map of "My Parents' Journeys," from *The Fiftieth Gate* by Mark Raphael Baker.

saga of one man's journey through the shifting European landscape of Communism, Nazism, Zionism, Nationalism and immigration." The memoir emphasizes the drama of survival, which the author says "depends on luck, who you know, and finding the friend beneath the foe." Reflecting on her complicated relationships with her own father, she documents how learning her father's story—about how he emerged from the horrors of war and death camps, the sole survivor of his once large family—humanizes him in her eyes. By narrating his story, she comes to reflect upon her own life in new ways. By understanding her father's story more fully, she comes to empathize with him in new ways and also, she tells us, "learns to let go."

Indeed, many of these memoirs describe how the process of storytelling creates new empathic bonds between survivor parents and children. Empathy requires the capacity to put yourself in someone else's story, and also, as psychologist and critic Elisabeth Young-Bruehl suggests, "put another person in yourself."[37] In coming to more fully understand parents' earlier lives, descendants find that they have a newfound appreciation for who their parents are, and the challenges they've faced. But in addition to requiring one to inhabit the life of another, at least temporarily, empathy also requires a capacity to differentiate oneself from that person, recognizing that you and they are different people. Indeed, a vast literature on descendants, which studied parent-child relationships at an earlier moment, described the blurred boundaries between children and parents: the child's internalization of his or her parent's traumatic past, and the difficulty that children have in establishing clear psychic boundaries with their traumatized parents.

Descendants' excavation projects, and their representation of these projects in the form of memoirs, emerged out a desire to fill in the void, conjure the past more concretely, and come to know their parents' better. By coming to this knowledge, they frequently were able to clarify the boundaries between their parents and themselves. Marianne Hirsch suggests that descendants grew up with "post-memories" of the traumatic past, with memories that tend to resist understanding and integration, and they come to identify with the victim or witness of trauma.[38] Learning the details of one's parents' story, often even after their death, becomes a way for descendants to develop a clearer sense of who they were as people. In some cases, as the previous memoir suggested, this leads to a de-idealization of a formerly larger-than-life parent, and a greater capacity to understand that a parents' story, while connected to them, belongs to their parents and not to them.

In keeping with the cultural penchant for redemptory endings, many of these memoirs transform tragic stories into thrilling adventures.

Piatka's memoir, we are told, "reminds us we can connect through our stories, that suffering can turn into celebration, and that the power of family and love endures beyond death." Similarly redemptive in tone is a memoir written by Joseph Finkelstein, a son of survivors, in collaboration with his parents, titled *I Choose Life*. It is described as "the true, first person account of two Jewish youths, Sol Finkelstein and Goldie Cukier Finkelstein, who survived Nazi concentration camps and transcended despair by choosing life." The book describes the author's parents' "idyllic childhoods in Radom and Sosnowiec, Poland, in warm and loving families imbued with Jewish pride and values; years of darkness, suffering, separation, loss and death; raids, selections, forced labor camps, cattle cars, and death marches; and survival in Auschwitz, Mauthausen and Bergen-Belsen."

We learn that Sol and Goldie met in a displaced persons camp in postwar Germany. The book explores "the challenges of restoration and rebirth, how two youths regained the ability to trust and love, to rebuild new lives after unimaginable losses, and to move to another continent to start a new family and live the American dream." Here, too, an unexpected development lends tension and drama. During the war, the author's father and grandfather had been separated from one another; for 60 years, Sol's father assumed his own father had been murdered. But during the writing of the book, the author learns of the existence of his grandfather's unmarked grave in Austria. As he describes it, "This astounding discovery gave Sol and his family emotional closure, after...60 years of uncertain guilt that Sol carried with him." These and other memoirs reckon with the past, construct an archive of family history that can be accessed by family members and others, and affirm a descendant's relationship with his or her parents.

As they matured, descendants used the memoir genre as a narrative template to create order out of the fragments and to share the fruits of their memory work with others. The process of developing knowledge and coming to know the past better, and all the attendant feelings involved in that experience, become part of the narrative. In trauma memoirs, survivors of rape, incest, child abuse, and of disease and disaster, narrate personal experiences. What binds these "I" stories of personal trauma is the secret, the dark and untold tale that can often be the centerpiece of a family. Such memoirs, by telling the story of a traumatic episode, naming it as such and claiming it as a part of one's experience, construct a life story with a clear trajectory, a before and an after; children of survivors' narratives followed this basic model.

A growing genre of films documented descendants' memory work and the journeys they took to accomplish it, as the following synopses of films by Italian, Israeli, Canadian, and American children of survivors suggest:

Is it possible to heal wounds and bitterness passed down through generations? An Orthodox Jewish father tries to alert his adult sons to the dangers of creating impenetrable barriers between themselves and those outside their faith. He takes them on an emotional journey to Poland to track down the family who risked their lives to hide their grandfather for more than two years during World War II. (*Hiding and Seeking: Faith and Tolerance after the Holocaust*, Oren Rudovsky and Menachem Daum, directors, 2004; Figure 5.2)

Trying to come to terms with her father's death in Israel, Hava Volterra undertakes a physical and intellectual journey that takes her to explore his Italian roots and the history of their family. With the help of her feisty eighty-two year old aunt, her father's sister, she travels relentlessly from city to city, digging through ancient manuscripts and interviewing a wide range of quirky scholars, to piece

Figure 5.2:
An image from the 2004 documentary *Hiding and Seeking: Faith and Tolerance after the Holocaust*, in which a father takes his adult sons to Poland, tracking down the family who hid their grandfather during World War II.
Courtesy of Menachem Daum.

together the fascinating story of her Italian Jewish ancestors. As Volterra continues her journey, her aunt begins to come to terms with her own past, and plans a journey to find and thank the family who hid her and the woman's father during WWII. Using both Monty Python-style animation and computer enhanced marionettes, the film tells the story of Jewish bankers, mystics, scientists and politicians, while reflecting on how one's parents and their roots affect our sense of belonging and identity. (*The Tree of Life*, Hava Volterra, director, 2008; Figure 5.3)

Still (Stille) looks back to the world of assimilated European Jews during the 1930s. Sixty years after the exile, Wendy Oberlander returned with her mother to Berlin—only to find the dissonance of her family's diaspora playing in real time. *Still (Stille)* transforms a collection of archival footage into an indelible montage of faces, piecing together the filmmaker's inheritance from her mother's story. (*Stille*, Wendy Oberlander, director, 2001; Figure 5.4)

Figure 5.3:
In *The Tree of Life* (2008), Hana Volterra travels to Italy to explore her father's roots, while contemplating broader issues of belonging and identity.
Courtesy of the filmmaker.

STILL (STILLE)

A film by WENDY OBERLANDER

Figure 5.4:
Still (Stille), a 2001 film by Wendy Oberlander, draws upon archival footage of home movies to document the filmmaker's trip to Berlin with her mother, and the inheritance of loss.
Courtesy of the filmmaker.

And *The Flat*, a 2011 documentary made in Israel by the grandson of survivors, suggested that members of the "third generation" were also beginning to produce quest narratives:

> At age 98, director Arnon Goldfinger's grandmother passed away, leaving him the task of clearing out the Tel Aviv flat that she and her husband shared for decades since immigrating from Nazi Germany in the 1930s. Sifting through a dense mountain of photos, letters, files, and objects, Goldfinger documents himself undertaking the arduous process of making sense of a lifetime's accumulation of possessions. In the process, he begins to uncover clues that seem to point to a greater mystery, and soon a complicated and shocking family history unfolds before his camera. What starts to take shape is the troubled and taboo history of Goldfinger's grandparents' lives in Germany in the tumultuous and difficult years before World War II, and the unexpected yet inevitable ethical ambiguities and repressed emotions that arise when everyday friendships suddenly cross enemy lines. In this emotionally riveting documentary, Goldfinger

follows the hints his grandparents left behind to investigate long-buried family secrets and unravel the mystery of their painful past.[39]

This is, of course, only a partial list, culled from what is now a burgeoning genre of films structured around encounters and meetings that are often accidental or unplanned, which often include reenactments of events in their ancestors' lives, including tours of the places where they once lived, or where they were taken to their deaths. One critic described "the post-Holocaust, return-to-Poland documentary as a subset of the road movie."[40] But sometimes the journeys remained closer to home.

Robert H. Lieberman, a Cornell University professor, grew up in Kew Gardens, Queens, in the 1950s, which was then home to a large population of mainly German and Viennese refugees, many of whom were survivors. He left for college and lived for years in the bucolic university town of Ithaca, New York, and never looked back, he said, until he grew older, and began to think about the old neighborhood, and about his parents. His 60-minute film *Last Stop Kew Gardens*, released in 2007, tells his story, his family's story, the story of other children of refugees in his neighborhood, and reflects on what members of the second generation have in common: a sense of unease—and a thirst for achievement, he says.

At a time when the survivor generation was rapidly fading away, in these films children of survivors tell stories about themselves by telling stories about their parents' pasts. Remembering becomes synonymous with recording and documenting. Telling a parent's story is a way of ordering the fragments, understanding them, making them one's own, and making them "real." They express a desire to address loss and, frequently, to work through and repair a broken or distant relationship with a parent. By putting a parents' story down on paper, or publishing books and films that document their quests to know, descendants seek to fill in the gaps of their own knowledge of the past, bringing some semblance of order to their fragmented, unruly family histories.

BACK TO THE GHETTO

I was bitten by this bug, too. When my father died in 1992, the wall he had constructed to keep the past at bay collapsed and I was suddenly faced with a set of questions about him that I could not answer. Who was this man, this virtual stranger to me? While his death had severed the primary route to his past, it lifted the emotional barriers he had carefully guarded. Suddenly, in ways that were surprising to me, I felt an enormous compulsion to learn more about the world he had lost and the loyalties and fears that shaped his life, and an overwhelming need to put the fragments of his life in some kind of order. I felt a powerful yet inexplicable urge for a narrative that predated my own birth, a story whose roots and branches extended back in time.

When I returned home to California after the funeral, I took his precious photographs with me and placed them in my own bedroom. Looking at them often, I wondered: Who were they? How did they live? How did they die? Who was my father? In search of clues, I gathered some of the scattered remains of his life: his address book, his passport, the papers he used to apply for German restitution, photographs from his years in Cuba after the war, while he was awaiting entry to the United States, along with a family history my brother wrote while he was in college. And then I decided to visit Poland.

The concept that there were once Jews who could trace their lineage back centuries to the same place was practically inconceivable. Poland was a dark, unknown place that had a strange unreality about it, at once contemporary and modern but also ancient, vanished. Its mysteriousness was exaggerated by fact that it had been obscured from the Western media eye for most of the postwar period, for most of my life. Largely because of this, and despite my parents' best efforts, Poland held a far greater fascination for me than Israel ever could. What did it look like? How did it smell?

Before he died, I told my father that I planned to visit Poland and I asked him to join me. Never one to talk very much of his wartime experiences, he declined. "The lousy Poles—they can keep their damned country," he said. What he didn't say was what I already knew: he would have wanted to make the journey, but it was too painful. It would have forced him to talk about his life and his losses. He would have been forced to reflect on the past and to cry. It was 1993, the year of the fiftieth anniversary of the Warsaw Ghetto Uprising, and the city, together with a number of Jewish organizations in Poland and abroad, had coordinated a series of events to commemorate that event—which was so resonant for my father. I decided to travel to Warsaw, the place of his birth: to see what it looked like, to continue his tradition of marking the uprising, and also (although I did not think of it in these terms at the time) to mourn his death.

Arriving in the city, the airport bus wound through miles of concrete blocks of housing projects and made its way to the central city. Almost immediately, I was struck by the mixture of strangeness and familiarity of the place. People were speaking a familiar language—the language of family gatherings, and of the late night conversations between my father and his uncle Joe. How strange it was to hear children speak this language—I

Figure 5.5:
Magazine welcoming tourists to Warsaw during the commemoration of the fiftieth anniversary of the Warsaw Ghetto Uprising, 1993.

had never heard anyone under the age of 50 speak Polish before. I had never heard people with Slavic faces and smooth skin speak this language. Where were the elderly Jewish men and women I knew?

As the week progressed, I had more of these experiences, more of this sense of *deja vu* mixed with the strange (Figure 5.5). I ate at restaurants that served borscht and kreplach, alongside ham. I saw men wearing hats much like my father wore, old-fashioned gray men's hats, but their wearers were taller, and larger than he. I saw the names of streets of which he talked: Dzielna, Swietorjerska, where he and his family lived in the heart of the old Jewish quarter, which once held a third of the city's population. But the old buildings were gone, replaced with modern communist-style housing projects.

And then I found myself on a bus hurtling toward Treblinka. I had both known and not known that this is where my father's family had been taken to their deaths when I read *Treblinka*, the 1967 book about the death camp written by Jean-Francois Steiner, as a seventh grader in the Bronx in the early 1970s. On a bus trip to the death camp, passing through villages that had changed little during the past century, I stared at the simple wooden houses inhabited by people, some of whom certainly witnessed the cattle cars passing through 50 years before. The tour, organized by the local host committee for the fiftieth anniversary of the Warsaw Ghetto Uprising, was filled with survivors and their children, including one highly enthusiastic descendant who decided to play the role of videographer. "So, how does it feel to be back in the Old Country?" she asked an elderly survivor, pushing a video camera into his face, who seemed a bit dumbstruck by it all, and then made her way through the bus asking each successive survivor, "So how does it feel to be going to Treblinka?" One woman said: "I came to pay respects to my parents." An elderly man responded curtly: "I would rather not be here. But I had no other choice."

The next day, I visited my father's cousin Irena, a spry 70-year-old concert pianist who had survived the war in hiding in Russia, like my father. But unlike him, Irena was captivated by communist ideals and decided to move back to Warsaw after the war to make a new life. In her cheerful sun-drenched home on the outskirts of the city, Irena fed me *piroshkes* and whitefish salad, which I devoured, along with scattered bits of information about my father's family. "I can't remember," she lamented in response to most of my questions, "that was so long ago." At times, my curiosity seemed to anger her. Irena had contained the past much as my father had done, storing it away in often deep and inaccessible places so that she could live her life and make a family. She had married a Gentile man, a trombonist with a hearty laugh and kind disposition, and gave birth to a daughter, Agneiszka, who did not learn her mother was Jewish until she was in her twenties. I was hesitant to probe deeper for fear that I would compromise the choices she had made. I returned home, to bury myself in books about the Shoah and attempt to piece together traces of my family history, with little success.

Several years later, however, when my great aunt Tola died, her death opened another gate to my father's past. Debbie, Tola's granddaughter, who helped her mother sort through the contents of her grandmother's apartment, called me immediately. "You must come over," she said excitedly, "I have something to show you." The next day, I watched as Debbie carefully opened a box containing scores of photographs of unnamed people—men, women, and children, posing individually and in groups, smiling and laughing—along with newspaper notices, marriage licenses, and, most astonishingly of all, dozens and dozens of letters, written in different hands, nearly all of them in Polish, some in Yiddish. Many of them were still in envelopes emblazoned with the dreaded swastika.

Debbie had known about this box for some time. Her grandmother had once caught her poking around in a closet where the box was well hidden. She chastised her granddaughter and quickly tucked it away. Now, more than 30 years later, we retrieved the box and went through its contents. Though we could not read the letters or identify the people in the photographs, their familiar chins, high foreheads, and distinguished noses immediately suggested that they were members of the Szliferstejn family.

Debbie's grandfather Joe was the youngest of ten siblings; my father's father David was the oldest. The letters were sent to Joe and Tola, who had immigrated to New York in 1938. What did the letters say—and why did Joe and Tola keep them hidden all those years? To find out, Debbie and I traveled to Washington, DC, and spent several days at the United States Holocaust Memorial Museum, sitting in a small cubicle as Teresa Pollin, a museum staffer, read the letters aloud in English while we took turns typing.

In early 1939, friends and relatives write about their desire to immigrate to the United States, pleading with Joe for assistance, sending their love and news of the goings-on in Poland, where members of the Szliferstejn family anticipated the future with a mixture of fear and hope. "Here everything is the same, and praise to God for that, but unfortunately there are no prospects for the future," Adam writes his brother Joe in early 1939. "I miss you very much and would like to be with you."

He and the others are preoccupied with their declining economic fortunes, the growing difficulties of making a living, and Hitler's movements on the continent. Joe's brother Arthur writes: "We have a gray reality. We have an aggressive neighbor who swallowed Austria and Czechoslovakia and he sharpens his teeth for everybody and everything that he wants to swallow. We hope that at the next bite he will choke. But at present we live on a volcano and everyday can bring a new unexpected event..." He reassures his brother that despite these dark times, he must think about himself. Irka, Joe and Tola's sister-in-law, tells them how much she misses them. "I really didn't expect that to such a degree I couldn't live without you," she writes, "You grew into my soul and blood. When will we dance together again?"

Through the letters we learn that the Szliferstejn family is relatively middle class and assimilated; that they live in Old Muranow, in the heart of Jewish Warsaw, speak Polish at home, and have little interest in the various political ideologies that captivate many Jews during the interwar period, except perhaps Zionism. Though they are not religiously observant, each Friday all of the siblings congregate with their spouses and children at their mother's apartment for Shabbat dinner. The letters document how profoundly close they are as a family. Joe's brother Arthur wrote him: "You know, you are a part of my being." As we transcribe the letters, I am struck by these expressions of closeness. *You know, you are a part of my being.* What a powerful declaration this is, expressing how deeply we are linked to those closest to us.

The Szliferstejn children were intensely devoted to their mother, Ita Ruchel. In the spring of 1939, after she was diagnosed with advanced leukemia, Arthur wrote to Joe:

> Today is the most tragic day in our household in our lives. The most ideal of mothers will be torn away from her children whom she loved her whole life with some incredible unearthly love.... What a great pity to lose such a great mother.

Transcribing the letters was a painstakingly slow process. At times Teresa stopped to clarify a word or a phrase and a discussion ensued about how best to translate it. By the second day, Debbie and I found ourselves becoming swept up in the world of the letter writers, with their lives, worries, flaws, passions, quirks, weaknesses. We began referring to them by their first names, as though we knew them. We read of intense love affairs and sibling rivalries; of their hopes, dreams, and fears; and especially their urgent requests for immigration papers, as well as talk of different business schemes that might ensure their survival.

Those hopes died in September 1939, as the Nazis entered Warsaw. My father, who was then 19 years old, quickly left the city with his uncle Arthur, the sole unmarried Szliferstejn sibling. They fled to Bialystok in Soviet-occupied Poland. My father had only a small suitcase containing some clothes and three precious photographs of his parents and sister. Under constant fire, the journey took a week by foot. They slept in peasants' barns at night and at one point were captured by German soldiers, but managed to escape.

Meanwhile, in Warsaw, a series of anti-Jewish laws were enacted by the Nazi occupiers. Primary schools for Jewish children were closed and Jews were forced to wear the yellow star. Food was rationed. In a letter from this period, David asked his brother Joe to send food packages: "Some tea, vanilla of good quality, all in cans or a kilo or half a kilo would be useful. If it is possible to do that, the sooner the better." This is the sole message from my grandfather among the letters. It is neatly typed and signed "David Szliferstejn." I stare at this letter for several minutes, losing the thread of Teresa's translation.

As far as I know, this is the only remaining physical evidence of my grandfather's existence, other than a photograph my father kept near his bed. I try to imagine these words emanating from the dignified, melancholy person in the image. I fantasize about David Szliferstejn knowing that many years after his death, three of us, including his son's daughter and his youngest brother's granddaughter, would be sitting three thousand miles away from Warsaw, in a museum dedicated to the memory of the Shoah, transcribing his words. I ask myself: Is he my grandfather if I never had a relationship with him? We break for lunch, and then the translating continues.

In November 1940, the Jewish ghetto is formed and sealed off from the rest of the city. Members of the Szliferstejn family who formerly lived in separate apartments are crowded into fewer apartments on Leszno Street. As conditions worsen, some members of the family try desperately to get out. In early 1941, Adam begs his brother Joe to arrange passage to America on the Hamburg-America Lines, asking him to get someone to cover the costs. "A journey now would be like winning a lottery." US immigration officials, however, are of little help.

As hope of immigration fades, the letters become preoccupied with the struggle for survival. Tensions and rivalries emerge among the previously close Szliferstejn siblings. Zygmunt sends a plea for food packages, questioning why Joe sent food to some brothers but not to him: "I just want to know what criteria did you use helping Adam, David and Ignac and bypassing me? Why do I deserve less help? Please do not exclude anybody." Bela, Tola's sister, describes the tensions that have emerged within couples and among the Szliferstejn brothers: "In this whole misery this is the worst evil, that if there is nothing to do the couples quarrel, and that is the way it is in every home. In your old apartment there are many people and each one has a temperament." She urges her brother-in-law to stop sending food packages, because they exacerbate tensions within the family: "Joe, I know that sending the food packages for your relatives is a tremendous effort, so do not do it. It would make sense if you could send to everybody, but this way there is only jealousy between them and they do not share the food." This dehumanization was, of course, part of the Nazi plan to pit family and friends against one another. Despite it all, however, romances blossomed—sometimes out of necessity.

On November 23, 1941, Zygmunt writes that he is to marry Tola's sister, Bela ("I found in her a good, honest and devoted soul. I believe that she will find in me a good friend.") and move in with her parents, happily leaving the Szliferstejn apartment, which had become a war zone. Two weeks later, Japan attacked Pearl Harbor, the United States entered the war, and the Nazi occupiers stopped all correspondence between the United States and Poland. Joe and Tola never again heard from their family in Warsaw.

Having translated the last letter, Teresa, Debbie, and I gather in the museum's cafeteria to debrief. We are physically tired and emotionally spent. I can barely eat. "The letters paint a skewed vision of family, a family in distress," says Teresa. "A pretty clear picture comes out: they were very close, but the circumstances made them go nuts. Of course jealousy exists in every family—the envy, the lack of justice—but these divisions were not natural." Debbie, Teresa, and I talk about how difficult it is for us to imagine how we would act toward one another if placed in such circumstances, if we were starving. "We have no clue, and no right to judge," says Teresa, and Debbie agrees: "We will never understand how it would feel." We say goodbye to Teresa.

On the car ride back to New York, Debbie and I reflect upon the letters and what they might tell us. Our understanding of the Szliferstejns' experiences during wartime is limited, we admit: the letters are marred by gaps, omissions, and the stamp of Nazi censors. "We piece them together hoping for an understanding of their lives," Debbie laments, "but it's like putting together the pieces of a puzzle that will never be finished, because so many pieces are lost." What we do understand better is why her grandparents kept those letters hidden all those years. We can appreciate the pain and shame surrounding Joe's fruitless efforts to help his family, a US government that turned its back on their desperate pleas for help, and the painful disintegration of a once powerfully close extended family. Tola and Joe saved the letters because they were the last tangible links to their family. Sixty years after the end of the war, we continue to live with these losses.

Paradoxically, the passing of the survivor generation created new openings to the past. As Debbie and I learned about the letter writers, recited their names out loud, and followed their movements, they became real, embodied individuals with names, faces, and lives. We began to think of them—for the first time—as our own. Those photographs sitting near my father's bed, which now sit near mine, have become my grandparents and aunt, David, Rosa, and Helina. Before the war, their world was filled with large family Sabbaths and Passover Seders, of Zionist hopes and fears of anti-Semitism. They laughed and they loved.

When I gaze upon these photographs now, I see family resemblances I had never before noticed, and I project onto them my hopes and fears, my nostalgia and longing—for wholeness and closeness—for a fantasy, perhaps, of a family that once was. My father had lost what I now know was a rich network that nurtured and anchored him in the world. I suspect that that sense of security and belonging he had lost was just too painful, making it impossible for him to share this story, even with his own children. But what my father never understood was that in my own way I, too, live with these losses, with all of the secrets and stories he never revealed. Finally, I am getting to know my ghosts.

By the turn of the millennium, we descendants traveled to our parents' places of origin, interviewing surviving relatives and excavating, piecing together, and refashioning our fractured family histories. On thousands of private expeditions, we tried to discover the contours of a history we knew intimately and yet not at all. By seeking, borrowing from, and selectively appropriating traces of the past, we reworked ideas of family, genealogy, loss, and history, using those traces as raw material in the production of new stories of ourselves. We searched for beginnings and endings, and for origin stories that offered continuous narratives rather than fractured familial histories. A veritable flood of documentation projects came forth: ranging from homemade or self-published books to moderately big-budget documentaries.

Through this memory work, descendants made sense of a past that was once deemed off limits, and by doing so, they made their own lives more intelligible. Excavating familial histories that were previously hidden, descendants filled in gaps in their knowledge of the past, narrated their parents' lives, and developed narratives of their own origins. They addressed the dramatic loss of memory and continuity wrought by genocide and searched for a greater understanding of the often hazy family contexts into which they had been born. They tried to assert control over an inheritance that was unassimilated and confusing. Excavating the past was often, too, an act of mourning. The traumatic manner of genocide created silence in families, denying mourning and creating barriers that separated the generations. Mourning demands that we slowly work through loss by repeatedly remembering the lost and integrating them into our own sense of self. Predominantly women, these post-Holocaust genealogists were doing "kin work," cultivating emotional ties among family members and building symbolic bridges across the generations.

These memory projects were enormously important to particular families, as my own story suggests.[41] Traveling to Poland and translating our family letters brought my cousin Debbie and I closer, and introduced us to our hidden history. These days, the names of Arthur, Zygmunt, Bela, and other lost ancestors occasionally make their way into our conversations, and they are part of living memory. Our efforts also inspired Debbie's 75-year-old mother, Dana, to visit Poland for the first time since she left as a young girl in 1938. Collectively, these memory projects were also important: they personalized the experiences of survivors and their families for non-survivor Jews, helped to integrate those experiences into American Jewish culture, and complicated the dominant progress narrative, which focused on the turn-of-the-century immigrant who had escaped the pogroms of Russia to make a life in the New World, whose descendants had prospered.

Still, some observers were ambivalent about whether these memory projects had any relevance beyond the families for whom they were created. In 1979 there were only "a few dozen" documentaries about the Holocaust in existence, but ten years later at least 69 new Holocaust-themed documentaries, many of them low-budget affairs, had appeared—a trend that showed few signs of abating. "Anyone with a relative who went through the Holocaust has a 'natural desire' to tell that story," one critic wrote, acknowledging that these documentaries are works of "moral witness." But, he added: "most movie audiences want to be entertained; they don't want to dwell on the sealed boxcars, extermination camps and mounds of corpses that are the staples of the Holocaust narrative." Are Holocaust documentaries, he wondered, "too much of a bad thing?"[42] As we will see in the next chapter, in the 1990s some began to wonder whether the proliferation of commemorative efforts had gone too far.

CHAPTER 6

Too Much Memory? Holocaust Fatigue in the Era of the Victim

In his 2007 novel, *Absurdistan*, Gary Shteyngart conjured an imagined memorial to the Holocaust. "Some of the world's most remarkable recent architecture has been built in commemoration of the Holocaust," the narrator proclaimed, "but much of it is too abstract and cerebral to inspire immediate Continuity." In Shteyngart's absurdist rendering of this out-sized memorial, in the main exhibition space "a broken matzoh leads to a titanium-clad lamb shank symbolizing both the forearm of the Almighty and our own newly found brute strength." There is also a "Holocaust for Kidz" exhibit, which promises to deliver "a carefully tailored miasma of fear, rage, impotence, and guilt for children . . . feelings that will be partly redeemed and partly thwarted by the ice-cream truck awaiting them at the end of the exhibit."

The novel offered a relentless, irreverent, critique of the "Holocaust industry" and the commodification of suffering, riffing on American Jewish organizations' deployment of Holocaust memory in the service of Jewish continuity—as a weapon of guilt. "Identity politics are a great boon to our quest for Continuity. Identity is born almost exclusively out of a nation's travails," proclaimed Shteyngart's narrator. "For us—a prosperous, unmolested people safely nuzzled in the arms of the word's last superpower (as of this writing, anyway)—this means Holocaust, Holocaust, Holocaust."[1]

By the new millennium, it certainly seemed as though Holocaust memory was everywhere. For schoolchildren across the country, Holocaust history became an integral part of the social studies curriculum, the United States Holocaust Memorial Museum joined the White House and the Smithsonian among the most popular attractions in Washington, DC, and Holocaust memory made its way into Christian liturgy and political discourse. If in an earlier moment survivors spoke of how others turned away from them, by the first decades of the new millennium, evidence of widespread identification with their suffering was not difficult to find.

The *New York Times*, for example, reported that a 47-year-old daughter of survivors decided to tattoo her arm with the number of a woman who had been in Auschwitz with her father, a woman she never knew, as a way of identifying with her story. "You can't go up to a stranger and tell your dark stories. But if she wore the number and people asked, she would give answers, at Starbucks, on the street, to anyone who asked. And she did—over and over." The reporter was sympathetic to the gesture: "In a culture of forgetting—of disposable cameras, diapers and memories," this daughter of survivors, wrote the *Times*, "made it her mission to swim relentlessly against the tide, back to 1944, to Poland, to Auschwitz to tell her father's story."[2]

That article generated a number of emotional letters to the editor, most of which were supportive of the woman's decision to mark her body. Some readers were touched by the image of descendants paying tribute to the suffering of their parents in such a visceral, embodied way. "The rolled-up sleeves with the numbers on the arms of the children in the concentration camps at liberation is a searing image," wrote one man, who admitted to being somewhat "puzzled" by such displays. Yet he acknowledged, "The reminder to the world that the Holocaust isn't ancient history can take many forms. We are surrounded by images and words on the Internet. The actual display permanently embedded on the skin is unequivocal. Perhaps that's more than words can say."[3]

Another letter writer saw the tattoo as an attempt to reclaim a once despised mark. "When I was a boy in the 1960s, there was an expression 'long sleeves in the summer.' It referred to Holocaust survivors who were so ashamed of their death camp tattoos that no matter how hot the weather became, they would not wear shirts that exposed their forearms." He continued: "It is inspiring to see how the grandchildren of those Holocaust survivors have turned a mark of shame and suffering into one of pride and remembrance."[4] He saw the tattoo as an affirmation of a once despised status.

But others were far less sympathetic to the prevalence of Holocaust representations. While reserving most of their ire for Jewish elites, whom they charged with erecting a "Holocaust industry" for their own political ends, they took survivors and their children to task for wallowing in melancholic identifications while doing little to address persistent suffering in far-flung parts of the globe today. Identifying himself as a child of survivors, British sociologist Frank Furedi registered regret that survivors and their children were speaking publicly at all. "As I know from my own childhood," he wrote, "many of the direct survivors of the death camps talked very little in public about their terrible experience. Their dignified, self-contained response stands in sharp contrast to the behavior of their children and grandchildren today: the so-called second- and third-generation survivors."

Criticizing descendants for encouraging an emotional politics and the "authority of feeling," Furedi was aghast that "some of the promoters of second-generation survivor groups have even criticized their parents for bottling up their emotions and refusing to embrace a victim identity."[5] The esteemed sociologist Zygmunt Bauman, himself a Polish Jew, similarly warned against the desire for "hereditary victimhood," a "zealous search for the collective Holocaust trauma, which would explain away...present genuine or putative personal troubles," brandishing it as a "certificate of moral righteousness."[6] Some went even further, comparing second generation memory workers to Binjamin Wilkomirski, who in a celebrated "memoir" later proven to be a fake, famously identified with survivors' suffering in order to falsely claim it as his own.[7]

In a controversial 1999 book, *The Holocaust in American Life*, historian Peter Novick charged that Holocaust memory had become an effective tool for coercing assimilated American Jews into retaining their Jewish identity. Holocaust memorial efforts, wrote Novick (mirrored by Shteyngart's fictional characterizations), are a ploy by Jewish leaders to consolidate their own power and provide collective meaning for Jewish identity at a time when it lacks depth, having lost the "bonds of shared language, shared religion, shared customs and traditions and shared persecution."[8] The memory of the Holocaust is "so banal, so inconsequential, not memory at all, precisely because it is so uncontroversial," he asserted; it is "removed from our time and place, and offers us few universal lessons."[9] His criticism extended to the increasing stature and moral authority of survivors, whose suffering, he lamented, had made them "exemplars of courage, fortitude, and wisdom."[10] How regrettable it is, he said, that "the cultural icon of the strong, silent hero" is replaced by "the vulnerable and verbose antihero." In a culture in which sensitivity replaces stoicism, instead of enduring in silence, one lets it all hang out.[11]

Just as the Holocaust emerged as a visible aspect of American culture and the subject of Hollywood films, national museums, and high school curricula, these and other critics proclaimed that, rather than dwelling on victimhood, it was time to move on. A sense of fatigue seemed to be setting in across a wide swath of the Jewish community and beyond, emanating from a number of different sources. Some on the Left charged that a preoccupation with Holocaust victimhood and the rise of a "Holocaust industry" narrowed Jewish loyalties, hardening Jews to the suffering of others, and instrumentalized Jewish suffering in the service of ethno-national identifications—and the embrace of a muscular Zionism. Political moderates, for their part, were more concerned with the fact that Holocaust memory seemed to be crowding out other sources of Jewish meaning, diminishing joy and celebration.

Though such arguments have some merit—it would indeed be a pity if Jewish identity were founded exclusively upon historical victimhood—they are curiously ahistorical, failing to recognize several crucial points: what a hard-won accomplishment Holocaust consciousness was, how much resistance those who tried to speak about the genocide during the early postwar decades often encountered, and how important it was for survivors and their children to finally be able to share their stories. Moreover, they fail to see that remembering the Jewish genocide does not necessarily further a narrow vision of ethno-racial solidarity but has in fact filtered into a broader consciousness of human rights.

HAUNTED ZION

It is the identification of Holocaust consciousness with Zionism that seems to trouble some critics most. Arguing that a preoccupation with victimhood is leading Jews down the wrong path, they fear that Holocaust consciousness represents a barbaric rejection of the deepest gains of the Enlightenment embrace of humankind against particularistic tribal loyalties—exemplified by the Jewish state. Of course, Israel has long played a central symbolic (and political) role in disaporic Jewish life. Carved out of the ashes of European Jewry (on land that was once part of the territory of Palestine), the Jewish state has often been seen as the redeemer of those losses. It is little coincidence, for example, that observers often date the rise of American Jewish Holocaust consciousness to 1967, when the Six Day War stoked fears among Jews worldwide of a second Holocaust. As the argument goes, when Israel dealt a crushing blow to its Arab enemies in the war, it enacted a kind of reparation of pain that liberated American Jews to reclaim their ethnic pride, spurring Holocaust memorialization.[12]

As I have suggested, many survivors (and their descendants) have embraced the view of Israel as redemption for Jewish suffering. If their attachments to Europe had been largely destroyed, Zion offered hope for the future—and a way to deflect attention from their own grievous losses and to keep the ghosts at bay. That was certainly the case in my own family, where nearly all of my parents' political loyalties were refracted through the lens of Zionism. In our household, the question "Is it good for the Jews?" was invariably answered by "if it is good for Israel." My parents' commitment to the state of Israel was deep and abiding, far exceeding even their religious convictions. In 1980, when they took my brother and me to Israel for the first (and only) time, my parents kissed the ground when our El Al flight landed, beaming with pride whenever they saw muscular young soldiers, or evidence of Israeli technological and military prowess. One can imagine the appeal of such displays of strength for those accustomed to weakness.

But it is precisely this understanding of Israel as reparation for past injuries that is so dangerous, say critics, because it casts Israeli policies as beyond reproach. Avraham Burg, a former speaker of the Knesset, Israel's parliament, describes his nation as Holocaust-obsessed, militaristic, xenophobic, and, like Germany in the 1930s, vulnerable to an extremist minority. Jewish martyrdom has hardened into a sectarian memory that is unable to acknowledge the pain of others, and which seeks reparation through violence. The historical suffering of Jews is being used to eclipse the suffering of the Palestinians and to gain a privileged moral position.[13] "You hear the conversation in the Knesset, you hear it in the public, you see the graffiti 'Arabs Out'—like *Juden raus*," he writes. "The seeds of national chauvinism are here and flourishing."[14] In this view, instead of encouraging a sense of broad empathy for the suffering of others, Holocaust consciousness has led to a destructive form of tribalism.

The specter of dead Jews haunts Israeli conceptions of self and sees Israeli militarism as reparation for having gone "like lambs to the slaughter."[15] Zionist nationalists picture Palestinians as Nazis who pose an existential threat to the Jewish people, at times collapsing distinctions among different sectors of the Islamic world. Israeli Prime Minister Benjamin Netanyahu regularly tells crowds that if we do not stop Iran, a new Nazi-like power will ascend, and appeasement will have disastrous consequences; "Pro-Israel" newsletters regularly warn American Jewish supporters of "Iran's Final Solution for Israel."[16] A group of children of Holocaust survivors in Los Angeles sponsors a talk entitled "Caliphate, Jihad, Sharia: Now What?" pronouncing that "Islam is constitutionally violent," that Islamic terrorists and ordinary Muslims are one and the same, and that "a Jihad-waging, sharia-enforcing caliphate represents a permanent, existential enemy— not a temporal foe that can be bought or pacified through diplomacy or concessions."[17]

The American Jewish establishment embraces this "grand drama of Jewish victimhood," according to Peter Beinart, in a recent book that is highly critical of contemporary forms of Zionism. For national Jewish organizations, much like neoconservatives, "it is always 1939," writes political analyst Michael Lind. Projecting the threat they instinctively understood as Jews onto America as a whole, rightwing Zionists argue for an aggressive defense of the country and its values; anything less is appeasement. Since Israel is the only democracy in the Middle East, they say, it deserves unqualified American support. The attack on the World Trade Center and the war on terrorism that commenced in its wake have only strengthened the view. Paradoxically, in Beinart's words, "we live in an age not of Jewish weakness, but of Jewish power" and without moral vigilance, he suggests, "Jews will abuse power just as hideously as anyone else."[18]

Today, the belief that Jews insist on wallowing in their own traumatic memories at the expense of the ongoing pain of others is common on the Left, as I discovered firsthand when I helped to sponsor a film program at my university several years ago. The two experimental films on the program, by a child of Holocaust survivors, who is also a close friend of mine, mixed personal narrative and found footage to explore her fractured family history and her parents' expulsion from Austria and Germany. The films were heartfelt, anguished examples of the kinds of family memory work I described in the previous chapter, a creative response to a history that had been buried and off limits.[19] After publicizing the event, I received a note from one of my colleagues, a sociologist, who thanked me for organizing it, but noted that at the university "we do already get a lot of movies, speakers, and other programs to help educate us about the history of Jewish culture."

He wondered whether the university would be showing any programs from "the Palestinian perspective." We all need to be "reminded of the horrors of the Holocaust," he acknowledged. "But I have yet to see even one commercial movie showing the tragic fate of all those Muslims who lost their homes in 1948." Please note, he implored me, "this is not meant in any way to criticize the showing of such programs as you are publicizing, but rather to try to achieve some balance on this painful and explosive issue. But are you aware of any events which are being planned which will in fact show an alternate perspective?"

I was taken aback by the message, which seemed to smack of unexamined anti-Semitism. There had been an undeniable paucity of discussion of the Middle East conflict on campus, and of the Palestinian experience in particular, to be sure, but the Holocaust is a central issue of human importance in its own right, and a film program on that subject should not be compelled to justify itself on some other grounds, I told him. To demand that every discussion of the Jewish world be tied to a discussion of the Palestinian conflict erroneously conflates diaspora Jews with Israel; they are not the same.[20] His reply came quickly: "We need to attempt at least some partial balance here, of which we currently have virtually none."

Years afterward, this exchange continues to unsettle me, as I suppose it was designed to do. If we suggest that talk of Palestinian suffering should accompany all discussions of the Holocaust, we conflate the Jewish diaspora with the Zionist project, collapsing historical specificity and homogenizing the Jewish world.[21] While there are certainly important symbolic and sometimes even political ties between American Jews and Israelis, the two groups are not the same. There are in fact an extraordinary range of different Jewish views (including ambivalence) toward the state of Israel; those who identify Jews with the state of Israel as if they were seamlessly the same are incorrect.[22]

And yet, even as we might wish to escape it, the Palestinian plight haunts the diaspora.[23] Once imagined as a source of refuge and a way to redeem and contain grievous loss, the Jewish state is now producing new forms of collective trauma, new silences, and new ghosts. In the wake of an Israeli incursion into Gaza, for example, a Jewish activist invoked Holocaust memories to highlight Palestinian suffering: "What can we say to all the mothers who are searching for bread for their children in the streets of Gaza and what can we say to ourselves? Only this: sixty years after Auschwitz the State of the Jews is confining people in ghettos." And yet, she lamented, invoking the name of the doctor who saved Jewish children in the Warsaw ghetto, who was sent to his death with them, "There is not a single Janusz Korczak among us who will go in and protect the children from the fire."[24]

Quick and easy Holocaust analogies are dangerous: Benjamin Netanyahu is not Hitler, and the Israeli occupation, even at its most aggressive, is not genocidal. Yet it is becoming more and more difficult to deny that Israel's occupation of the territories captured during the 1967 war has led to the protracted, unconscionable suffering of so many uprooted people—even the former heads of Israel's security forces have admitted as much in a recent documentary.[25] And as some see it, growing consciousness of the Holocaust, by placing victimization at the core of Jewish identity, is partially at fault, setting the stage for victims to become victimizers, and diverting them from their historical obligation to recognize the pain of others.[26]

Another, related, strain of Holocaust fatigue registers ambivalence about the fact that the genocide has emerged as a core element of Jewish identity. These critics argue that the Jewish people should be an ethnic group like any other—neither a "chosen people," nor one defined mainly by pain and suffering.[27] They charge that Holocaust consciousness leads to a preoccupation with death and a lachrymose conception of Jewish identity that robs Jews of "the joy and replenishment that Jewish identity has always offered."[28]

THE LURE OF BEING NORMAL

A number of years ago, I sat in Carnegie Hall listening to a performance by the Klezmatics, an American musical group that is part of the klezmer revival, melding the music of the shtetl with contemporary folk and other musical genres. At one point during the performance, the band performed a song in Yiddish that spoke of a mass murder during the Holocaust. As one of the performers translated the lyrics for the audience, a man sitting in front of me turned to his wife and said facetiously, "Oh *that's* very uplifting." A song about the genocide jarred his sense of what is suitable to perform in public, and what constitutes entertainment. As this incident suggests, today, even in the midst of a robust memorial culture, the Holocaust remains forbidden territory. We distance ourselves from it, bathing it in Hollywood homilies to the power of human kindness. We draw boundaries around it, housing it in concrete structures, hoping to contain it.

On the site of the former Jewish ghetto in Warsaw, a museum commemorating centuries of Polish Jewry has risen. Organizers of the museum say they wish to recall the vibrant Jewish communities that flourished in Poland despite anti-Semitism and discrimination. "This will not be another Holocaust museum," said Marian Turski, president of the Jewish Historical Institute Association in Poland. "It will be a museum of life."[29] She and others are critical of what they see as a communal preoccupation with Jewish suffering, exemplified by the annual organized tours that take young Jews to the sites of Auschwitz, Birkenau, Treblinka, Majdanek, and other death camps. "The implied emotional bind of the March of the Living—'be Jewish, for had you been Jewish then, they would have killed you' is hardly worthy of a great civilization," a critic of these marches argues. "There are many better reasons to be Jewish. We are, as the name of the march itself implies, a civilization of life, not death."[30]

Antimemory has long accompanied Holocaust memorialization efforts, calling upon us to "replace devastation, resentment, and guilt with reconciliation, forgiveness, and closure."[31] Today, in a period of heightened Holocaust consciousness, antimemory often appears in the guise of a desire for Jewish normalization. "Human beings need to get to grips with the horrors of their shared past," writes critic Micha Odenheimer. "I sympathize with those who are desperate to ensure none of it is forgotten, and yet I still find my heart sinks a little. First, I am one of those Jews who prefers his Jewishness to be rooted in culture, tradition, or customs that can be lived, enjoyed, and celebrated." The alternative is, he says, "Five Thousand Years of Bitterness." While the Nazi period "remains seared into the collective mind like no other," he noted, "it casts a long shadow—and sometimes we need to step aside it."[32] "I'm sick of the Holocaust as a shorthand for 'We suffered more than you, so we should get the piece of the cake with the rosette on it,'" writes a woman in her twenties. While her parents' generation tried this tactic, she said, her generation embraces a more "open" relationship to their Jewishness—and rejects a politics of victimhood.[33]

We hear laments, too, that Jews' everyday losses are increasingly overshadowed by memories of mass trauma. Visiting Yaffa Eliach's monumental "Tower of Faces" exhibit at the United States Holocaust Memorial Museum in Washington, DC, which assembles thousands of family photographs to commemorate the Jewish dead of a single Polish town, an American Jewish scholar suggests that it is emblematic of how "the grander vision of devastation and loss that is the Holocaust" dwarfs the "ordinary losses" of American Jews, making it difficult to process individual loss, such as the "normal" deaths of loved ones.[34]

"Trauma is not just the result of major disasters," says Mark Epstein, a psychiatrist and Buddhist practitioner. "It does not happen to only some people. An undercurrent of trauma runs through ordinary life, shot through as it is with the poignancy of impermanence." Trauma is not something that simply happens to those who are caught in the crossfire of war or disaster: it happens to everyone who has ever lost someone they deeply loved.[35] Epstein describes the experience of his 88-year-old mother, who two years ago lost her husband of almost 60 years and still suffers from that loss, while those around her tell her that she must move on. Our culture frowns on those who would wallow in our grief. We are expected to mourn, work through, and move toward closure, tying it all up very neatly and handily. And yet loved ones and painful episodes linger on in our memory, pulling us away from our daily lives.

While recognizing that psychic injuries, such as the death of a loved one, can be painfully destructive, the experience of genocide is of a different order of magnitude, constituting a rupture with the everyday that exists "outside the range of human experience." Trauma, writes Eva Hoffman, "is produced by persecution of subjects to whom all agency and principle have been denied. Tragic struggle may entail moral agony, but it leaves the sense of identity and dignity intact. Violent abuse can lead to a deeper penetration and fragmentation of the psychic cells, of the victim's self and soul."[36] Trauma, says Hoffman, "is suffering in excess of what the psyche can absorb."[37] So while the death of a loved one can certainly be traumatizing, living through events such as mass violence creates lasting injuries and fundamentally changes the way one sees the world.

"I was a different person before the [fill in the blank] event that changed my life" is the typical refrain of the traumatized. If trauma is, by its very definition, caused by an exceptionally jarring event, then the notion that common events such as joblessness, homophobia, or even losing a loved one (through a typical death) are traumatic makes little sense—however painful they may be for those who experience them. "We are all suffering from "pre-traumatic stress disorder," say some.[38] But tell that to the thousands of soldiers returning from Iraq and Afghanistan, who suffer from painful flashbacks, nightmares, and an inability to speak of their experiences. And tell that to the survivors of genocides—or to survivors of rape. While modern life brings uncertainties to which we are all vulnerable, trauma is an exceptional state.

I would much rather live in a society that over-diagnoses trauma than in one that denies trauma and fails to care for those who suffer from it; we did live in such a society until fairly recently. Before the advent of the diagnosis of "post-traumatic stress," beginning in the 1970s, trauma was often met with incomprehension—or denial.[39] Holocaust survivors, we thought, simply needed jobs and families to get over their experiences, and to become "normal" again. Rape victims had endured bad sexual experiences, and would quickly heal. Today, we know that these experiences often have enduring effects that haunt individuals for the rest of their lives.

And yet during the past few decades, an unprecedented focus on mourning and memory has converged with the belief, writes Marita Sturken, "that one can always heal, move on, and place the past in its proper context, and do so quickly."[40] We assume that closure is desirable and necessary, and that grief is bad and must end in order for individuals to adapt and for life to resume. We are assured that "someday things will just be a memory," and we are encouraged to "move on." Closure offers order and predictability instead of ambiguity and uncertainty. It allows us to "get on with our lives" and to resume expectations of productivity and forward trajectories. Looking clearly into the eye of unimaginable horror can certainly make us crazy. How can one enter that place of mass death without being driven to despair? How can Jews, in particular, build clear-headed connections to their murdered cousins while affirming the value of life in the present and alleviating the suffering of others? These questions haunt many of us who have grown up in the shadow of the Holocaust as we try to grapple with its ongoing significance.

The permanent association of Jewish identity with victimization is highly problematic, to be sure. Jews, particularly in the United States, are no longer collectively powerless, even if they consistently perceive anti-Semitism to be more endemic to American society than public opinion polls say it is.[41] And yet those who say that the past is behind us, and that we need to move on, are also mistaken. Calls for normalization, for Jews to become an ethnic group like any other, where the bonds of tradition are celebrated with special foods, festive occasions, and unique rituals, rather than by memorials to death and suffering, are premature. Indeed, a recent national survey of American Jews found they are divided as to whether they see following religious law or feeling connected to Israel as central to their Jewishness. However, large majorities of American Jews, across different age groups and denominational groups, agree on two things: that remembering the Holocaust and working for justice and equality are essential to what it means to be Jewish.[42] Indeed, remembering the Holocaust can be a profoundly ethical act if such remembering is embedded in a larger set of commitments.

Dina Rosenfeld was part of the initial conversations that helped establish the "second generation" as a collective identity in the 1970s. Decades later, when we spoke, she was no longer a young woman trying to make sense of her parents' legacy, but was now solidly in middle age, a mother, social worker, and college professor. When I asked her what she thought of the growing visibility of the Holocaust in American life, she told me that while she welcomes the fact that the Holocaust is now widely recognized in this country, she worries that "there's a little oversaturation."

The Holocaust is "such a narrow vision of Jewish identity," she told me. Rosenfeld understands the allure of victimhood: "There's something very appealing about being such an obvious victim and of being in this grand tragedy, where its so clear what is right and what is wrong, versus the rest of our lives which are very gray. So in terms of those absolutes, I think there's a lot of attraction right now to the topic. Absolute evil, absolute victimization, in our much more relativistic society, is appealing." And yet she rejects the belief that Holocaust consciousness has been constructed by some as a means of consolidating power. That's too "premeditated, too cynical."

These days, Rosenfeld helps to organize Holocaust commemorations at a progressive Jewish school in New York, but her connection to that legacy is just one aspect of a rich, varied life. She just does not think about it as much as she used to, she says. And yet she is grateful that Holocaust stories, no longer repressed, are now "part of the language, and part of the culture."[43] Her stance suggests that, rather than causing us to embrace normalization or a sense of victimization that hardens us to the suffering of others, Holocaust consciousness can also permit us to imagine a different set of possibilities, ways of thinking that acknowledge past injuries while moving us toward a broader set of identifications.

TOWARD AN ETHICS OF REMEMBERING

As I have shown, during the first few decades after World War II, there was little space for Jewish survivors to articulate their experiences of collective trauma, and be recognized by others. Talking was an exceedingly difficult task. The survivors, who did not yet define themselves as such, experienced a great deal of guilt for surviving when most did not, and for not being able to do more to save their loved ones. American Jews often felt guilty, too, for their powerlessness or inaction in the face of the genocide, and often turned away. Shame was a powerful barrier to speaking, and listening. Struggling to integrate their pasts into their new lives, survivors consequently faced difficulties building intimate ties with those closest to them, including their own children.

It took a series of shifts to make the recognition of collective victimhood possible. Psychiatrists who worked with Vietnam veterans publicized the existence of post-traumatic stress. Social movements altered the status of victims in American culture, sometimes even valorizing them as the bearers of privileged insights. Generational change pushed descendants into the role of audiences and coaxers of their parents' stories. Empowered by the cultural changes around them and by the mobilization of a collective identity as the second generation, children of survivors carved out cultural space for discussing the ongoing impact of the Holocaust upon their families, and they began to elicit their parents' stories.

Where there were often blurred boundaries between parents and children, the formation of support groups enabled descendants to see themselves as both separate from and connected to their parents' histories. If there were once ghosts who shared the dinner table, through their memory projects descendants transformed those ghosts into ancestors. Those who were able to coax their parents to speak often found that it allowed them to create deeper intimate ties with them and greater empathy for their experiences. By excavating their parents' lost worlds, they built symbolic ties to grandparents and other relatives and mourned their losses, often for the first time. By narrating their losses they were able to gain greater control over them, rather than being controlled by them.

Today, thanks to this legacy of activism, coupled with rise of social media, I am in contact with distant relatives in Poland, Argentina, and

Canada and now have an extended family of sorts—at least virtually. When I log into my Facebook account, I learn about the daily activities of my cousins Agnieszka and Ewa in Warsaw, Pablo in Buenos Aires, and Taya, who lived for many years in Moscow and is now in Toronto. On my newsfeed, I hear about new babies, job transitions, and upcoming travels, and have a window into the lives of people to whom I am connected through history and genealogy. My digital family tree now visualizes branches of my family that I had little knowledge of until only a few years ago. It is a broken family tree, filled with names of relatives, mainly dead, whom I have never met, and also some of whom are now familiar to me. And while I've never relied exclusively on biological definitions of family to define my intimate circle, these connections, however tenuous, are important to me, helping me to symbolically repair a sense of generational continuity that had been severed by the genocide. My own experience suggests that, rather than hardening us to the suffering of others, grappling with loss and suffering can reweave sustaining relations and can deepen a sense of ethical obligation.

Today, the Jewish genocide, no longer the exclusive reference point for mass death, is overshadowed by the tragic accumulation of other episodes. Samantha Power, writing about the recurring incidents of genocide across the globe, notes: "We gradually came to accept the depravity of the Holocaust, but then slotted it in our consciousness as 'history'; we resisted acknowledging that genocide was occurring in the present."[44] And yet Holocaust memory has also furthered the development of a more global, cosmopolitan form of identity. It is precisely my intimate knowledge of the effects of war and mass violence and their impact on subsequent generations that motivates me, to the extent that I can, to try to work to prevent violence from occurring.

The United States Holocaust Memorial Museum's Committee of Conscience has, for example, organized campaigns on American college campuses to end the genocide in Sudan. In campaign literature, students are informed, "tens of thousands of civilians have been murdered and thousands of women raped in Sudan's western region by Sudanese government soldiers and members of the government-supported militia sometimes referred to as the Janjaweed. Over 1.5 million civilians have been driven from their homes, their villages torched, and their property stolen by the Sudanese military and allied militia." Such campaigns draw symbolic parallels with the genocide of European Jewry.

The term "genocide," students are informed, was coined by Raphael Lemkin, a Jewish refugee who in 1944 fled to the United States from Poland, to describe what was happening in Nazi-occupied Europe.[45] They

Figure 6.1:
Brochure prepared by the Committee on Conscience of the United States Holocaust Memorial Museum, Washington DC, 2005.

are urged to mobilize on local campuses to build awareness of this humanitarian crisis. A flyer (Figure 6.1) juxtaposed images of fleeing villagers next to a quote from Elie Wiesel: "How can a citizen of free country not pay attention? How can anyone, anywhere not feel outraged? How can a person, whether religious or secular, not be moved by compassion? And above all, how can anyone who remembers remain silent?"

Some years ago, when I was teaching in England, a student, a Bosnian refugee, told me about the atrocities she had witnessed: about the people who came into her village and killed her uncles and cousins in the dark of night. She looked at me plaintively, embarrassed, wondering how I would respond, and whether the discussion was out of place in an academic office overlooking green rolling hills. When I told her that I understood, and that my parents had survived Nazism, she shot me a knowing look, softly uttering, "so of course you know." At that moment, she felt less alone in her grief, and I did as well.

Then, several years later, in Australia in 2008, I witnessed "Sorry Day," when the prime minister apologized for the centuries-long mistreatment of its indigenous population, and heard members of the Stolen Generation—victims of the Australian government's policy of forced relocation—speak about how those policies had personally impacted them. One woman described how her mother had been taken from her own mother, placed in a church-run dormitory, and refused permission to visit her parents, and how her great-grandfather, an indigenous man who fought for Australia in World War I, returned from battle only to be enslaved by his own country. When I heard her talk about her own efforts to excavate her familial past—her own mother never shared those stories with her—I immediately saw myself in her experience of having grown up with ghosts. The parents' generation knew all too well what they had lost, but their children, removed from the traumatic episode, had only traces of the past—names mentioned in hushed tones, photographs retrieved from hidden boxes—hauntings and gaps. It was a story that sounded eerily familiar to me, about how trauma silenced a generation, leaving their descendants with many questions and a good deal of shame.

In a world characterized by ever-increasing saturation of media images of violence, the experience of being haunted by events that predate one's birth, and excavating the past in order to understand it, is becoming ever more common. The memory practices undertaken by the Holocaust second generation are becoming a template for other post-genocide descendant groups who travel to their parents' and grandparents' places of origin, conducting oral histories with surviving relatives, and producing films and memoirs describing this memory work. Because the Armenian genocide "was so methodically suppressed and merely ignored," one woman writes, remembering it has an "almost bizarre urgency for Armenian survivors and descendants, actually increasing as that original generation of survivors slowly and steadily diminishes."[46] American descendants of slaves travel to Africa to fill in the blank spaces of the historical record and to represent the lives of those deemed unworthy of being remembered.[47]

Descendants of Punjabi Hindu refugees after the Indian Partition experience the "presence of absence" and yearn to know about their parents' and grandparents' past.[48] Sikh activists in the diaspora mobilize on the Internet, invoking memories of the Holocaust to make claims for their own suffering.[49] A child of a Korean War survivor speaks of the way gaps in knowledge of her family history, much like children of Holocaust survivors, turns secrets into phantoms that haunt her generation.[50] These and other descendants, who grow up dominated by events that occurred before their birth, often develop an enormous hunger to fill in the missing pieces of their histories; some become coaxers, and carriers, of their parents' memories.

Collapsing distinctions among different traumatic histories is not a particularly fruitful exercise; every incident of mass victimization takes place in a specific context. The Bosnian genocide is not equivalent to the forced removal of Australian aborigines; nor are the experiences of Punjabi refugees wholly comparable to those who witnessed the genocide of European Jewry. Moreover, power politics determines which conflicts, and which mass tragedies, we become aware of, and how they come to be addressed, if they are addressed at all. Suffering populations can, and do, frequently become pawns in larger games of power. And still they endure many common experiences: traumatic shocks upend their places in the world; they feel betrayed by those around them; after the event, they must reconstruct their lives, practically from scratch; and they must figure out how to convey a sense of the past to their children—to link their own lives to the future—though others may prefer that they move on. Regrettably, these experiences are becoming more commonplace. At the same time, the acceleration of global information flows means that there are many more potential encounters, points of contact, and possibilities for witnessing the pain of others, forging bonds between different populations who have endured mass violence.[51]

Contacts across groups are potentially transformative if the memory of the Holocaust, and of mass trauma in general, can be used to develop a "species awareness" to prevent future holocausts from occurring.[52] Such is the philosophy behind Holocaust educational programs that draw connections to other strains of intolerance and bigotry.[53] Rather than hardening us to the suffering of others, these projects suggest that by acknowledging the ongoing legacy of collective trauma, we can create greater empathy for the suffering of others—and work toward alleviating future suffering.

The philosopher Emmanuel Levinas has suggested that to live an ethical life we must truly see the "other" and converse with her, get to know her, look her in the face, and make her part of our moral universe. In fact, survivors, who were once strangers and were disavowed by many of those around them, have become valued witnesses. Rather than turn away from them, Americans increasingly welcome them into their midst. Thanks to this growing public discussion, the families of survivors have been able to reintegrate lost parts of their fractured histories, Jewish communities have been able to renew emotional connections with pre-war Eastern and Central European Jewry, and American Jews have been able to build bridges to other victimized groups.[54]

Recently, Cambodian refugees living in the United States established the Cambodian American Heritage Museum and Killing Fields Memorial, which seeks to memorialize the more than two million Cambodians who were murdered during the brutal reign of the Khmer Rouge and to document the stories of those who fled to America. The bulk of the funding came from Jewish donors in Chicago.[55] By giving money to a group that has also experienced mass death, these donors acknowledge that they have a special relationship with Cambodians, and that as Jews they share a tragic history with them.

Such efforts, which speak of the possibility of building bridges across victimized groups, transforming painful legacies into acts of empathy and recognition, must be applauded.[56] But radical remembering must also lead to self-criticism. So while it may be easy for Jews to commit support for a memorial to a genocide in Cambodia, or Sudan, places where they have little direct emotional or political investment, it may be much more difficult to subject their own identifications and political loyalties to scrutiny. Feeling sympathy for others may enable us to imagine ourselves as innocent bystanders. But our privileges may in fact be implicated in the suffering of others, and they may at times facilitate that suffering, sometimes in ways that are unknown to us. So while we remember the past, we must, in Paul Gilroy's words, engage in a "principled and methodical cultivation of a degree of estrangement from [our] own culture and history."[57] A truly ethical approach to memory, in other words, brings to light the repressed or forgotten while sustaining a critical and questioning attitude toward the past and working to alleviate suffering in the present.

The historical memory of the Holocaust will be made and remade, appropriated and re-appropriated—particularly as we move further and further away from firsthand memory. Today, as the number of original tellers of Holocaust stories rapidly diminishes, and as the second generation and their children become the last links to living memory, mediated and institutionalized forms of memory are becoming the primary ways we know about the Holocaust. These memories now belong, in a sense, to everyone. Some may question whether this is a good thing, suggesting that it is time to move on, and that the time of remembering is long gone. But the past is not yet completely behind us, and we can never expect it to be so.

ACKNOWLEDGMENTS

I've accumulated many debts to friends, family, and colleagues while writing this book. Judith Gerson and Diane Wolf organized a conference at Rutgers where I first tested out some of the ideas that appear here; Annelise Orleck and Marianne Hirsch invited me to Dartmouth, and Deborah Gould hosted me at the University of Pittsburgh. At a historical sociology conference at Berkeley, Brian Donovan and Nancy Whittier offered useful feedback, and Ellen Herman hosted me at a workshop on therapeutic culture at the University of Oregon, where Rebecca Jo Plant, Jennifer Freyd, and others were generous critics.

I had the good fortune to be in residence at the Humanities Center of Australian National University during the initial stages of this project. Thanks to the Freilich Foundation, Renata Grossi, Carolyn Strange, Richard Sandell, Rosemary Hollow, Rosanne Kennedy, Susan Andrews, and Shannon Woodcock for stimulating company down under. A Silberman Faculty Seminar at the United States Holocaust Memorial Museum was invaluable, as was a fellowship year at the Institute for Research on Women at Rutgers with Dorothy Hodgson at the helm; Rutgers University also provided a small faculty grant that aided my work. I am also thankful to Deborah Carr and Lisa Iorillo of the Rutgers Department of Sociology, who insured that the trains ran on time.

At various points, Fran Bartkowski, Nancy Chodorow, Beth Cohen, Ann Cvetkovich, Cynthia Eller, Helen Epstein, Judith Gerson, Doug Greenberg, Mary Hawkesworth, Krista Hegburg, Allan Horwitz, Roger Lancaster, Jeff Land, Erica Lehrer, Ishani Maitra, Rachel Pfeffer, Ken Plummer, Jeffrey Prager, Zakia Salime, Richard Williams, Eviatar Zerubavel, and Phil Zuckerman offered useful feedback, as did members of the Psychoanalytic Sociology group in New York, especially Lynn Chancer and Catherine Silver. My students at Rutgers reflected on suffering and its aftermath with me: Shruti Devgan, Tom DeGloma, Daina Harvey, Ghassan Moussawi, Vikash Singh, and Kirsten Song. Karen Cerulo, Lisa Kramer, Eliza Kentridge,

Jeremy Krikler, Jodi O'Brien, Theresa Hammond, Polly Thistlethwaite, and Liz Snyder offered advice and encouragement at crucial moments.

I am very grateful to the survivors and descendants whose words appear in this book, some of whom are identified by name, but many of whom are not. The Oral History collection of the United States Holocaust Memorial Museum in Washington, DC, kindly provided transcripts of interviews, as did the Transcending Trauma Project in Philadelphia; special thanks to Nancy Isserman for her assistance with the latter. I could not have written this book without them. Dori Laub, Yael Danieli, and the late Dan Bar-On generously shared their time, as did Ellen Blalock, Director of Survivor Affairs at the United States Holocaust Memorial Museum.

I also owe a great deal to the relatives, colleagues, and friends who helped me excavate my family history, fragments of which appear in these pages. My brother David Evan conducted an interview with our father that proved invaluable, and he was always supportive of my efforts. My cousin Debbie Nadolney traveled with me to present-day Warsaw and to the Warsaw of memory. Debbie and her mother Dana Williams shared letters written to Joe and Tola Stein and understood the importance of this project from the start; I am grateful to them in so many ways. My cousins Irena Pietrachowia (of blessed memory) and her husband Julek, and Agneiszka and Piotr, hosted me in Warsaw, and cried and laughed with me. Nancy Solomon lived with me and with this project for many years, journeyed with me to Poland, and always supported my efforts, as did Lewis, our son.

Teresa Pollin of the United States Holocaust Memorial Museum helped Debbie and me translate our family letters, and understood their importance. Molly Wesling and Dorota Szymkowiak translated additional Polish archival materials. In Berlin, my friends Sabine Hark and Ilona Pache appreciated our strange, linked twists of historical fate; in Vancouver, Wendy Oberlander, and in Copenhagen, Karin Lutzen, shared their family excavation projects and encouraged me to undertake my own. Thanks to *Bridges, Jewish Social Studies, Qualitative Sociology*, and *Symbolic Interaction* for publishing earlier versions of parts of this book, to anonymous reviewers who made them better, and to James Cook of Oxford University Press, who ably shepherded the book to publication. Finally, I am deeply indebted to Cynthia Chris, who convinced me to complete this book and helped in so very many ways.

Methodological Notes

How can we study the lives of those who have survived a terrible history? As much as we might try to fix the object of such a study, it remains complex and elusive. When I met with him a few years ago, Menachem Rosensaft, a descendant of survivors who has long been a leader in Holocaust commemorative efforts and whose parents were leaders before him, admitted as much, cautioning against generalizing about survivors and their descendants. "The victims of the Holocaust, both the dead and the survivors, represented the entirety of European Jewry, from the orthodox to the assimilated, from the Zionist to the communist, the rich to the poor," he said. "They included the banker from Paris, and the rabbi and pickpocket from Warsaw, the Jewish mother from Krakow and the Jewish prostitute from Paris." Because the Nazis did not differentiate between rich and poor, educated and uneducated, assimilated or not, he told me, the group of survivors is exceedingly diverse.

The same is true of children of survivors, Rosensaft insisted. "It's a completely heterogeneous group that goes across the spectrum and in large measure we are a reflection of our parents and the upbringing we received from our parents," he said. "All we really have in common is the fact that our parents went through a particular historical experience," he cautioned. "But even there those who were in Auschwitz had a different way of relating a story than someone who was in the Bielski brigade, who survived in the forest, who again had a different experience than someone who was in hiding on a farm or who passed on Aryan papers." Because of this, he said: "any generalization about these populations is dangerous."

His comments gave me pause. And yet we sociologists are in the business of generalization; I've spent my career looking at how societies pattern human experience, and I was not yet ready to throw in the towel. But how, I wondered, could I possibly write a book about a group that encompasses such a vast array of different people, and such divergent responses to trauma? Could generalizations suffice? The challenges have been daunting. This qualitative, interpretive study of survivors and their children, and the making of Holocaust consciousness, uses multiple research methods: participant observation, secondary analyses of archived interviews, interviews, content analyses of films and memoirs, and auto-ethnography. I began this project in an autobiographical vein, trying to figure out my relationship to a painful past; it became a sociological project somewhat later.

At the start of this project, I proceeded along two parallel tracks, excavating my family's hidden past, and trying to understand the lives of descendants and what, if anything, they shared in common. At first this was a personal project; over time, it became more than that. When, for nearly a year beginning in 1997, I participated in an Internet listserv for children of survivors, I wondered, what did descendants of survivors discuss on the Internet? What, if anything did they have in common? Although mainly composed of North Americans, the discussion list drew some international participation, and was focused on a variety of issues facing descendants as they made sense of the continuing impact of the Holocaust legacy.

Forums such as these have become a common way for members of different victim groups, from survivors of child abuse to political violence, to mobilize in a relatively safe, accessible way. They are sites of communication among individuals with particular shared experiences, but also archives of memory as individuals have come to use new technologies to create virtual remembering communities. As a participant in this virtual community, I made a list of recurring themes that came up in discussions online. I rejoined the listserv seven years later, for six months during 2004, to see whether the concerns of participants had changed from the earlier period. (I can't say that I fully embraced membership in the 2G identity. During my youth and early adulthood, I was too busy to dwell on painful aspects of my familial legacy, and had put that on hold. And yet, as a member of the baby boom cohort, and influenced by therapeutic currents moving through the culture via feminism, I believed it was important of confront one's demons—and to do so collectively, if possible. Eventually, I became part of the wave of self-reflection that others had already embarked on.)

Eventually, I also became more interested in the lives of the survivor generation, too, and decided to consult survivors' life histories as well. There are a number of archives of survivor testimonies in the United States, including the Fortunoff Archives at Yale University, the United States Holocaust Memorial Museum Oral History collection, and the Shoah Foundation Institute at the University of Southern California. (The latter now contains videotaped oral testimonies with nearly 52,000 Holocaust survivors and witnesses that were collected mainly in the second half of the 1990s.) Because of ease of access, and because I needed a collection of interviews that focused on survivors' postwar lives, I consulted the Oral History collection of the United States Holocaust Memorial Museum in Washington, DC

In the 1990s, the museum conducted oral histories with 520 survivors, broadly defining them as persons who were victims of Nazi policy 1933–1945, including those who had escaped the war years in the Soviet Union. Of these, museum staff members and local journalists interviewed 105 individuals about their postwar lives. At the time of my research, the museum's collection was among the most extensive archive of interviews focusing on survivors' postwar lives, and particularly on the dynamics of the families they created. These oral histories were structured as a conversation between the survivor and the interviewer in which the interviewer tried to engage people in telling their story. While interviews were originally conducted on video, some subjects were chosen for audio interviews as well. The museum transcribed the interviews, and these transcripts average 80 typewritten pages each; from these I randomly selected 23 interviews to analyze.

From these interviews, we can gain considerable insight into survivors' impressions of how family members, social workers, and others greeted them upon arrival in the United States, how they saw themselves in relation to these groups over time, and how they devised strategies of self-presentation in daily life, including with their children. Using a grounded theory approach, I made note of common, recurring themes that came up, and used these as the basis for my chapter outlines. I also tried, to the best of my capability, to capture the gestalt of the subject—to understand his or her wartime experiences in relation to the biography of a life that began before the war, and extended after it was over.

Because I had not conducted these interviews myself, and was dependent upon how the interviewers had structured the oral history, I could not probe to gain additional insights, or follow lines of inquiry they had opened up. Interviews tend to offer accounts of lives that accentuate consistency and suppress contradiction, and guard against painful feelings, such as anxiety or shame. These interviewees undoubtedly did so as well. While the relationship between interviewee and interviewer, and the bonds that are constructed between them, can be an important source of insight, I had little access to them. Much the same was true of the interviews with children of survivors completed by a group of Philadelphia psychologists in the 1990s, which I analyzed.

The Transcending Trauma Project, part of the Council of Relationships' Research Department, conducted 100 in-depth life history interviews with children of survivors, along with 35 grandchildren, and non-survivor spouses. These interviews were conducted by a team of psychologists, beginning in the early 1990s, who had a particular interest in communication patterns in Holocaust survivor households, and in patterns of "coping and adaptation." Working within the framework of trauma but diverging from models that focus on pathology, their interviews focus on "the process of recovery" and on individuals' adaptive, resilient responses.[1]

These interview subjects, gathered through a snowball sample, had at least one parent who survived the Holocaust, and at the time of interview they were generally in their thirties and forties. Approximately 60 percent of interviewees were female, 75 percent were born in the United States, and most were married at the time of the interview. They were based primarily in the Northeast, particularly in the Philadelphia area. From among these subjects, I randomly selected 27 life histories to focus on. I was interested in the ways descendants described how their parents communicated with them about their traumatic experiences, and how they conveyed knowledge of the past to them. Using a snowball sample, I also conducted an additional series of open-ended interviews with 15 children of survivors living in the New York City area, half of whom had been active in the "second generation" movement, and some of whom were recognizable leaders.

Rather than analyze these interviews as a succession of facts about an individual's life, I was interested in the stories the tellers told about these events. What shape did their narrative take? To interpret the data, I read the transcripts of the testimonies, interviews, and virtual conversations repeatedly, categorizing the data and searching for evidence of analytically important themes, using ethnographic material to situate the life histories within a broader historical/cultural context. I also read numerous memoirs written by children of survivors, which are listed in the bibliography. I used a methodology similar to the one I first used in my earlier study of women's sexual identities—simultaneously tracing the trajectory of one generational cohort alongside the movement and the culture that its members helped to create.

REFLEXIVITY AND INDIVIDUALITY

Autobiographical experience is a powerful source of sociological insight. Auto-ethnography, in sociologist Patricia Clough's words, gives "a personal accounting of the location of the observer," which is typically disavowed in traditional social science writing. "It does so by making the ethnographer the subject-object of observation, exploring experience from the inside of the ethnographer's life."[2] In telling the story of my family, to the extent that I was able to come to know it, I am also telling a story of knowledge production, and reflecting on why excavating the past has been so important for many members of my cohort.

My family background also aided me in interpreting these archived interviews, and allowed me to better understand the gaps, the emotional register of the discussions, and the stories that were told between the lines. I have woven my own family's story—captured though recollections, photos, and fragments—into this varied mix of data, using it to illustrate the larger trends I saw, and to situate myself as the author of this text. I tell my family's story, focusing mainly on my father—through recollections, photos, and fragments—not necessarily because I believe that my own experiences are somehow representative of the population of descendants of survivors, but because they illustrate many of the themes that came up in other interviews I analyzed.

By tapping into my own experiential knowledge, I also hoped to disrupt some of the unspoken power dynamics of social science research, and to expand our notion of what counts as evidence. As a discipline, sociology remains committed to an objective notion of truth unencumbered by subjectivity. Because it examines the experience of tremendous suffering, a book about the Holocaust can never in my view be a dispassionate, disinterested analysis, and I question whether "value-free" social science is an effective route to understanding such an event and its impact on individual lives.

While individuals participate in collective meaning making, and are influenced by the social contexts in which they live, they are also unique individuals. In this project, while emphasizing collective patterns, I have tried to be attuned to the varied ways in which individuals respond to the same event or situation. While trauma imprints itself on individuals, for example, they do not react in uniform or predictable ways. Some are overcome by their losses, while others retain a sense of agency, exercising resilience.

For example, Nancy Chodorow describes the variability of families of survivors, who exhibit "a range from ebullient optimism and a claim that all is right with the world, to simple relief at having survived, to emotional frozenness and painful depression." In some families, she writes, "there is silence and occlusion of a loss that is too painful to acknowledge. Other families, by contrast, rather than mourning their losses, celebrate survival and make cheerful, positive thinking a goal."[3]

In my own research on the postwar lives of survivors, I, too, found considerable variation in how individuals coped with trauma. Some individuals strongly identified with their pasts, surrounding themselves with those who shared their experiences, and became willing spokespersons for the collectivity of survivors. At the opposite extreme were those who fled these kinds of identifications, distancing themselves from their pasts, some even renouncing their Jewishness, or emphasizing their French nationality, for example. While some welcomed the newfound visibility of survivors in the 1980s, others felt deeply ambivalent about it—wondering why anyone would "air their dirty laundry." Some questioned themselves whether they in fact were survivors, or even victims. Their identification with the dead, and their feelings of guilt for having survived when so many did not, made it difficult to see themselves as victims, too.

Descendants also varied in how they processed their traumatic inheritance, and how salient they made it in their lives. While culture and context clearly mediate how individuals experience trauma, individual experiences vary within the same cultural context, and even children growing up in the same family have different experiences. Within families, it was typical for one child to take a keen interest in their family history, and to become, in effect, the instigator of memory work, to see it as a kind of calling; other siblings often had little or no interest in such endeavors, and were at times quite uncomfortable with a sibling's interest in them. Some actively participated in therapy groups made up of other children of survivors; others had little interest in participating in such efforts. Those who participated were more likely to be women, to have been influenced by feminism and by therapeutic discourse, and to be of Eastern European parentage, but these demographic characteristics did not, in the end, determine who did or didn't participate; this was a much more individual question.

While there is a great deal of variability in individual experiences, and how individuals respond to those experiences, we should not overstate the capacity of the individual to stand apart from his or her environment. Burying oneself in one's work and developing an extraordinary drive to succeed may look on the surface like evidence of resilience but can in fact be a different form of denial, a way of escaping one's past rather than integrating it into one's life. Cultural contexts place limits on individual variation, encouraging certain patterns of response, and discouraging others. So while how people will respond to a given event is ultimately highly variable, culture places limits on individual variation, encouraging certain patterns of response, and discouraging others. Ideally, we need to understand all of these dimensions—the cultural, the interpersonal, and the individual. My study focuses on the cultural and interpersonal dimensions.

LIMITS OF KNOWLEDGE

I have tried to the best of my ability to paint a picture that is accurate in its broadest outlines, which captures the patterns I observed. But like all sociological studies, and indeed all studies, this is a partial rendering of reality. For example, my sample of survivors and descendants is certainly biased in favor of those for whom such identifications are salient. Descendants who participate in organized activities where they identify as a member of the "second generation," such as the listserv I participated in and observed, are but a small subset of the total number of children of survivors. This and other electronic communities draw people who may otherwise be too geographically dispersed, or not highly motivated enough, to participate in face-to-face discussions. But even people who participate in an online forum of this sort may not define themselves as part of a collectivity of children or descendants of Holocaust survivors. Moreover, if they do possess a shared identity, it may be fleeting, and not relevant to other areas of their lives. These caveats notwithstanding, the tenor of the online discussions suggested that most participants in them find them to be very personally meaningful.

A number of critics have cautioned against viewing archived survivor testimonies as being representative of the larger population of survivors.[4] The survivor population is exceedingly diverse, coming from many countries, and possessing many different class backgrounds, ideologies, and life experiences. The United States Holocaust Memorial Museum often recruited interviewees from among people with whom it had prior contact—survivor volunteers, for example, and people who contacted the museum to offer themselves as subjects. It also did some outreach through its survivors' registry, targeting particular categories of persons who were under-represented among its interviewees—Greek Jews, for example. Generally, interviews were conducted in Washington, DC, and occasionally in New York; there were also a number of outreach efforts to other parts of the United States.

My study therefore over-represents survivors who settled in the mid-Atlantic United States, who were affiliated with Jewish and Holocaust-related organizations, and who had previously spoken about their wartime and postwar lives in non-family contexts. It under-sampled those who lacked any connection to organized Jewish communities, or who did not have children or grandchildren who coaxed them to speak. Those who had never before spoken about their wartime experiences to strangers were also less likely to be represented. Moreover, many, if not most, survivors refused to speak. My father, whose reticence to share his story infuses the narrative of this book, may be more representative of the population of survivors than those who do speak.

The sample is also biased against highly religious survivors, who were probably less inclined to offer their stories to secular institutions such as the United States Holocaust Memorial Museum, or even to think of

Holocaust memory outside religious terms. Collectively, I would specu-late that they would have an interpretation of events that lay outside the parameters of the story I am telling here. Women are also over-represented among survivors and descendants, for a number of reasons. In my random sample of United States Holocaust Memorial Museum interviews with sur-vivors, over half of those interviewed were women, reflecting to a great extent the demographics of the postwar oral histories held by the museum. This gender disparity is greater among my random sample of individuals interviewed by the Transcending Trauma Project: about two-thirds are women, which mirrors the larger sample. The gender disparity is most pro-nounced in the discussion lists I studied, where more than three-quarters of all participants were women, and where women were by far the most active members in terms of frequency of posts. As I argue in this book, women are more likely to be memory workers, and are disproportionately represented among descendants who engage in excavation projects of the sort I documented in Chapter 5. They are also more likely to work in the helping professions and to be familiar with therapeutic discourse, which probably makes them more likely to participate in such memory practices.

Interpreting these interviews was at times highly challenging. Oral his-tories collected by archivists such as the United States Holocaust Memorial Museum encourage interviewees to plot their lives in terms of linear tra-jectories, downplaying the messiness and incoherence of lives. We know that when people talk about their lives, they actively frame their experi-ence to suit their own needs, as well as the needs of the interviewer. In keeping with the tendency to value biographical consistency, they tend to downplay ambiguity and flux. To a great extent, survivors' stories were all about ambiguity, flux, and uncertainty. Yet the structure of the interview often emphasizes such narratives' linearity. The nature of the interview process leads individuals to "recast the past," telling their story in light of the present.

Moreover, archived interviews give the researcher access to only one side of an interaction: the survivor's story. Discerning the context of the inter-action requires one to analyze "around" interviews, and to be conscious of emotional exchanges and facial expressions. Since I was mainly analyz-ing written transcripts of interviews conducted by others, this was very difficult to do. It is for that reason that I decided to conduct a number of interviews of my own, to supplement the archived interviews. Moreover, interviews are snapshots of a moment in time: they are as much about the present as the past. Ideally, if I had had the time, I would have built an ongoing relationship with the interview subject, interviewing him or her at different points, again and again—a difficult, time-consuming task, particularly as many of the interviewees I've written about are now at the end of their lives, or are deceased.

As one can imagine, listening to the stories of survivors of genocide entails a great deal of emotional labor. This may be particularly true for someone whose own biography is so deeply implicated in that history. This is hardly a set of "data" from which I can easily distance myself, and I encountered considerable emotional challenges in writing this book. Particularly at the beginning of the research process, before I had become acclimated to reading, speaking, and thinking about the Holocaust, when much of this material was still new to me, I found myself overcome with emotion at times. Over the course of the many years I spent reading and analyzing the transcripts of Holocaust survivors and their descendants, I was able to (partially) "work through" my relationship to this traumatic past, and to develop a clearer analytic distance. Writing this book also allowed me to develop a great deal more empathy with my parents, particularly my father. When I began this book, I hardly knew the details of his history. By the end, I had developed a much greater understanding of the sources of his pain—and his resilience, too.

Janet Jacobs has written of the problem of "double vision": of having a personal connection to one's research subjects, while maintaining the distance needed to analyze social science "data." As a Jewish woman studying Holocaust memory, Jacobs describes herself as "both a witness to crimes against humanity and an ethnographic observer in search of qualitative data," echoing earlier discussions of the tension between a feminist ethnographer's dual roles as participant and observer.[5] Jacobs struggled with her deep emotional connection with her subjects, and her engagement in so-called "value-free" social science research. Although I have never considered myself a neutral observer, and have always had deep personal investments in the subjects I have chosen to study, the study of something as personal and overwhelming as the legacy of genocide, particularly one that was so formative in my own life, posed new challenges, eliciting inevitable sadness and loss, but also the possibility of working through those losses.

In many respects, this has been the most difficult project I have ever undertaken. Particularly at the beginning, writing and reading about mass trauma that was both close and far from my own life elicited feelings of sorrow and pain. While I have not "gotten beyond" and banished feelings of loss, or have achieved "closure"—if that were even possible—by writing this book I have found a way to acknowledge these feelings of loss and to weave them into the story of my life and my family. I have also, I hope, told a larger story that will be useful to others, about the enduring presence of difficult pasts.

Finally, I also encountered ethical dilemmas around issues of privacy and risk, particularly when it came to deciding whether or not to identify the survivors by name.[6] Sociological convention calls for researchers to protect the anonymity of their research subjects by assigning them pseudonyms. But many of these individuals, who had never before spoken publicly about their experiences, were developing a sense of agency and dignity, and reconstructing a sense of self through acts of storytelling. If I disguised their names, and disconnected their stories from their person, was I silencing them once again? Was I, in effect, wiping out their identities, at least metaphorically, and failing to portray them as complete humans?

I decided to use to the actual names of my survivor respondents, having been granted permission to do so by the United States Holocaust Memorial Museum's Oral History collection; many of the oral histories are now available online, and individual subjects can therefore be easily identified. To protect individuals' privacy, and to comply with the wishes of the Transcending Trauma Project, I assigned pseudonyms to descendants. For the 15 interviews with children of survivors that I conducted myself, I used the real names of public figures, and asked others whether they wished to be identified by their real names. If I could not locate them, I assigned them pseudonyms. To protect the identities of participants on second generation listservs, I refer to individuals by first names, although many of these first names have been changed.

INTERVIEWEES

Survivors

Survivors	Year interviewed	Year of birth	Country of origin
Esther Adler	1992	1924	Germany
Harry Alexander	1992	1921	Germany
Erwin Baum	1994	1926	Warsaw
Thomas Blatt	1983	1927	Poland
Thomas Buergenthal	2001	1934	Czechoslovakia
Aron Derman	1997	1922	Poland
Lisa Derman	1997	1926	Poland
Eva Edmands	1990	1929	Austria
Florence Eisen	1994	1928	Poland
Barbara Farkas	1990	1920	Romania
Nesse Godin	1995	1928	Lithuania
Rene Goldberg*	1994	1928	Czechoslovakia
Sylvia Green	1999	1924	Germany
Irene Hizme	1992	1937	Czechoslovakia

(Continued)

Survivors	Year interviewed	Year of birth	Country of origin
Lucine Horn	1994	1926	Poland
Anna Kleinhaus	1990	1936	Belgium
Dorianne Kurz	1990	1936	Austria
William Loew	1995	1925	Poland
Lily Margules	1990	1924	Lithuania
Edwarda Rorat	1994	1935	Poland
Laura Simon	1993	1928	Hungary
Daniel Simon	1993	1927	Hungary
Rene Slotkin	1992	1937	Czechoslovakia
Bella Tovey	1992	1926	Poland

*Conducted by the Holocaust Documentation and Education Center, Miami, accessed through U.S. Holocaust Memorial Museum. All others held in Oral History Collection of U.S. Holocaust Memorial Museum.

Descendants

Descendants	Year interviewed	Year of birth
United States Holocaust Memorial Museum, Oral History Collection:		
Esther Dezube	2000	
Transcending Trauma Project (listed by pseudonym):		
Ann Bander	1995	1956
Theo Berg	1995	1948
Stanley Glassberg	1996	1951
Renee Grinspan	1995	1964
Sally Gross	1996	1955
David Halbert	1995	1967
Jennifer Holland	1996	1955
Janet Horwath	1994	1958
Jodi Kahn	1999	1953
Jesse Klapholz	1998	1954
Lisa Kramer	1999	1974
Melody Landsman	1995	1949
Joan Loeb	1994	1952
Jesse Klaman	1998	1954
Sandra Malkin	1994	1952
Sharon Miller	1994	1951
Sarah Moen	1994	1958
Pam Neuborne	1994	1950
Laura Pfeffer	1996	1955
Isaac Rosen	1996	1947
Julie Schwartzman	1999	1951

(Continued)

Descendants	Year interviewed	Year of birth
William Simon	1994	1967
Barbara Samuels	1996	1953
Susan Stern	1994	1958
Ron Solomon	1994	1943
Eve Stiller	1996	1947
Jonathan Keller	1996	1950
Author Interviews (*pseudonym)		
Harvey Brint*	2004	1953
Martin Fellner	2004	1959
Eva Fogelman	2004	
Jeanette Friedman	2004	1947
Sandi Goodman	2004	1956
Sylvia Hennig*	2003	1957
Janet Hollander*	2003	1950
Jack Jacobs	2005	1953
Anita Norich	2008	1952
Dina Rosenfeld	2004	1949
Menachem Rosensaft	2009	1948
Alan Sadovnik	2004	1953
Andrew Shear	2005	1967
Mel Simon*	2006	1955

NOTES

INTRODUCTION

1. See Nanette C. Auerhahn and Dori Laub, "Intergenerational Memory of the Holocaust," in *International Handbook of Multigenerational Legacies of Trauma*, ed. Yael Danieli (New York: Plenum Press, 1978), 21; Cathy Caruth, "Introduction," in *Trauma: Explorations in Memory*, ed. Cathy Caruth (Baltimore: Johns Hopkins University Press, 1995); and Judith Herman, *Trauma and Recovery: The Aftermath of Violence from Domestic Abuse to Political Terror* (New York: Basic Books, 1997), x. While Herman described the difficult challenges facing those who tell stories about trauma, she was one of a number of psychologists in the 1980s and 1990s who, influenced by feminism and other social movements, worked to change the terms by which we understand trauma and open up a public conversation about its effects.

2. See Annie Rogers, *The Unsayable: The Hidden Language of Trauma* (New York: Random House, 2008). According to the *Diagnostic and Statistical Manual of Mental Disorders, Fourth Edition*: "The trauma may involve direct personal experience of an event that involves actual or threatened death or serious injury, or other threat to one's physical integrity; or witnessing an event that involves death, injury, or a threat to the physical integrity or another person; or learning about unexpected or violent death, serious harm, or threat of death or injury experienced by a family member or other close associate. The person's response to the event must involved intense fear, helplessness, or horror. The characteristic symptoms resulting from the exposure to the extreme trauma include persistent re-experiencing of the traumatic event, persistent avoidance of stimuli associated with the trauma and numbing of general responsiveness, and persistent symptoms of increased arousal" (American Psychiatric Association, *DSM-IV-TR*, 1994). This does not address the symptoms experienced by children of survivors of trauma or the mechanisms of the possible intergenerational transmission of the effects of trauma. See also Robert Lifton, *Home from the War: Learning from Vietnam Veterans* (Boston: Beacon, 1973); Herman, *Trauma and Recovery*; Paul Lerner and Mark S. Micale, "Trauma, Psychiatry, and History," in *Traumatic Pasts: History, Psychiatry, and Trauma in the Modern Age, 1870–1930*, ed. Paul Lerner and Mark S. Micale (Cambridge: Cambridge University Press, 2001), 2.

3. David Dobbs, "A New Focus on the 'Post' in Post-Traumatic Stress," *New York Times*, December 24, 2012, accessed March 13, 2013, http://www.nytimes.com/2012/12/25/science/understanding-the-effects-of-

social-environment-on-trauma-victims.html. Kai Erikson, researching the aftermath of floods and other natural disasters, similarly observes that "it is *how people react* to them rather than *what they are* that give events whatever traumatic quality they can be said to have." Trauma, he says, results from a "constellation of life experiences as well as from a discrete happening, from a persisting condition as well as an acute event." Kai Erikson, "Notes on Trauma and Community," in *Trauma: Explorations in Memory*, ed. Cathy Caruth (Baltimore: The Johns Hopkins University Press, 1995), 184.

4. Erikson, "Notes on Trauma and Community," 184 (emphasis in original).
5. Dobbs, "A New Focus on the 'Post' in Post-Traumatic Stress."
6. Selma Leydesdorff, Graham Dawson, Natasha Burchardt, and T. G. Ashplant, "Introduction: Trauma and Life Stories," in *Trauma: Life Stories of Survivors*, ed. Kim Lacy Rogers and Selma Leydesdorff (with Graham Dawson) (New Brunswick, NJ: Transaction, 2004), 9, 10.
7. While my focus is on Jewish survivors, I recognize that non-Jewish Roma, leftists, homosexuals, and members of other groups also suffered. I focus on the Jewish Holocaust not to privilege Jewish suffering, but because that is where my personal and intellectual investments begin, and because the scope of the Jewish genocide overshadowed the mass murders of other groups during the Nazi period. I am also mindful of the ways that a focus on Jewish loss may at times inadvertently obscure other groups' (such as Roma) search for memory and recognition today.
8. Eva Hoffman, *After Such Knowledge: Memory, History, and the Legacy of the Holocaust* (New York: Public Affairs, 2004), 16. See also Annette Kuhn, *Family Secrets: Acts of Memory and Imagination* (London: Verso, 1995). Feminists, people of color, and immigration scholars have illuminated the frequent, yawning gaps between social norms and emotional lives, and the ways that official, dominant, interpretive devices of a culture often exclude whole swaths of populations.
9. Ken Plummer discusses the importance of story coaxers in *Telling Sexual Stories: Power, Culture, and Social Worlds* (New York: Routledge, 1995).
10. See, for example, Ann Cvetkovich, *An Archive of Feelings* (Durham, NC: Duke University Press, 2003).
11. See Alyson Cole, *The Cult of True Victimhood: From the War on Welfare to the War on Terror* (Stanford, CA: Stanford University Press, 2007), 1.
12. Leonard Dinnerstein, *America and the Survivors of the Holocaust* (New York: Columbia University Press, 1982); William Helmreich, "Don't Look Back: Holocaust Survivors in the US," Jerusalem Center for Public Affairs, 1991.
13. Erik Erikson, cited by Nancy Chodorow, "Born into a World at War: Listening for Affect and Personal Meaning," *American Imago* 59, no. 3 (2002).
14. Television in this period, from the 1961 Eichmann trial to the *Holocaust* miniseries, brought the events into the homes of millions of Americans, but often transformed tragic stories into tales of heroism and moral uplift.
15. Barbara Ehrenreich, *Bright-Sided: How the Relentless Promotion of Positive Thinking Has Undermined America* (New York: Metropolitan Books, 2009), 56. On the tendency to look on the bright side, also see Karen Cerulo, *Never Saw It Coming: Cultural Challenges to Imagining the Worst* (Chicago: University of Chicago Press, 2006); Marita Sturken, *Tourists of History: Memory, Kitsch, and Consumerism from Oklahoma City to Ground Zero* (Durham, NC: Duke University Press, 2007).
16. See Bruno Bettleheim, *Surviving and Other Essays* (New York: Knopf: 1979).

17. William G. Niederland, "Clinical Observations on the 'Survivor Syndrome,'" *International Journal of Psycho-Analysis* 49 (1968): 313–315.

18. Yael Danieli, "Introduction: History and Conceptual Foundations," in *International Handbook of Multigenerational Legacies of Trauma*, ed. Yael Danieli (New York: Plenum, 1998).

19. Primo Levi, "Shame," in *The Drowned and the Saved* (New York: Random House, 1989), 81–82. See also Henry Greenspan, *On Listening to Holocaust Survivors* (Westport, CT: Praeger, 1998), 33. As Greenspan puts it, "it is easier for us to accommodate the guilty survivor." The pain that the guilty survivor directs inward "neither directly shames us nor shames the world. Survivors' guilt remains their problem, not ours." On Sylvan Tompkins's view of shame, see Eve Kosofsky Sedgwick, "Shame, Theatricality, and Queer Performativity: Henry James' *The Art of the Novel*," in *Gay Shame*, ed. David M. Halperin and Valerie Traub (Chicago: University of Chicago Press, 2009), 49. For a sophisticated theoretical survey of the move from a focus on guilt to shame in the conceptualization of trauma, see Ruth Leys, *From Guilt to Shame: Auschwitz and After* (Princeton, NJ: Princeton University Press, 2007). On shame in the context of sexuality, see my *Shameless: Sexual Dissidence in American Culture* (New York: New York University Press, 2007).

20. *Exploring Affect: The Selected Writings of Silvan S. Tompkins*, ed. Virginia E. Demos (Cambridge, UK: Press Syndicate of the University of Cambridge, 1995). I am not going to wade into debates about the distinction among feelings, emotions, and affect here; I leave that to others.

21. Thomas Scheff, "Shame in Self and Society," *Symbolic Interaction* 26, no. 2 (2003): 239–262; Thomas Scheff and Suzanne Retzinger. "Shame as the Master Emotion of Everyday Life," *Journal of Mundane Behavior* 1, no. 3 (2000), accessed March 13, 2013, http://www.mundanebehavior.org/issues/v1n3/scheff-retzinger.htm.

22. Geoffrey Hartman, cited in Froma Zeitlin, "The Vicarious Witness: Belated Memory and Authorial Presence in Recent Holocaust Literature," *History and Memory* 10, no. 2 (Fall 1998), 5–42.

23. The figure of 250,000 is cited by Helen Epstein in *Children of the Holocaust* (New York: Putnam, 1979) and is probably a conservative estimate. The number is derived from the estimated 140,000–150,000 survivors who settled in the United States between 1945 and 1951. It does not include subsequent immigrants from the former Soviet Union, Hungary, Romania, and Israel, many of whom were survivors but whose postwar experiences are often quite different from those I discuss here. Nor does it include those who were denied entry to the United States, who waited elsewhere until they were eventually admitted. My father, for example, who lived in Cuba for five years until he was granted a United States visa, would not have been included in this tally.

24. Dori Laub, "The Empty Circle: Children of Survivors and the Limits of Reconstruction," *Journal of the American Psychoanalytic Association* 46, no. 2 (1998): 509, 521.

25. Nadine Fresco, "Remembering the Unknown," *International Journal of Psychoanalysis* 11 (1984): 421.

26. Helen Epstein, *Where She Came From: A Daughter's Search for Her Mother's Story* (New York: Penguin, 1997); Hoffman, *After Such Knowledge*; Marianne Hirsch, *Family Frames: Photography, Narrative, and Postmemory* (Cambridge, MA: Harvard University Press, 1997); Zeitlin, "The Vicarious Witness."

27. Epstein, *Children of the Holocaust*; Aaron Haas, *In the Shadow of the Holocaust: the Second Generation* (London: Cambridge University Press, 1990); Hoffman, *After Such Knowledge*; Samuel Slipp, "Intergenerational Transmission of Psychic Trauma," in *Object Relations* (New York and London: Jason Aronson, 1991), 163–173; Henry Krystal and William G. Niederland, "Clinical Observations on the Survivor Syndrome," in *Massive Psychic Trauma*, ed. Henry Krystal (New York: International Universities Press, 1968), 327–348; Judith Kestenberg, "Psychoanalytic Contributions to the Problems of Children of Survivors from Nazi Persecution," *Israeli Annals of Psychiatry and Related Disciplines* 10 (1972), 311–325; Dina Wardi, *Memorial Candles: Children of the Holocaust* (New York: Routledge, 1992).

28. Literary critic Annette Kuhn, who grew up in post–World War II Britain, described the ways "possibility and loss are written into [the] world [her] generation inherited." She, like others of her generation experienced "the traces present all around us of a war we did not live through—traces in our physical surroundings, in our parent's talk, in so many aspects of our daily lives." More recently, Grace M. Cho has documented the experiences of the children of American servicemen and Korean prostitutes. "An unspeakable trauma does not die out with the person who first experienced it," she writes. "Rather it takes on a life of its own, emerging from the spaces where secrets are concealed." Though Korean comfort women tried to maintain silence about their sexual enslavement, their secrets were already being transmitted to the next generations, and would haunt the Korean diaspora. Grace M. Cho, *Haunting the Korean Diaspora: Shame, Secrecy, and the Forgotten War* (Minneapolis: University of Minnesota, 2008), 6.

29. Avery Gordon, *Ghostly Matters: Haunting and the Sociological Imagination* (Minneapolis: University of Minnesota, 1997), 21.

30. Kuhn, *Family Secrets*; Hirsch, *Family Frames*; Marianne Hirsch and Valerie Smith, "Feminism and Cultural Memory: An Introduction," *Signs* 28, no. 1 (2002), 1–19.

31. Avishai Margalit, *The Ethics of Memory* (Cambridge, MA: Harvard University Press, 2002), 7.

32. Nancy Whittier, *The Politics of Sexual Abuse: Emotion, Social Movements, and the State* (New York: Oxford University Press, 2009).

33. Hasia Diner, *We Remember with Reverence and Love: American Jews and the Myth of Silence after the Holocaust, 1945–1962* (New York: New York University Press, 2009).

34. http://www.pewforum.org/2013/10/01/jewish-american-beliefs-attitudes-culture-survey/.

35. On the "trauma process" see, for example, Ron Eyerman, "Cultural Trauma: Slavery and the Formation of African American Memory," in *Cultural Trauma and Collective Memory*, ed. Jeffrey Alexander et al. (Berkeley: University of California Press, 2004).

36. Peter Novick, *The Holocaust in American Life* (New York: Houghton Mifflin, 1999), 10, 280. Norman Finkelstein similarly criticized an emerging "Holocaust industry" for exploiting past Jewish suffering and evading moral and historical responsibility for ongoing mass violence occurring across the globe. See his book *The Holocaust Industry: Reflections on the Exploitation of Jewish Suffering* (London: Verso, 2000). For similar temporalizations, see Arthur Hertzberg, "The First Encounter: Survivors and Americans in the Late 1940s" (Washington, DC: United States Holocaust Memorial Museum, 1996); Alvin H. Rosenfeld, "The Americanization of the Holocaust," *Commentary* 6 (June 1995); Annette Wieviorka, *The Era of the Witness* (Ithaca, NY: Cornell University Press, 2006).

37. See, for example, the recent Pew poll of American Jews: http://www.pewforum.org/2013/10/01/jewish-american-beliefs-attitudes-culture-survey/.

38. Arthur Frank describes the way the ill narrate their lives. They tell stories of the bodies that have failed them, which are subjected to medical expertise; quest narratives, stories of just suffering, of suffering for others, and for a particular purpose; and restitution narratives, which say: "Yesterday I was well; today I am sick; tomorrow I will be well again." There is a clear cultural preference for restitution and quest narratives. See Arthur Frank, *Wounded Storytellers: Body, Illness, and Ethics* (Chicago: University of Chicago Press, 1995).

39. I am influenced by the symbolic interactionist tradition in sociology, which looks at social life as a series of open-ended negotiations, in which people make meanings in relation to those around them, sometimes by telling stories about their lives. The social world is made up by people using the symbols and languages at our disposal; stories are among these symbolic tools. On the narrative turn in sociology, see Plummer, *Telling Sexual Stories*; Francesca Polletta, *It Was Like a Fever: Storytelling in Protest and Politics* (Chicago: University of Chicago Press, 2006); Arlene Stein, *Sex and Sensibility: Stories of a Lesbian Generation* (Berkeley: University of Chicago Press, 1993); Mary Jo Maynes, Jennifer L. Pierce, and Barbara Laslett, *Telling Stories: The Use of Personal Narratives in the Social Sciences and History* (Ithaca, NY: Cornell University Press, 2008). I am also influenced by those who are seeking to meld sociological and psychoanalytic perspectives, who see human subjects as simultaneously the products of their own unique psychic worlds and a shared social world, such as Wendy Hollway and Tony Jefferson, *Doing Qualitative Work Differently* (London: Sage, 2013).

40. Chodorow, "Born into a World at War," 298.

41. Gordon, *Ghostly Matters*.

42. Jessica Benjamin, *The Bonds of Love: Psychoanalysis, Feminism, and the Problem of Domination* (New York: Pantheon, 1988).

CHAPTER 1

1. Erving Goffman documented the great lengths members of stigmatized groups go to in order to present themselves to others in public, manage their identities, and downplay mutual discomfort. While these threats can be imagined or anticipated, shame is a continuing threat in most social interactions: we are always desperately worried about our image in the eyes of the other, and we try to present ourselves in the best possible light. See his *Stigma: Notes on the Management of Spoiled Identity* (New York: Touchstone, 1986), first published in 1963.

2. The interviews analyzed in this chapter, with two exceptions, were conducted in the 1990s by the United States Holocaust Memorial Museum's Oral History Division.

3. Ruth Kluger, *Still Alive* (New York: The Feminist Press, 2003), 177.

4. As Article II of the United Nations Convention on the Prevention and Punishment of the Crime of Genocide defines it, genocide encompasses a variety of acts intended to "destroy in whole or in part, a national, ethnical, racial or religious group." See United Nations, Convention on the Prevention and Punishment of the Crime of Genocide (New York, United Nations, 1991). See also Samantha Power, *A Problem from Hell: America and the Age of Genocide* (New York: Harper Perennial, 2007).

5. Christopher Lasch, *The Minimal Self: Psychic Survival in Troubled Times* (New York: Norton), 198, 100.

6. On the transnationalization of Holocaust memory discourse, see Andreas Huyssen, *Present Pasts: Urban Palimpsests and the Politics of Memory* (Stanford, CA: Stanford University Press, 2003); on its Americanization, see Peter Novick, *The Holocaust in American Life* (New York: Houghton Mifflin, 1999); Michael Berenbaum, "The Nativization of the Holocaust," *Judaism* 35, 1986.

7. "Before It Had a Name," *This American Life*, Chicago Public Radio, October 26, 2001.

8. See, for example, "Editors' Condemn Nazis' Brutality," *New York Times*, May 6, 1943. Also see Jeffrey Shandler, *While America Watches: Televising the Holocaust* (New York: Oxford University Press, 1999); Beth Cohen, *Case Closed: Holocaust Survivors in Postwar America* (New Brunswick, NJ: Rutgers University Press, 2007), 28–29.

9. Hannah Arendt. "The Jew as Pariah: A Hidden Tradition," in *The Jew as Pariah: Jewish Identity and Politics in the Modern Age*, ed. Ron H. Feldman (New York: Grove Press, 1978).

10. Karen Brodkin, *How Jews Became White Folks* (New Brunswick, NJ: Rutgers University Press, 1998).

11. Yuri Slezkine, *The Jewish Century* (Princeton, NJ: Princeton University Press, 2006), 207. See also Richard D. Alba and Victor Nee, *Remaking the American Mainstream: Assimilation and Contemporary Immigration* (Cambridge, MA: Harvard University Press, 2005).

12. Philip Roth, *The Plot Against America* (New York: Houghton Mifflin, 2004).

13. Susan A. Glenn, "The Vogue of Jewish Self-Hatred in Post-World War II America," *Jewish Social Studies* 12, no. 3 (Spring–Summer 2006). For a cogent discussion of the conflict between Jewish particularism and universalism, see Michael E. Staub, *Torn at the Roots: The Crisis of Jewish Liberalism in Postwar America* (New York: Columbia University Press, 2002).

14. David Biale, "The Melting Pot and Beyond: Jews and the Politics of American Identity," in *Insider/Outsider: American Jews and Multiculturalism*, ed. David Biale et al. (Berkeley: University of California Press, 1998), 26.

15. Cited by Staub, *Torn at the Roots*; see also Novick, *The Holocaust in American Life*; Shani Orgad, "The Survivor in Contemporary Culture and Public Discourse: A Genealogy," *Communication Review* 12, no. 2 (2009).

16. See Hasia Diner, *We Remember with Reverence and Love: American Jews and the Myth of Silence after the Holocaust, 1945–1962* (New York: New York University Press, 2009).

17. Goffman, *Stigma*.

18. This interview was conducted by the Transcending Trauma Project; additional interviews in this chapter were conducted and archived by the United States Holocaust Memorial Museum.

19. Goffman, *Stigma*, 5.

20. Kirsten Fermaglich, *American Dreams and Nazi Nightmares* (Waltham, MA: Brandeis University Press, 2006), notes that Erving Goffman's *Asylums*, which analyzes "total institutions," draws analogies to Nazi concentration camps, mentioning Jews in passing. Likewise, *Stigma* mentions Jews briefly, but Holocaust survivors not at all.

21. Thomas Scheff, "Shame in Self and Society," *Symbolic Interaction* 26, no. 2 (2003): 239–262.

22. Leonard Dinnerstein, *America and the Survivors of the Holocaust* (New York: Columbia University Press, 1982).

23. Julia Epstein, "Between Exiles: Parenting and Cultural Memory," in *Shaping Losses: Cultural Memory and the Holocaust*, ed. Julia Epstein and Lori Hope Lefkowitz (Urbana: University of Illinois, 2001), 215; Goffman's *Stigma* describes forms of quackery or unsound medical practices through which the stigmatized minimize their abject status. Homosexuals visit therapists hoping to "cure" themselves; black people consume skin lighteners.

24. Ferenc Eros, Julia Vajda, and Eva Kovacs, "Intergenerational Responses to Social and Political Changes: Transformation of Jewish Identity in Hungary," in *International Handbook of Multigenerational Legacies of Trauma*, ed. Yael Danieli (New York: Plenum, 1998).

25. Helen Fremont, *After Long Silence: A Memoir* (New York: Delacourt, 1999), 47.

26. Eva Hoffman, *After Such Knowledge: Memory, History, and the Legacy of the Holocaust* (New York: Public Affairs, 2004), 46.

27. J. M. Chaumont, *The Competition of Victims: Genocide, Identity, Recognition* (Paris: La Decouverte and Syros, 1997), cited in Orgad, "The Survivor in Contemporary Culture," 137.

28. It was essentially passivity and lack of agency, Bettleheim believed, that enabled survival. Most survivors, including himself, "survived because the Gestapo chose to set them free, and for no other reason." See Bruno Bettleheim, *Surviving and Other Essays* (New York: Knopf, 1979), 288.

29. Translated into English by Elliot Palevsky, the hymn is widely known by its Yiddish title, *Zog Nit Keyn Mol!*

30. Bettleheim, *Surviving and Other Essays*.

31. Today, the United States Holocaust Memorial Museum defines survivors as: "any persons, Jewish or non-Jewish, who were displaced, persecuted, or discriminated against due to the racial, religious, ethnic, social, and political policies of the Nazis and their collaborators between 1933 and 1945. In addition to former inmates of concentration camps, ghettos, and prisons, this definition includes, among others, people who were refugees or were in hiding." United States Holocaust Memorial Museum website, http://www.United Stateshmm.org/remembrance/registry/.

32. Marilyn Henry. *Confronting the Perpetrators: A History of the Claims Conference* (Middlesex, England: Vallentine Mitchell, 2007).

33. Goffman, *Stigma*.

34. Erik Erikson, "The Human Life Cycle," in *A Way of Looking At Things* (New York: Norton, 1995), 194, 198.

35. Diner, *We Remember with Reverence and Love*.

36. Sam E. Bloch and Samuel R. Mozes, eds., *From Holocaust to Redemption Bearing Witness: A Documentary Volume Depicting the Proceedings and Events of the World Gathering of Jewish Holocaust Survivors, Israel* (New York: World Gathering of Holocaust Survivors, 1984), 3.

37. Saul Friedlander, "Trauma, Transference and 'Working Through' in Writing the History of the Shoah," *History and Memory* 4 (1992): 47.

38. Primo Levi, *The Drowned and the Saved* (New York: Random House, 1989).

39. Cohen, *Case Closed*, 158.

40. See Jack Kugelmass and Jonathan Boyarin, *From a Ruined Garden: The Memorial Books of Polish Jewry* (Bloomington: Indiana University Press, 1998); Eviatar Zerubavel, *Time Maps: Collective Memory and the Social Shape of the Past* (Chicago: University of Chicago Press, 2003), 52–53.

CHAPTER 2

1. On the social conventions of family photography, see Robert Zussman, "Picturing the Self: My Mother's Photo Albums," *Contexts* 5, no. 4 (2006): 28–34; Jo Spence and Patricia Holland, eds. *Family Snaps: The Meaning of Domestic Photography* (London: Virago, 1991); Marianne Hirsch, *Family Frames:Photography, Narrative, and Postmemory* (Cambridge, MA.: Harvard University Press, 1997).

2. Hans Pols, "War Neurosis, Adjustment Problems in Veterans, and an Ill Nation," *Osiris* 22 (2007), 74.

3. Beth Cohen, *Case Closed: Holocaust Survivors in Postwar America* (New Brunswick, NJ: Rutgers University Press, 2007), 117; see also David Wyman, *The Abandonment of the Jews: America and the Holocaust 1941–1945* (New York: New Press, 2007).

4. Report to the Annual Meeting of the United Service for New Americans, New York City, January 11, 1948.

5. See Elaine Tyler May, *American Families in the Cold War Era* (New York: Basic Books, 1988), xxv; Philip A. Wylie, *A Generation of Vipers* (New York: Holt, Rhinehart, and Winston, 1942).

6. Emily Nussbaum, "Tune in Next Week," *The New Yorker*, July 30, 2012, 72. A "mass public" was also beginning to emerge, due in part to the growing popularity of social science, which set its sights on defining the "average" American. Solidifying the notion that there was in fact such a thing as a "normal" American—defined in statistical terms—it helped to construct an image of an America that was far more homogeneous than that which existed in reality. See Sarah Igo, *The Averaged American: Surveys, Citizens, and the Making of a Mass Public* (Cambridge, MA: Harvard University Press, 2008), 18–19. Also see Lila Corwin Berman, "Sociology, Jews, and Intermarriage in Twentieth Century America," *Jewish Social Studies* 14, no. 2 (Winter 2008): 32–60.

7. Elaine Tyler May, *Homeward Bound: American Families in the Cold War Era* (New York: Basic Books 1988).

8. See, for example, Judith Gerson's study of German refugee families, "Family Matters," in *Jewish Masculinities*, ed. Benjamin Maria Baader, Sharon Gillerman, and Paul Lerner (Bloomington: Indiana University Press, 2012).

9. See Dina Wardi, *Memorial Candles: Children of the Holocaust* (New York: Routledge, 1992).

10. Ellen Herman, *The Romance of American Psychology: Political Culture in the Age of Experts* (Berkeley: University of California Press, 1995).

11. Dan Bar-On, "Legacy of Silence in Nazi Perpetrators' and Holocaust Survivors' Families," paper presented at Henry Schwartzman Faculty Seminar, Rutgers University, September 2005. See also Ruth Wajnryb, *The Silence: How Tragedy Shapes Talk* (Crow's Nest, New South Wales: Allen & Unwin, 2001).

12. Barbara Finkelstein, "Return to Poland," in Philipa Kafka, *Lost on the Map of the World* (New York: Peter Lang, 2001), 35, 76.

13. There is an extensive psychological literature on survivor families' coping strategies. For example, Yael Danieli observed four adaptational styles in her clinical work with families of survivors: "numb," "victim," "fighters," and "those who made it." See Yael Danieli, "The Group Project for Holocaust Survivors and the Children," Appendix A, "Therapists' Difficulties in Treating Survivors of the Nazi Holocaust and Their Children," PhD dissertation, New York University, 1981.

14. This interview is archived at the US Holocaust Memorial Museum; all other descendant interviews in this chapter are from the Transcending Trauma Project.

15. Lily Brett, "Half There," in *Nothing Makes You Free: Writings by Descendants of Holocaust Survivors*, ed. Melvin Jules Bukiet (New York: W.W. Norton, 2002), 232.

16. See, for example, some of the work contained in Bukiet, ed. *Nothing Makes You Free*, as well as the celebrated comic-memoir by Art Spiegelman, *Maus I: A Survivor's Tale: My Father Bleeds History* (New York: Pantheon, 1986).

17. Gabriele Rosenthal, *The Holocaust in Three Generations* (London: Cassell, 1998), 20.

18. Lisa Appignanesi, *Losing the Dead* (Toronto: McArthur & Co., 1999), 18.

19. Finkelstein, "Return to Poland," 82.

20. Dan Bar-On, *Fear and Hope: Three Generations of the Holocaust* (Cambridge, MA: Harvard University Press, 1998).

21. Aaron Haas, *In the Shadow of the Holocaust: The Second Generation*. London: Cambridge University Press, 1990.

22. Eva Hoffman, *After Such Knowledge* (New York: Public Affairs, 2004), 58. See also Nadine Fresco, "Remembering the Unknown," *International Journal of Psychoanalysis* 11 (1984): 417–427.

23. Appignanesi, *Losing the Dead*, 21

24. Hasia Diner, *We Remember with Reverence and Love: American Jews and the Myth of Silence after the Holocaust* (New York: New York University Press), 316.

25. Lawrence Langer, *Holocaust Testimonies: The Ruins of Memory* (New Haven, CT.: Yale University Press, 1991).

26. Avery Gordon, *Ghostly Matters: Haunting and the Sociological Imagination* (Minneapolis: University of Minneapolis Press, 1999), 21.

27. This is similar to what has been called "flashbulb memories." See Roger Brown and James Kulik, "Flashbulb Memories," *Cognition* 5, no. 1 (1977): 73–99.

28. C. Fred Alford, "Why Holocaust Testimony Is Important, and How Psychoanalytic Interpretation Can Help…But Only to a Point," *Psychoanalysis, Culture & Society* 13 (2008), 226. See also Langer, *Holocaust Testimonies*.

29. Arthur Frank, *Wounded Storytellers: Body, Illness and Ethics* (Chicago: University of Chicago Press, 1995), 60.

30. Carl Friedman, *Nightfather: A Novel*, trans. Arnold Pomerans and Erica Pomerans (New York: Persea, 1995).

31. Hoffman, *After Such Knowledge*, 10.

32. Hoffman, *After Such Knowledge*, 9.

33. Quoted in Hans Pols, "War Neurosis, Adjustment Problems in Veterans, and an Ill Nation," 92.

34. Cohen, *Case Closed*, 137.

35. See Martin S. Bergmann and Milton E. Jucovy, eds., Introduction, *Generations of the Holocaust* (New York: Basic Books, 1982), 8.

36. W. G. Niederland, "Clinical Observations on the 'Survivor Syndrome," *International Journal of Psycho-Analysis* 49 (1968): 313–315.

37. William Helmreich, "Don't Look Back: Holocaust Survivors in the US" (Jerusalem Center for Public Affairs, 1991).

38. Kai Erikson, "Notes on Trauma and Community," in *Trauma: Explorations in Memory*, ed. Cathy Caruth (Baltimore: The Johns Hopkins University Press, 1995), 187.

39. See Marilyn Henry, *Confronting the Perpetrators: A History of the Claims Conference* (Vallentine Mitchell, 2007).

40. See W. H. Engel, "Reflections on the Psychiatric Consequences of Persecution," *American Journal of Psychotherapy* 2 (1962): 191–203.

41. Engel, "Reflections on the Psychiatric Consequences of Persecution.

CHAPTER 3

1. On the American Jewish counterculture, see Norman L. Friedman, "Social Movement Legacies: The American Jewish Counterculture, 1973–1988," *Jewish Social Studies* 50, nos. 3–4 (Summer 1988–Fall 1993): 127–146.
2. Lucy Y. Steinitz and David M. Szonyi, eds., *Living after the Holocaust: Reflections by Children of Survivors in America*, rev. 2nd ed. (New York: Block Publishing Company, 1979), 33.
3. Steinitz and Szonyi, *Living after the Holocaust*, 21.
4. Steinitz and Szonyi, *Living after the Holocaust*, 46.
5. Steinitz and Szonyi, *Living after the Holocaust*, 49.
6. Steinitz and Szonyi, *Living after the Holocaust*, 50.
7. Steinitz and Szonyi, *Living after the Holocaust*, 51.
8. Steinitz and Szonyi, *Living after the Holocaust*, 11.
9. E-mail correspondence with Helen Epstein, February 17, 2011.
10. Helen Epstein, *Children of the Holocaust* (New York: Putnam, 1979), 5.
11. E-mail correspondence with Helen Epstein, February 17, 2011.
12. Epstein, *Children of the Holocaust*, 26.
13. Epstein, *Children of the Holocaust*, 7.
14. Louisa Passerini, in *Autobiography of a Generation* (Hanover, NH: Wesleyan University Press, 1996), suggested that members of the Italian New Left chose to become "orphans."
15. Ruklhl Shaechter, "Remembering the Hair Tangle of the 1960s," *The Forward*, May 11, 2007, B3.
16. Melvin Jules Bukiet, "Introduction," in *Nothing Makes You Free: Writings by Descendants of Jewish Holocaust Survivors*, ed. Melvin Jules Bukiet (New York: W. W. Norton, 2002), 14.
17. On relational individualism, see Nancy Julia Chodorow, "Toward a Relational Individualism," in *Reconstructing Individualism: Autonomy, Individuality, and the Self in Western Thought*, ed. Thomas C. Heller, Morton Sosna, and David Wellbery (Stanford, CA: Stanford University Press, 1986); Carol Gilligan, "Mapping the Moral Domain: New Images of Self in Relationship," in *Reconstructing Individualism: Autonomy, Individuality, and the Self in Western Thought*, ed. Thomas C. Heller, Morton Sosna, and David Wellbery (Stanford, CA: Stanford University Press, 1986).
18. On the basis of my research, I would speculate that those who became involved in the second generation movement, particularly its more psychological variants, were disproportionately female, highly educated, of Eastern European parentage, had more secular but not wholly assimilated Jewish identities, and lived in households where their parents were relatively silent about their wartime experiences.
19. Eva Hoffman, *After Such Knowledge: Memory, History, and the Legacy of the Holocaust* (New York: Public Affairs, 2004), 27–28.
20. Ellen Herman, *The Romance of American Psychology: Political Culture in the Age of Experts* (Berkeley: University of California Press, 1995).
21. Alice Echols, *Daring to be Bad: Radical Feminism in America* (Minneapolis: University of Minnesota Press, 1989); Joan Scott, "The Evidence of Experience," *Critical Inquiry* 17, no. 4 (Summer 1991): 773–797.
22. On silence as a form of communication within survivor families, see Ruth Waynryb, *The Silence: How Tragedy Shapes Talk* (Sydney: Allen & Unwin, 2001). On silence in everyday life, see Eviatar Zerubavel, *The Elephant in the Room: Silence and Denial in Everyday Life* (Oxford, UK: Oxford University Press, 2006).

23. Interview with author, May 14, 2004.
24. Interview with author, May 14, 2004.
25. Yael Danieli, "The Group Project for Holocaust Survivors and the Children," Appendix A, "Therapists' Difficulties in Treating Survivors of the Nazi Holocaust and Their Children," PhD dissertation, New York University, 1981. There is an extensive psychological literature on children of survivors. See, for example, Judith Kestenberg, "Psychoanalytic Contributions to the Problems of Children of Survivors from Nazi Persecution," *Israeli Annals of Psychiatry and Related Sciences*, 10 (1972): 311–325; Aaron Haas, *In the Shadow of the Holocaust*; Yael Danieli, ed., *International Handbook of Multigenerational Legacies of Trauma* (New York: Plenum, 1988); Dori Laub, "The Empty Circle: Children of Survivors and the Limits of Reconstruction," *Journal of the American Psychoanalytic Association* 46, no. 2 (1998): 507–529; Marinus H Van Ijzendoorn, M. Bakermans-Kranenburg, and A. Sagi-Schwartz, "Are Children of Holocaust Survivors Less Well Adapted?" *Journal of Traumatic Stress*, vol. 16, no. 5, (October 2003): 459–469.
26. Jonathan Woocher, *Sacred Survival: The Civil Religion of American Jews* (Bloomington: Indiana University Press, 1986), 200.
27. Terrence Des Pres, "Lessons of the Holocaust," *New York Times*, April 27, 1976.
28. Jeffrey Shandler, *While America Watches: Televising the Holocaust* (New York: Oxford University Press, 1999).
29. Judith Herman, *Trauma and Recovery: The Aftermath of Violence from Domestic Abuse to Political Terror* (New York: Basic Books, 1997).
30. According to sociologist Eva Illouz, the therapeutic "emotional style," which emerged in the relatively short period from World War I to World War II and was popularized after the 1960s, offered "a new lexicon to conceptualize and discuss emotions and self in the realm of ordinary life and new ways of handling emotional life." This emotional style overlapped with feminism, blurring the boundaries between private and public life, and calling upon individuals to contemplate the basis of their consciousness and transform it reflexively. Eva Illouz, *Saving the Modern Soul: Therapy, Emotions, and the Culture of Self-Help.* (Berkeley: University of California Press, 2008), 15. For a discussion of therapeutic culture and its relationship to politics, see my "Therapeutic Politics—An Oxymoron?" *Sociological Forum* 26, no. 1 (March 2011): 187–193.
31. Herman, *Trauma and Recovery*.
32. See Jessica Grogan, *Encountering America: Humanistic Psychology, Sixties Culture, and the Shaping of the Modern Self* (New York: Harper Perennial, 2012).
33. I am paraphrasing based on my recollections of the time.
34. Hoffman, *After Such Knowledge*.
35. Arlene Stein, *Sex and Sensibility: Stories of a Lesbian Generation* (Berkeley: University of California Press, 1993).
36. *Breaking the Silence: The Generation after the Holocaust*, Edward Mason, director, 59 minutes, Public Broadcasting System.
37. *Breaking Silence*, directed by Theresa Tollini, 58 minutes, New Day Films, 1984.
38. Janice Haaken, *Pillar of Salt: Gender, Memory, and the Perils of Looking Back* (New Brunswick, NJ: Rutgers University Press, 1988).
39. The term "transformative remembering" is from Haaken, *Pillar of Salt*, 14–15.
40. Ken Plummer, *Telling Sexual Stories: Power, Change, and Social Worlds* (New York: Routledge, 1995), 76.
41. Haaken, *Pillar of Salt*, 272–273.
42. *Separate Skin* (1987), directed by Deirdre Fishel, 28 minutes.

43. Shane Phelan, *Getting Specific: Postmodern Lesbian Politics* (Minneapolis: University of Minnesota Press, 1994), 11.

44. Andrew Heinze, *Jews and the American Soul: Human Nature in the Twentieth Century* (Princeton, NJ: Princeton University Press, 2004), 267. On identity politics and the move toward specificity, see my article: "The Incredible Shrinking Lesbian World and Other Queer Conundra," *Sexualities* 13, no. 1 (2010): 21–32.

45. Epstein, *Children of the Holocaust*, 88.

46. Des Pres, *The Survivor.*

47. Steinitz and Szonyi, *Living after the Holocaust*, ii.

48. Epstein, *Children of the Holocaust*, 178.

49. See Wendy Brown, *States of Injury: Power and Freedom in Late Modernity* (Princeton, NJ: Princeton University Press, 1995).

50. Sigmund Freud (1917 [1915]) "Mourning and Melancholia." *Standard Edition* 14: (London: The Hogarth Press and the Institution of Psychoanalysis), 242–260.

51. Newsletters published by second generation groups in San Francisco and Los Angeles in 1986–1992, personal collection of author.

52. Second Generation Conference, December 27–30, 1987, University of California, Los Angeles, organized by the International Network of Jewish Holocaust Survivors and Second Generation of Los Angeles, which I attended.

53. Todd Gitlin, *The Sixties: Years of Hope, Days of Rage* (New York: Random House, 1993), 25.

54. Rebecca Klatch, *A Generation Divided: The New Left, the New Right, and the 1960s* (Berkeley: University of California Press, 1999), 56.

55. Quoted in Klatch, *A Generation Divided*, 56.

56. Mark Rudd, *Underground: My Life with SDS and the Weathermen* (New York: Harper Collins, 2009), 11.

57. Rudd, *Underground*, 23, 189.

58. Matthew Frye Jacobson, *Roots Too: White Ethnic Revival in Post-Civil Rights America* (Cambridge, MA: Harvard University Press, 2006), 9–10.

59. Combahee River Collective, "A Black Feminist Statement." in *Home Girls: A Black Feminist Anthology*, ed. Barbara Smith (New Brunswick, NJ: Rutgers University Press, 2000), 267.

60. Nancy Fraser and Axel Honneth, *Redistribution or Recognition? A Political-Philosophical Exchange* (London: Verso, 1998); Charles Taylor, "The Politics of Recognition," in *Multiculturalism: Examining the Politics of Recognition*, ed. Amy Gutmann (Princeton, NJ: Princeton University Press, 1993).

61. *Second Generation Newsletter*, Jewish Federation Council of Greater Los Angeles, May/June 1987.

62. Anne Karpf, *The War After: Living with the Holocaust* (London: Minerva, 1996), 286.

63. A number of critics have taken the "second generation" to task for over-identifying with their parents' suffering. In her ethnographic account of a support group of descendants of Holocaust survivors in Israel, Carol Kidron suggested that descendants utilize the discursive frame of PTSD in order to fashion a sense of self as survivors of the distant traumatic past. She disputed whether individuals can be constituted by historical events that occurred prior to their birth, and many times removed. She charged them with undertaking identity work in order to "constitute their emergent identities as authentic carriers of Holocaust memory" for the emotional and political benefits they might reap in exchange.

simply to transform themselves into "survivors" and reap the supposed benefits of such trauma-descendant identities. For every descendant of survivors who over-identified with his or her parents, there were many more who fled such identifications, avoiding associating themselves with the Holocaust legacy. Carol A. Kidron, "Surviving a Distant Past: A Case Study of the Cultural Construction of Trauma Descendant Identity," *Ethos* 31, no. 4 (1999): 516.

64. Hirsch and Smith, "Feminism and Cultural Memory: An Introduction," *Signs* 28, no. 1 (2002): 10. See also Elisabeth Young-Bruehl, "The Biographer's Empathy With Her Subject," in *Subject to Biography: Psychoanalysis, Feminism, and Writing Women's Lives* (Cambridge, MA: Harvard University Press, 1998).

65. C. Fred Alford, "Why Holocaust Testimony Is Important, and How Psychoanalytic Interpretation Can Help...But Only to a Point," *Psychoanalysis, Culture & Society* 13 (September 2008): 231.

66. Charles Figley, ed., *Trauma and Its Wake: The Study and Treatment of Post-Traumatic Stress Disorder* (New York: Brunner/Mazel, 1985), 399, cited by Orgad, "The Survivor in Contemporary Culture and Public Discourse: A Geneology," *Communication Review* 12, no. 2 (2009): 138.

CHAPTER 4

1. According to my own, admittedly primitive, content analysis of the *New York Times*, the term "Holocaust survivor" was first associated with the Jewish survivors of Nazi persecution in 1959. Before, it was used to describe survivors of fires, and the term "Holocaust" was not capitalized. The number of mentions of the term exploded during the period 1981 to 1995. There were several different ways stories about survivors were framed during this period. There were: (1) stories about gatherings of Holocaust survivors, such as the 1981 World Gathering of Holocaust Survivors in Jerusalem, commemorations such as the annual remembrance of the Warsaw Ghetto Uprising, or protests in which survivors appeared, such as 1985 in Bitburg, Germany; (2) profiles of notable survivors such as Elie Wiesel, especially around the time of Yom Ha Shoah each year; and (3) stories about educational and archival projects that elicited the participation of survivors. On the trajectory of Holocaust memory, see Jeffrey Alexander et al., eds., *Cultural Trauma and Collective Identity* (Berkeley: University of California Press, 2004); Margalit, *The Ethics of Memory*, 7.

2. Avishai Margalit, *The Ethics of Memory* (Cambridge, MA: Harvard University Press, 2002).

3. On the double function of storytelling, see "Introduction," *Trauma: Life Stories of Survivors*, ed. Kim Lacy Rogers, Selma Leydesdorff, and Graham Dawson (New Brunswick, NJ: Transaction, 2004), 8.

4. Werner Weinberg, *Self-Portrait of a Holocaust Survivor* (Jefferson, NC: McFarland, 1985), 150. Thanks to Krista Hegburg for bringing this to my attention.

5. Andrew Heinze, *Jews and the American Soul: Human Nature in the Twentieth Century* (Princeton, NJ: Princeton University Press, 2004), 329.

6. Rosalyn Kliot, e-mail correspondence, June 23, 2010.

7. Bruno Bettelheim, *Surviving and Other Essays* (New York: Knopf, 1979).

8. Lawrence Langer, *Holocaust Testimonies: The Ruins of Memory* (New Haven, CT: Yale University Press, 1979), 5–6.

9. On the latter point, see especially Shani Orgad, "The Survivor in Contemporary Culture and Public Discourse: A Genealogy," *Communication Review* 12, no. 2 (2009): 132–161.

10. Robert Lifton, quoted in Christopher Lasch, *The Minimal Self: Psychic Survival in Troubled Times* (New York: Norton, 1984), 120.

11. As Beth Cohen shows, the case files and survivors' oral histories reveal a different sentiment: "They are filled, loud and clear, with the refugees' desire and need to address the past. This need at times seems uncontrollable and at other times ambivalently expressed." See *Case Closed: Holocaust Survivors in Postwar America* (New Brunswick, NJ: Rutgers University Press, 2007), 117.

12. Netty Gross, "Finding the Words," *The Jerusalem Report*, May 26, 2008. On the memoir boom more generally, see Ben Yagoda, *Memoir: A History* (New York: Riverhead Books, 2010).

13. Lucy Steinitz and David M. Szonyi, *Living after the Holocaust: Reflections by Children of Survivors in America*, rev. 2nd ed. (New York: Bloch Publishing Company, 1979), 40.

14. Annette Wieviorka, *The Era of the Witness* (Ithaca, NY: Cornell University Press, 2006).

15. Erikson, "Notes on Trauma and Community," in *Trauma: Explorations in Memory*, ed. Cathy Caruth (Baltimore: The Johns Hopkins University Press, 1995), 186.

16. Quoted in Ruth Leys, *From Guilt to Shame: Auschwitz and After* (Princeton, NJ: Princeton University Press, 2009), 127.

17. Quoted in Leys, *From Guilt to Shame*, 130.

18. "Nesse Godin," Wikipedia, accessed March 24, 2013, http://en.wikipedia.org/wiki/Nesse_Godin.

19. Eva Hoffman, *After Such Knowledge* (New York: Public Affairs, 2004), 172. See also Susan Andrews, "Holocaust Remembrance in Australia: Gender, Memory, and Identity Between the Local and the Transnational," doctoral dissertation, Australian National University, August 2007.

20. Deborah Lipstadt, *Denying the Holocaust: The Growing Assault on Truth and Memory* (New York: Plume, 1994).

21. Lipstadt, *Denying the Holocaust*.

22. Interview, United States Holocaust Memorial Museum.

23. Wieviorka, *The Era of the Witness*, xii.

24. Wieviorka, *The Era of the Witness*, xiii.

25. Langer, *Holocaust Testimonies*, xvii. Scattered oral history projects preceded the establishment of the Yale archive, including one that was directed by a professor of journalism at Columbia, funded by the National Endowment of Humanities, archived in the William E. Wiener Oral History Library of the American Jewish Committee. See "U.S. Immigrants Tape-Record Grim Memories of Nazi Holocaust," *New York Times*, May 11, 1976.

26. Cited by Diane Wolf, "Holocaust Testimony: Producing Post-memories, Producing Identities," in *Sociology Confronts the Holocaust: Memories and Identities in Jewish Diasporas*, ed. Judith M. Gerson and Diane L. Wolf (Durham, NC: Duke University Press, 2007), 157.

27. In some scenarios, we demand that survivor testimonies are intense and explicitly emotional before they are considered credible. If the survivor does not cry when she tells her story, she will not be believed. In other scenarios, the emotional content of survivor discourse has to be toned down in order to be acceptable. See Linda

Alcoff and Laura Gray, "Survivor Discourse: Transgression or Recuperation?" in *Signs* 18, no. 2 (Winter 1993): 260–290.

28. Arthur Frank, *Wounded Storytellers: Body, Illness and Ethics* (Chicago: University of Chicago Press, 1995), 138.

29. Geoffrey Hartman, *The Longest Shadow: In the Aftermath of the Holocaust* (Bloomington: Indiana University Press, 1996), 153–154.

30. Herman, *Trauma and Recovery: The Aftermath of Violence from Domestic Abuse to Political Terror* (New York: Basic Books, 1997), 175.

31. Ruth Waynryb, "The Holocaust as Unspeakable: Public Ritual Versus Private Hell," *Journal of Intercultural Studies* 20, no.1 (1999), 91.

32. Amelia Klein found that few family members ever watch these video testimonies, in a paper given at Association for the Psychoanalysis of Culture and Society Conference, October 22, 2010, Rutgers University.

33. See Wieviorka, *The Era of the Witness*, 120, xiv, 90. On the limits of experience, see Joan Scott, "The Evidence of Experience," *Critical Inquiry* 17, no. 4 (Summer 1991), 797.

34. See Edward T. Linenthal's discussion of Raul Hilberg, in "The Boundaries of Memory: The United States Holocaust Memorial Museum," *American Quarterly* 46, no. 3 (September 1994): 425.

35. Frank, *Wounded Storytellers*, 101.

36. Langer, *Holocaust Testimonies*, 61.

37. Joanne Weiner Rudof, "A Yale University and New Haven Community Project: From Local to Global," October 2007, accessed March 24, 2013, www.library.yale.edu/testimonies.

38. Wolf, "Holocaust Testimony," 175n5.

39. Robert Fulford, *The Triumph of the Narrative: Storytelling in the Age of Mass Culture* (Toronto: House of Anansi Press, 1999), 14, 17.

40. See also Tim Cole, *Selling the Holocaust: From Auschwitz to Shindler: How History is Bought, Packaged, and Sold* (New York: Routledge, 2000).

41. Barbara A. Misztal, *Theories of Social Remembering* (Philadelphia: Open University Press, 2003), 147.

42. Barbie Zelizer, *Remembering to Forget: Holocaust Memory Through the Camera's Eye* (Chicago: University of Chicago Press, 1998).

43. Eva Illouz, *Saving the Modern Soul: Therapy, Emotions and the Culture of Self-Help* (Berkeley: University of California Press, 208), 128.

44. Cited by Jeffrey Shandler, *Jews, God, and Videotape: Religion and Meaning in America* (New York: New York University Press, 2009), 131.

45. Orgad, "The Survivor in Contemporary Culture," 279; Marita Sturken, *Tourists of History: Memory, Kitsch, and Consumerism from Oklahoma City to Ground Zero* (Durham, NC: Duke University Press, 2007); Cole, *Selling the Holocaust*, 88.

46. Orgad, "The Survivor in Contemporary Culture."

47. Orgad, citing the ideas of Rose, in "The Survivor in Contemporary Culture," 151.

48. Arlene Stein, *The Stranger Next Door: The Story of a Small Town's Battle over Sex, Faith, and Community* (Boston: Beacon, 2001).

49. Robert Lifton, *Home from the War: Learning from Vietnam Veterans* (Boston: Beacon Press, 1973), 63.

50. Langer, *Holocaust Testimonies*.

51. Theodora Kroeber and Karl Kroeber, *Ishi in Two Worlds: A Biography of the Last Wild Indian in North America* (Berkeley: University of California Press, 2002).

52. Resistance to identity lies at the very heart of psychic life, according to Judith Butler in *The Psychic Life of Power: Theories of Subjection* (Stanford, CA: Stanford University Press, 1997), 17.

53. Niza Yanay, *The Ideology of Hatred: The Psychic Power of Discourse* (New York: Fordham University Press, 2013).

54. Orgad, "The Survivor in Contemporary Culture," 152.

55. Fulford, *The Triumph of the Narrative*, 14, 17; Leys, *From Guilt to Shame*, 54.

CHAPTER 5

1. Helen Fremont, *After Long Silence: A Memoir* (New York: Delacourt, 1999), 34.

2. Anthony Giddens, *Modernity and Self-Identity* (Stanford, CA: Stanford University Press, 1991).

3. Michael Erben, "Genealogy and Sociology: A Preliminary Set of Statements and Speculations." *Sociology* 25 (1991): 280. Eyerman, "Cultural Trauma," in *Cultural Trauma and Collective Identity*, ed. Jeffrey Alexander, Ron Eyerman, Bernhard Giesen, Neil J. Smelser, and Piotr Sztompka (Berkeley: University of California Press, 2004), 123.

4. B. J. Lifton, *The Adoption Experience* (New York: Harper and Row, 1979), 47. See also Janet Carsten, "Knowing Where You've Come From: Ruptures and Continuities of Time and Kinship of Adoption Reunions," *Journal of the American Anthropological Institute* 6, no. 4 (December 2000): 696, 687–703.

5. B. J. Lifton, "The Adopted Self," in *Trauma and the Self*, ed. Charles B. Strozier and Michael Flynn (New York: Rowman and Littlefield, 1996), xii.

6. Dina Wardi, *Memorial Candles: Children and the Holocaust* (New York: Routledge, 1992).

7. Anthony Giddens, *Modernity and Self-Identity* (Stanford, CA: Stanford University Press, 1991); Rosenwald and Ochberg, *Storied Lives: The Cultural Politics of Self-Understanding* (New Haven, CT: Yale University Press, 1992); Dan McAdams, "Identity and the Life Story," in *Autobiographical Memory and the Construction of a Narrative Self*, ed. Catherine A. Haden, John W. Dimmick, and Robyn Fivush (Mahwah, NJ: Lawrence Ehrlbaum, 2003).

8. Micaela di Leonardo, "The Female World of Cards and Holidays: Women, Families, and the Work of Kinship," *Signs* 12, no. 3 (1987): 440–453.

9. Illouz, *Saving the Modern Soul: Therapy, Emotions, and the Culture of Self-Help* (Berkeley: University of California Press, 2008).

10. Erikson, "The Human Life Cycle," in *A Way of Looking at Things* (New York: W. W. Norton, 1995).

11. See also Laub, "The Empty Circle": Children of Survivors and the Limits of Reconstruction," *Journal of the American Psychoanalytic Association* 46, no. 2 (1998): 507–529; Ruth Waynryb, *The Silence: How Tragedy Shapes Talk* (Crow's Nest, New South Wales: Allen & Unwin), 2001.

12. Helena Janaczek, "Joemi's Table," in *Nothing Makes You Free: Writings by Descendants of Jewish Holocaust Survivors*, ed. Melvin Bukiet (New York: W.W. Norton, 2002), 261; see also Sturken, *Tourists of History: Memory, Kitsch, and Consumerism From Oklahoma City Tto Ground Zero* (Durham, NC: Duke University Press, 2007).

13. H. Loewald, quoted in Nancy Chodorow, "The Psychoanalytic Vision of Hans Loewald," *International Journal of Psychoanalysis* 84 (2003): 907.

14. Anna Fodorova, "Mourning by Proxy: Notes on a Conference, Empty Graves and Silence," *Psychodynamic Practice* 11, no. 3 (August 2005): 303. Also, Marianne

Hirsch describes the second generation's "post-memory," in which a connection to the past is mediated not by recall but by "imaginative investment, projection, and creation"; see *The Generation of Postmemory: Writing and Visual Culture after the Holocaust* (New York: Columbia University Press, 2012), 5.

15. Zerubavel, *Time Maps: Collective Memory and the Social Shape of the Past* (Chicago: University of Chicago Press, 2003), 42.

16. Maria Tumarkin, *Traumascapes* (Melbourne: Melbourne University Press, 2005), 13.

17. Jack Kugelmass, "The Rites of the Tribe: American Jewish Tourism in Poland," in *Museums and Communities: The Politics of Public Culture*, ed. Ivan Karp et al. (Washington, DC: Smithsonian Institution Press, 1992), 403, 415. On the tourist's search for authenticity, see Dean MacCannell, *The Tourist: A New Theory of the Leisure Class* (New York: Schocken, 1976).

18. Pierre Nora, "Between Memory and History: *Les Lieux de Memoire*," trans. Marc Roudebush, *Representations* 26 (Spring 1989): 7–25.

19. Andrea Louie, *Chineseness across Borders: Renegotiating Chinese Identities in China and the US* (Durham, NC: Duke University Press, 2004).

20. Monka Adamczyk-Garbowska, *Patterns of Return Survivors' Postwar Journeys to Poland* (Washington, DC: United States Holocaust Memorial Museum, Center for Advanced Holocaust Studies, 2007).

21. Interview conducted December 7, 2000.

22. McAdams, "Identity and the Life Story."

23. Kuhn, *Family Secrets: Acts of Memory and Imagination* (London, Verso, 1995), 1; see also Hirsch, *Family Frames: Photography, Narrative, and Postmemory* (Cambridge, MA: Harvard University Press, 1997); Margaret Homans, "Adoption Narratives, Trauma and Origins," *Narrative* 14, no. 1 (2006): 4–26; Zussman, "Picturing the Self: My Mother's Photo Albums," *Contexts* 5, no. 4 (2006): 28–34.

24. Carol A. Kidron, "Toward of Ethnography of Silence," *Current Anthropology* 50, no. 1 (February 2009): 13.

25. Cited in Claire Kahane, "Dark Mirrors: A Feminist Reflection on Holocaust Narrative and the Maternal Metaphor," in *Feminist Consequences: Theory for a New Century*, ed. Elisabeth Bronfen and Misha Kavka (New York: Columbia University Press, 2001), 32.

26. Appignanesi, *Losing the Dead* (Toronto: McArthur & Co., 1999), 108.

27. Toby Saltzman, "The Birds of Auschwitz: Walking Through Poland in the Footsteps of Ancestors," travelterrific, December 2003, accessed March 15, 2013, http://www.travelterrific.com/dec2003/europeauschwitz_dec03.html.

28. Finkelstein, "Return to Poland," 53.

29. Interview conducted September 27, 2004.

30. Svetlana Boym, *The Future of Nostalgia* (New York: Basic Books, 2001), 55.

31. Epstein, *Where She Came From: A Daughter's Search for Her Mother's Story* (New York: Penguin, 1997).

32. Naomi Berger, "Coming Full Circle," in *Second Generation Voices: Reflections by Children of Survivors and Perpetrators*, ed. Alan L. Berger and Naomi Berger (Syracuse, NY: Syracuse University Press, 2001); Barbara, Finkelstein, "Return to Poland"; Michal Govrin, "The Journey to Poland," in *Second Generation Voices: Reflections by Children of Survivors and Perpetrators*, ed. Alan L. Berger and Naomi Berger (Syracuse, NY: Syracuse University Press, 2001); Irena F. Karafilly, *Ashes and Miracles: A Polish Journey* (Malcolm Lester Books: 1998); Elaine Kalman Naves, *Journey to Vaja: Reconstructing the World of a Hungarian-Jewish Family*

(Montreal: McGill-Queen's University Press, 1996); Theo Richmond, *Konin: One Man's Quest for a Vanished Jewish Community* (New York: Vintage, 1996); Daniel Asa Rose, *Hiding Places: A Father and His Sons Retrace Their Family's Escape from the Holocaust* (New York: Simon & Schuster, 2000); Sarah Silberstein Swartz, "Return to Poland: In Search of My Parents' Memories" in *From Memory to Transformation: Jewish Women's Voices*, ed. Sarah Silberstein Swartz and Margie Wolfe (New York: Second Story Press, 1998); Andrew Kolin, *One Family: Before and During the Holocaust* (Lanham, MD: University Press of America, 2000). This is but a small sampling of a large, growing body of literature.

33. Lev Raphael, *My Germany: A Jewish Writer Returns to the World His Parents Escaped* (Madison: University of Wisconsin Press, 2009).

34. Mimi Schwartz, *Good Neighbors, Bad Times: Echoes of My Father's German Village*.

35. Kolin, *One Family*.

36. Leslie Gilbert-Lurie and Rita Lurie, *Bending Toward the Sun* (New York: HarperColins, 2009).

37. Young-Bruehl, "The Biographer's Empathy with Her Subject," in *Subject to Biography: Psychoanalysis, Feminism, and Writing Women's Lives* (Cambridge, MA: Harvard University Press, 1998).

38. Hirsch and Smith, "Feminism and Cultural Memory: An Introduction," *Signs* 28, no. 1 (2002), 10.

39. http://www.tribecafilm.com/filmguide/flat-film42535.html#.UTe-Vxy1814. For another example of a "third generation" genealogical project, see Andrea Simon, *Bashert: A Granddaughter's Holocaust Quest* (Jackson: University Press of Mississippi, 2002).

40. Stuart Klawans, "Europa, Europa," *The Nation*, February 16, 2004, 34.

41. Our family letters are archived at the US Holocaust Memorial Museum in Washington, DC, and are listed as the "Szliferstejn and Mitelsbach family collection, 1938–1943," RG-10.248.

42. Barry Gewen, "Holocaust Documentaries: Too Much of a Bad Thing?" *New York Times*, June 15, 2003, accessed March 15, 2013, http://www.nytimes.com/2003/06/15/movies/holocaust-documentaries-too-much-of-a-bad-thing.html.

CHAPTER 6

1. Gary Shteyngart, *Absurdistan* (New York: Random House, 2007). http://forward.com/articles/1324/from-eabsurdistane-by-gary-shteyngart/.

2. Peter Applebome, "Numbers Prompt a Story Told in Words," *New York Times*, November 1, 2006. http://www.nytimes.com/2006/11/01/nyregion/01towns.html?_r=0.

3. Steven A. Ludsin, Letters, *New York Times*, October, 8, 2012.

4. Edward S. Hochman, Letters, *New York Times*, October, 8, 2012.

5. Frank Furedi, "The 'Second Generation' of Holocaust Survivors," *Spiked*, January 24, 2002, accessed March 16, 2013, http://www.spiked-online.com/Articles/00000000545B.htm. A number of critics across the political spectrum similarly warned that America was becoming a "nation of victims."
See Wendy Brown, *States of Injury: Power and Freedom in Late Modernity* (Princeton, NJ: Princeton University Press, 1995); Jeffrey Prager, *Presenting the Past: Psychoanalysis and the Sociology of Misremembering* (Cambridge, MA: Harvard University Press, 1998);

Christopher Lasch, *The Minimal Self: Psychic Survival in Troubled Times* (New York: Norton, 1984); Charles J. Sykes, *A Nation of Victims: The Decay of the American Character* (New York: St. Martins, 1992); Lauren Berlant, *The Queen of America Goes to Washington City: Essays on Sex and Citizenship* (Durham, NC: Duke University Press, 1997); Roger Lancaster, *Sex Panic and the Punitive State* (Berkeley: University of California Press, 2011). On the genealogy of victim discourse, see Alyson Cole, *The Cult of True Victimhood: From the War on Welfare to the War on Terror* (Stanford, CA: Stanford University Press, 2007).

6. Zygmunt Bauman, "The Holocaust's Life as a Ghost," in *The Holocaust Ghost: Writings on Art, Politics, Law and Education*, ed. F. C. Decoste and Bernard Schwartz (Edmonton: University of Alberta Press, 2000), 6.

7. Furedi, "The 'Second Generation' of Holocaust Survivors." See also Ruth Franklin, "Identity Theft," *New Republic*, May 31, 2004.

8. Peter Novick, *The Holocaust in American Life* (New York: Houghton Mifflin, 1999), 279. In *After Such Knowledge: Memory, History and the Legacy of the Holocaust* (New York: Public Affairs, 2004), Eva Hoffman similarly warns of individuals and groups "rush[ing] in to lay claim to histories of calamity and victimization," 169.

9. Novick, *The Holocaust in American Life*, 279.

10. Novick, *The Holocaust in American Life*, 279, 68.

11. Novick, *The Holocaust in American Life*, 8.

12. Yuri Slezkine makes this argument in *The Jewish Century* (Princeton, NJ: Princeton University Press, 2006), as do Norman Finkelstein, *The Holocaust Industry: Reflections on the Exploitation of Jewish Suffering* (London: Verso, 2000); Tim Cole, *Selling the Holocaust: From Auschwitz to Shindler: How History is Bought, Packaged, and Sold* (New York: Routledge, 2000); and Novick, *The Holocaust in American Life.*

13. Mordechai Gordon, "The United States and Israel: Double Standards, Favoritism, and Unconditional Support," in *The Miseducation of the West: How Schools and the Media Distort Our Understanding of the Islamic World*, ed. Joe Kincheloe and Shirley Steinberg (Westport, CT: Praeger, 2004), 113.

14. Quoted in David Remnick, "Letter from Jerusalem: The Apostate," *The New Yorker* July 30, 2007.

15. Quoted in James Young, *Writing and Rewriting the Holocaust* (Bloomington: Indiana University Press, 1988), 15.

16. Andrew Bostom, "Iran's Final Solution for Israel," March 6, 2012, *Israel Advocate* (first published in *National Review Online*, February 10, 2012).

17. Raymond Ibrahim, a conservative of Egyptian Coptic heritage, in a talk sponsored by Children of Jewish Holocaust Survivors and the David Horowitz Freedom Center on April 12, 2011. For an analysis of right-wing Islamophobia that deploys this kind of rhetoric, see Zakia Salime and Arlene Stein, "Mediating Homophobia and Islamophobia: The "Paranoid Style" Revisited," unpublished paper. See also Niza Yanay, *The Ideology of Hatred: The Psychic Power of Discourse* (New York: Columbia University Press, 2013), 102, for an argument that hatred is a defense against (re)experiencing trauma.

18. Peter Beinart, *The Crisis of Zionism* (New York: Times Books, 2012), 32–33.

19. Wendy Oberlander, *Nothing To Be Written Here* (1996) and *Still (Stille)* (2001).

20. See Lisa Duggan, "A New Consensus on Public Space and 'Free' Speech on Israel/Palestine in New York City," *The Nation*, February 22, 2013, accessed March 16, 2013, http://www.thenation.com/article/173073/new-consensus-public-space-and-free-speech-israelpalestine-new-york-city.

21. Ann Cvetkovich, *An Archive of Feelings* (Durham, NC: Duke University Press, 2003), 16.

22. Testifying to this ideological diversity is the existence of a small but growing movement among American Jews that is highly critical of many Israeli policies, at the same time as it defends the existence of the state of Israel. This movement coalesces, to a great extent, around the belief that Israel's survival as a secure, democratic homeland of the Jewish people depends upon the establishment of a Palestinian state. On the difficulty of criticizing Israel, see Judith Butler, "The Charge of Anti-Semitism: Jews, Israel, and the Risks of Public Critique," in *Precarious Life: The Powers of Mourning and Violence* (London: Verso, 2004), 101–127.

23. See Judith Butler's Remarks to Brooklyn College on BDS [movement for Boycott, Divestment, and Sanctions in Israel], reprinted in *The Nation*, February 7, 2013, accessed March 16, 2013, http://www.thenation.com/article/172752/judith-butlers-remarks-brooklyn-college-bds.

24. Nurit Peled-Elhanan, "At the Gates of Gaza," http://www.jewishvoiceforpeace.org/publish/article_955.shtml, 2008.

25. Dror Moreh, director, *The Gatekeepers (Shomerei Ha'saf)*, 2012.

26. This politics of narrowed obligations was on display at an event that purported to be about precisely the opposite: "Genocide: Do the Strong Have an Obligation to Protect the Weak?" The panel discussion was sponsored by This World: The Values Network and was organized by Shmuley Boteach, the self-proclaimed "America's Rabbi." Held in New York City on September 29, 2013, it featured Elie Wiesel and Paul Kagame, president of Rwanda. Though framed as a panel about universal human rights, the speakers drew an equivalence between Rwanda, which has recently elicited fierce criticism for its incursions into Congo, and Israel. If Rwanda and Israel must occasionally engage in violence against others to protect their people, the panelists suggested, they have little choice in the matter—they are simply trying to avoid another Holocaust. The evening made full use of the trope of Israel as reparation for the Holocaust, and it did so (regrettably, in my opinion) by giving *carte blanche* to the activities of muscular nation-states. It was Holocaust memory mobilized toward neoconservative ends, rather than toward ethical remembering.

27. Beinart, *The Crisis of Zionism*; see also David Biale, *Power and Powerlessness in Jewish History* (New York: Schocken Books, 1986).

28. Deborah Lipstadt, quoted in Steven M. Cohen and Arnold M. Eisen, *The Jew Within: Self, Family, and Community in America* (Bloomington: Indiana University Press, 2000).

29. Lawrence Van Gelder, "Groundbreaking in Warsaw for Jewish Museum," *New York Times*, June 25, 2007, accessed March 15, 2013, http://www.nytimes.com/2007/06/25/arts/25arts.html.

30. Tad Taube, "March of the Living Must Embrace Life," *The Jewish Daily Forward*, May 5, 2006.

31. Geoffrey Hartman, quoted in Froma Zeitlin, "The Vicarious Witness: Belated Memory and Authorial Presence in Recent Holocaust Literature," *History & Memory* 10 (1998): 5–42.

32. Micha Odenheimer, "Jerusalem Is Still Burning," *Guilt and Pleasure* 4 (Spring 2007), 33.

33. Marjorie Ingall, "My Generation: New Identity," *The Jewish Daily Forward*, August 11, 2006, 25.

34. Laura Levitt, *American Jewish Loss after the Holocaust* (New York: New York University Press, 2007).

35. Mark Epstein, "The Trauma of Being Alive," *New York Times*, August 3, 2013, 8. http://www.nytimes.com/2013/08/04/opinion/sunday/the-trauma-of-being-alive.html?pagewanted=all&_r=0.

36. Hoffman, *After Such Knowledge*, 41.

37. Hoffman, *After Such Knowledge*, 54.

38. Epstein, "The Trauma of Being Alive."

39. Thanks to psychiatrist Robert Lifton and others who worked with Vietnam vets and others who endured war, and Judith Herman, who added intimate violence, such as rape and incest, to the mix.

40. Marita Sturken, *Tourists of History: Memory, Kitsch, and Consumerism from Oklahoma City to Ground Zero* (Durham, NC: Duke University Press, 2007), 14. See also Nancy Berns, *Closure: The Rush to End Grief and What It Costs Us* (Philadelphia: Temple University Press, 2011).

41. Biale, *Power and Powerlessness in Jewish History*, 199.

42. http://www.pewforum.org/2013/10/01/chapter-3-jewish-identity/.

43. Steven Seidman makes a parallel argument about the cultural recognition of homosexuality. Once a matter of fear and loathing, an aspect of the self one was compelled to conceal, same-sex desires are now increasingly routinized and incorporated into American culture. While this integration is partial and homophobia persists, many gays and lesbians now live, says Seidman, beyond the closet. See Seidman, Chet Meeks, and Francie Traschen, "Beyond the Closet? The Changing Social Meaning of Homosexuality in the United States," in *Sexuality and Gender*, ed. Christine L. Williams and Arlene Stein (Cambridge, UK: Blackwell, 2002), 427–445.

44. Samantha Power, *A Problem from Hell: America and the Age of Genocide* (New York: Harper Perennial, 2007), 505.

45. Committee on Conscience, US Holocaust Memorial Museum, "Organizing on Campus to End the Genocide in Sudan," February 2005.

46. Lisa Siraganian, "'Is This My Mother's Grave?': Genocide and Diaspora in Atom Egoyan's *Family Viewing*," *Diaspora* 6, no. 2 (Fall 1997), 129; Dhooleka Raj, "Ignorance, Forgetting and Family Nostalgia: Partition, the Nation State and Refugees in Delhi," *Social Analysis* 44 (2000).

47. Saidya Hartman, *Lose Your Mother: A Journey along the Atlantic Slave Route* (New York: Farrar, Strauss and Giroux, 2007).

48. Raj, "Ignorance, Forgetting and Family Nostalgia."

49. Shruti Devgan, "Crevices in Dominant Memories: Virtual Commemoration and the 1984 Anti-Sikh Violence," *Identities: Global Studies in Culture and Power* (2013), 1–29.

50. Grace M. Cho, *Haunting the Korean Diaspora: Shame, Secrecy, and the Forgotten War*. Minneapolis: University of Minnesota, 2008.

51. Despite the haunting nature of images of famine, genocide, and disease, Susan D. Moeller writes, "we seem to care less and less about the world around us." See her *Compassion Fatigue: How the Media Sell Disease, Famine, War and Death* (New York: Routledge, 1999), 2.

52. Robert Jay Lifton, *The Protean Self* (New York: Basic Books, 1993), 217. See also Judith Butler, "Violence, Mourning, Politics," *Studies in Gender and Sexuality* 4, no. 1 (2003): 9–37.

53. "Facing History and Ourselves," among the most prominent of these efforts, is a nonprofit foundation that trains teachers to incorporate the Holocaust into curricula about history and individual moral choices.

54. On cosmopolitan memory, see Daniel Levy and Natan Sznaider, "Memory Unbound: The Holocaust and the Formation of Cosmopolitan Memory," *European Journal of Social Theory* 5, no. 1 (2002): 87–106.

55. Aviya Kushner, "Donors Open Pockets for a Cambodian Museum," *The Jewish Daily Forward,* January 7, 2005.

56. On truth and reconciliation commissions as vehicles for addressing collective victimization, see, for example, Martha Minow, *Between Vengeance and Forgiveness: Facing History after Genocide and Mass Violence* (Boston: Beacon Press, 1998). Such dialogues between descendants of survivors and their German counterparts represent a kind of reconciliation project, though they are much more limited than in South Africa, and more therapeutic in emphasis. See, for example, Dan Bar-On, *Tell Your Life-Story: Creating Dialogue Between Jews and Germans, Israelis and Palestinians* (Budapest: Central European University Press, 2006).

57. Paul Gilroy, *Postcolonial Melancholy* (New York: Columbia University Press, 2005), 67. See also Susan Sontag, *Regarding the Pain of Others* (New York: Picador, 2004).

APPENDIX

1. Bea Hollander-Goldfein, Nancy Isserman, and Jennifer Goldenberg, eds., *Transcending Trauma: Survival, Resilience, and Clinical Implications in Survivor Families* (New York: Routledge, 2012), 3.

2. Patricia Clough, *Autoaffection: Unconscious Thought in an Age of Teletechnology* (Minneapolis: University of Minnesota, 2000), 16.

3. Nancy Chodorow, "Born into a World at War: Listening for Affect and Personal Meaning," *American Imago* 59, no. 3 (2002), 307.

4. Douglas Greenberg, "Historical Memory of the Shoah: The Use of Survivor Testimony," conference on The Shoah and Mass Violence in the 20th Century, January 2008, Florence, Italy.

5. Janet Jacobs, "Women, Gender, and Memory: The Ethics of Feminist Ethnography in Holocaust Research," *Gender and Society* 18 (2004): 227

6. Rachel Einwohner, "Ethical Considerations on the Use of Archived Testimonies in Holocaust Research: Beyond the IRB Exemption," *Qualitative Sociology* 34 (2011): 415–430.

REFERENCES

Adamczyk-Garbowska, Monka. *Patterns of Return Survivors' Postwar Journeys to Poland*. Washington, DC: United States Holocaust Memorial Museum, Center for Advanced Holocaust Studies, 2007.

Alba, Richard D., and Victor Nee. *Remaking the American Mainstream: Assimilation and Contemporary Immigration*. Cambridge, MA: Harvard University Press, 2005.

Alcoff, Linda, and Laura Gray. "Survivor Discourse: Transgression or Recuperation?" *SIGNS* 18, no. 2 (1993): 260–290.

Alexander, Jeffrey. "Toward a Theory of Cultural Trauma," in *Cultural Trauma and Collective Identity*, ed. Jeffrey Alexander, Ron Eyerman, Bernhard Giesen, Neil J. Smelser, and Piotr Sztompka. Berkeley: University of California Press, 2004.

Alexander, Jeffrey. "On the Social Construction of Moral Universals: The "Holocaust" from War Crime to Trauma Drama," *in Cultural Trauma and Collective Identity*, ed. Jeffrey Alexander, Ron Eyerman, Bernhard Giesen, Neil J. Smelser, and Piotr Sztompka, 196–263. New Haven, CT: Yale University Press, 2004.

Alexander, Jeffrey. *The Meanings of Social Life*. Oxford, UK: Oxford University Press, 2003.

Alford, C. Fred. "Why Holocaust Testimony is Important, and How Psychoanalytic Interpretation Can Help . . . But Only to a Point," *Psychoanalysis, Culture & Society* 13 (2008): 221–239.

Andrews, Susan. "Holocaust Remembrance in Australia: Gender, Memory, and Identity Between the Local and the Transnational," doctoral dissertation, Australian National University, August 2007.

Antze, Paul, and Michael Lambek, eds. *Tense Past*. Thousand Oaks, CA: Sage, 1996.

Appignanesi, Lisa. *Losing the Dead*. Toronto: McArthur & Co., 1999.

Applebome, Peter. "Numbers Prompt a Story Told in Words," *New York Times*, November 1, 2006, accessed March 13, 2013, http://www.nytimes.com/2006/11/01/nyregion/01towns.html.

Arendt, Hannah. "The Jew as Pariah: A Hidden Tradition," in *The Jew as Pariah: Jewish Identity and Politics in the Modern Age*, ed. Ron H. Feldman, 67–90. New York: Grove Press, 1978.

Auerhahn, Nanette C., and Dori Laub. "Intergenerational Memory of the Holocaust," in *International Handbook of Multigenerational Legacies of Trauma*, ed. Yael Danieli, 21–41. New York: Plenum, 1978.

Balakian, Peter. *Black Dog of Fate*. New York: Broadway Books, 1997.

Bar-On, Dan. *Tell Your Life-Story: Creating Dialogue among Jews and Germans, Israelis and Palestinians*. Budapest: Central European University Press, 2006.

Bar-On, Dan. "Legacy of Silence in Nazi Perpetrators' and Holocaust Survivors' Families." Paper presented at Henry Schwartzman Faculty Seminar, Rutgers University, September 2005.

Bar-On, Dan. *Fear and Hope: Three Generations of the Holocaust*. Cambridge, MA: Harvard University Press, 1998.

Bauman, Zygmunt. "The Holocaust's Life as a Ghost," in *The Holocaust Ghost: Writings on Art, Politics, Law and Education*, ed. F. C. Decoste and Bernard Schwartz, 3–15. Edmonton: University of Alberta Press, 2000.

Bauman, Zygmunt. *Modernity and the Holocaust*. Ithaca, NY: Cornell University Press, 1989.

Beinart, Peter. *The Crisis of Zionism*. New York: Times Books, 2012.

Benjamin, Jessica. *The Bonds of Love: Psychoanalysis, Feminism and the Problem of Domination*. New York: Pantheon, 1988.

Berenbaum, Michael. "The Nativization of the Holocaust," *Judaism* 35 (1986): 447–457.

Berger, Alan L., and Naomi Berger, eds. *Second Generation Voices: Reflections by Children of Survivors and Perpetrators*. Syracuse, NY: Syracuse University Press, 2001.

Berger, Naomi. "Coming Full Circle," in *Second Generation Voices: Reflections by Children of Survivors and Perpetrators*, ed. Alan L. Berger and Naomi Berger, 92–109. Syracuse, NY: Syracuse University Press, 2001.

Bergmann, Martin S., and Milton E. Jucovy, eds. *Generations of the Holocaust*. New York: Basic Books, 1982.

Berlant, Lauren. *The Queen of America Goes to Washington City: Essays on Sex and Citizenship*. Durham, NC: Duke University Press, 1997.

Berlant, Lauren. "The Subject of True Feeling: Pain, Privacy, and Politics" in *Feminist Consequences: Theory for a New Century*, ed. Elisabeth Bronfen and Misha Kavka, 126–60. New York: Columbia University Press, 2001.

Berman, Lila Corwin. "Sociology, Jews, and Intermarriage in Twentieth Century America," *Jewish Social Studies* 14, no. 2 (Winter 2008): 32–60.

Berns, Nancy. *Closure: The Rush to End Grief and What It Costs Us*. Philadelphia: Temple University Press, 2011.

Bettleheim, Bruno. *Surviving and Other Essays*. New York: Knopf, 1979.

Biale, David. "The Melting Pot and Beyond: Jews and the Politics of American Identity," in *Insider/Outsider: American Jews and Multiculturalism*, ed. David Biale, Michael Galchinsky and Susan Heschel, 17–33. Berkeley: University of California Press, 1998.

Biale, David. *Power and Powerlessness in Jewish History*. New York: Schocken Books, 1986.

Bloch, Sam E., and Samuel R. Mozes, eds. *From Holocaust to Redemption, Bearing Witness: A Documentary Volume Depicting the Proceedings and Events of the World Gathering of Jewish Holocaust Survivors, Israel*. New York: World Gathering of Holocaust Survivors, 1984.

Boss, Pauline. *Ambiguous Loss*. Cambridge, MA: Harvard University Press, 1999.

Bostom, Andrew. "Iran's Final Solution for Israel," March 6, 2012, *Israel Advocate* (first published in *National Review Online*, February 10, 2012).

Boyarin, Jonathan, and Jack Kugelmass. *From a Ruined Garden: The Memorial Books of Polish Jewry*. New York: Schocken Press, 1983.

Boym, Svetlana. *The Future of Nostalgia*. New York: Basic Books, 2001.

Brett, Lily. "Half There," in *Nothing Makes You Free: Writings by Descendants of Holocaust Survivors*, ed. Melvin Jules Bukiet, 230–254. New York: W. W. Norton, 2002.

Brodkin, Karen. *How Jews Became White Folks*. New Brunswick, NJ: Rutgers University Press, 1998.

Brown, Roger, and James Kulik. "Flashbulb Memories," *Cognition* 5, no. 1 (1977): 73–99.

Brown, Wendy. *States of Injury: Power and Freedom in Late Modernity*. Princeton, NJ: Princeton University Press, 1995.

Bukiet, Melvin Jules. "Introduction," *Nothing Makes You Free: Writings by Descendants of Jewish Holocaust Survivors*, ed. Melvin Jules Bukiet, 11–25. New York: W. W. Norton, 2002.

Butler, Judith, "Remarks to Brooklyn College on BDS [movement for Boycott, Divestment, and Sanctions in Israel]," reprinted in *The Nation*, February 7, 2013.

Butler, Judith. *Giving an Account of Oneself*. New York: Fordham University Press, 2005.

Butler, Judith. "The Charge of Anti-Semitism: Jews, Israel, and the Risks of Public Critique," in *Precarious Life: The Powers of Mourning and Violence*, 101–127. London: Verso, 2004.

Butler, Judith. *Precarious Life: The Powers of Mourning and Violence*. London: Verso, 2004.

Butler, Judith. "Violence, Mourning, Politics," *Studies in Gender and Sexuality* 4, no. 1 (2003): 9–37.

Butler, Judith. 1997. *The Psychic Life of Power: Theories of Subjection*. Stanford, CA: Stanford University Press.

Carsten, Janet. "Knowing Where You've Come From: Ruptures and Continuities of Time and Kinship of Adoption Reunions," *Journal of the American Anthropological Institute* 6, no. 4 (December 2000): 687–703.

Caruth, Cathy, ed. *Trauma: Explorations in Memory*. Baltimore: Johns Hopkins University Press, 1995.

Cerulo, Karen. *Never Saw It Coming: Cultural Challenges to Imagining the Worst*. Chicago: University of Chicago Press, 2006.

Cho, Grace M. *Haunting the Korean Diaspora: Shame, Secrecy, and the Forgotten War*. Minneapolis: University of Minnesota, 2008.

Chodorow, Nancy Julia. "Toward a Relational Individualism," in *Reconstructing Individualism: Autonomy, Individuality, and the Self in Western Thought*, ed. Thomas C. Heller, Morton Sosna, and David Wellbery, 197–207. Stanford, CA: Stanford University Press, 1986.

Chodorow, Nancy. "The Psychoanalytic Vision of Hans Loewald," *International Journal of Psychoanalysis* 84 (2003): 897–913.

Chodorow, Nancy. "Born into a World at War: Listening for Affect and Personal Meaning," *American Imago* 59, no. 3 (2002): 297–315.

Clough, Patricia. *Autoaffection: Unconscious Thought in an Age of Teletechnology*. Minneapolis: University of Minnesota, 2000.

Cohen, Beth. *Case Closed: Holocaust Survivors in Postwar America*. New Brunswick, NJ: Rutgers University Press, 2007.

Cohen, Stanley. *States of Denial: Knowing about Atrocities and Suffering*. Cambridge, UK: Polity, 2001.

Cohen, Steven M., and Arnold M. Eisen. *The Jew Within: Self, Family, and Community in America*. Bloomington: Indiana University Press, 2000.

Cole, Alyson. *The Cult of True Victimhood: From the War on Welfare to the War on Terror*. Stanford, CA: Stanford University Press, 2007.

Cole, Tim. *Selling the Holocaust: From Auschwitz to Shindler: How History Is Bought, Packaged, and Sold*. New York: Routledge, 2000.

Combahee River Collective. "A Black Feminist Statement," in *Home Girls: A Black Feminist Anthology*, ed. Barbara Smith, 264–274. New Brunswick, NJ: Rutgers, 2000.

Cvetkovich, Ann. *An Archive of Feelings*. Durham, NC: Duke University Press, 2003.

Danieli, Yael. "Introduction: History and Conceptual Foundations," in *International Handbook of Multigenerational Legacies of Trauma*, ed. Yael Danieli, 1–20. New York: Plenum, 1998.

Danieli, Yael. "The Group Project for Holocaust Survivors and the Children," Appendix A, "Therapists' Difficulties in Treating Survivors of the Nazi Holocaust and Their Children," PhD dissertation, New York University, 1981.

Davidman, Lynn. *Motherloss*. Berkeley: University of California Press, 2000.

Davis, Joseph. "Victim Narratives and Victim Selves: False Memory Syndrome and the Power of Accounts," *Social Problems* 52, issue 4 (2005): 529–548.

Davoine, François, and Jean-Max Gaudillière. *History Beyond Trauma*. New York: Other Press, 2004.

Des Pres, Terrence. *The Survivor: An Anatomy of Life in the Death Camps*. New York: Pocket Books, 1977.

Des Pres, Terrence. "Lessons of the Holocaust," *New York Times*, April 27, 1976.

Devgan, Shruti. "Crevices in Dominant Memories: Virtual Commemoration and the 1984 Anti-Sikh Violence," *Identities: Global Studies in Culture and Power* 20, no. 2 (2013): 207–233.

di Leonardo, Micaela. "The Female World of Cards and Holidays: Women, Families, and the Work of Kinship," *Signs* 12, no. 3 (1987): 440–453.

Diner, Hasia. *We Remember with Reverence and Love: American Jews and the Myth of Silence after the Holocaust, 1945–1962*. New York: New York University Press, 2009.

Dinnerstein, Leonard. *America and the Survivors of the Holocaust*. New York: Columbia University Press, 1982.

Dobbs, David. "A New Focus on the 'Post' in Post-Traumatic Stress," *New York Times*, December 24, 2012, accessed March 13, 2013, http://www.nytimes.com/2012/12/25/science/understanding-the-esffects-of-social-environment-on-trauma-victims.html.

DuBois, W. E. B. (1903) "Double Consciousness and the Veil," in *Social Theory: The Multicultural and Classic Readings*, ed. Charles Lemert, 177–182. Boulder: Westfield, 1993. Originally published in W. E. B. DuBois, *The Souls of Black Folk* (Chicago: A. C. McClurg, 1903).

Duggan, Lisa. "A New Consensus on Public Space and 'Free' Speech on Israel/Palestine in New York City," *The Nation*, February 22, 2013, accessed March 16, 2013, http://www.thenation.com/article/173073/new-consensus-public-space-and-free-speech-israelpalestine-new-york-city.

Echols, Alice. *Daring to Be Bad: Radical Feminism in America*. Minneapolis: University of Minnesota Press, 1989.

Ehrenreich, Barbara. *Bright-Sided: How the Relentless Promotion of Positive Thinking Has Undermined America*. New York: Metropolitan Books, 2009.

Einwohner, Rachel. "*Ethical Considerations on the Use of Archived Testimonies in Holocaust Research: Beyond the IRB Exemption*," *Qualitative Sociology* 34 (2011): 415–430.

Eng, David L., and Shinhee Han. "A Dialogue on Racial Melancholia," in *Loss*, ed. David L. Eng and David Kazanjian, 343–371. Berkeley: University of California Press, 2003.

Engel, W. H. "Reflections on the Psychiatric Consequences of Persecution," *American Journal of Psychotherapy* 2 (1962): 191–203.

Engelking, Barbara. *Holocaust and Memory*. London: Leicester University Press, 2001.

Epstein, Helen. *Children of the Holocaust*. New York: Putnam, 1979.

Epstein, Helen. *Where She Came From: A Daughter's Search for Her Mother's Story*. New York: Penguin, 1997.

Epstein, Julia. "Between Exiles: Parenting and Cultural Memory," in *Shaping Losses: Cultural Memory and the Holocaust*, ed. Julia Epstein and Lori Hope Lefkowitz, 207–219. Urbana: University of Illinois, 2001.

Epstein, Mark. "The Trauma of Being Alive," *New York Times*, August 3, 2013, 8. http://www.nytimes.com/2013/08/04/opinion/sunday/the-trauma-of-being-alive.html?pagewanted=all&_r=0.

Erben, Michael. "Genealogy and Sociology: A Preliminary Set of Statements and Speculations," *Sociology* 25 (1991): 275–292.

Erikson, Erik. "The Human Life Cycle," in *A Way of Looking At Things*. New York: Norton, 1995.

Erikson, Erik. *Childhood and Society*. New York: Norton, 1950.

Erikson, Kai. "Notes on Trauma and Community," in *Trauma: Explorations in Memory*, ed. Cathy Caruth, 183–199. Baltimore: The Johns Hopkins University Press, 1995.

Eros, Ferenc, Julia Vajda, and Eva Kovacs. "Intergenerational Responses to Social and Political Changes: Transformation of Jewish Identity in Hungary," in *International Handbook of Multigenerational Legacies of Trauma*, ed. Yael Danieli, 315–324. New York: Plenum, 1998.

Eyerman, Ron. "Cultural Trauma: Slavery and the Formation of African American Identity," in *Cultural Trauma and Collective Identity*, ed. Jeffrey Alexander, Ron Eyerman, Bernhard Giesen, Neil J. Smelser, and Piotr Sztompka, 60–111. Berkeley: University of California Press, 2004.

Faye, Esther. "Missing the 'Real' Trace of Trauma: How the Second Generation Remember the Holocaust," *American Imago* 58, no. 2 (2001): 525–544.

Felman, Shoshana, and Dori Laub. *Testimony: Crises of Witnessing in Literature, Psychoanalysis and History*. New York: Routledge, 1992.

Fermaglich, Kirsten. *American Dreams and Nazi Nightmares: Early Holocaust Consciousness and Liberal America, 1957–1965*. Waltham, MA: Brandeis University Press, 2006.

Finkelstein, Barbara. "Return to Poland," in *Lost on the Map of the World*, ed. Phillipa Kafka. New York: Peter Lang, 2001.

Finkelstein, Norman. *The Holocaust Industry: Reflections on the Exploitation of Jewish Suffering*. London: Verso, 2000.

Fivush, Robyn, and Catherine Haden, eds. *Autobiographical Memory and the Construction of a Narrative Self: Developmental and Cultural Perspectives*. Mahwah, NJ: Lawrence Erlbaum, 2003.

Fodorova, Anna. "Mourning by Proxy: Notes on a Conference, Empty Graves and Silence," *Psychodynamic Practice* 11, no. 3 (August 2005): 301–310.

Frank, Arthur. *Wounded Storytellers: Body, Illness, and Ethics*. Chicago: University of Chicago Press, 1995.

Franklin, Ruth. "Identity Theft," *New Republic*, May 31, 2004.

Fraser, Nancy, and Axel Honneth. *Redistribution or Recognition? A Political- Philosophical Exchange*. London: Verso, 1998.

Fremont, Helen. *After Long Silence: A Memoir*. New York: Delacourt, 1999.

Fresco, Nadine. "Remembering the Unknown," *International Journal of Psychoanalysis* 11 (1984): 417–427.

Freud, Sigmund. (1917 [1915]) "Mourning and Melancholia." *The Standard Edition of the Complete Works of Sigmund Freud* 14. London: The Hogarth Press: 242–260.

Freyd, Jennifer. *Betrayal Trauma: The Logic of Forgetting Childhood Abuse*. Cambridge, MA: Harvard University Press, 1996.

Friedlander, Saul. "Trauma, Transference and 'Working Through' in Writing the History of the Shoah," *History and Memory* 4 (1992): 39–55.

Friedman, Carl. *Nightfather: A Novel*. Trans. Arnold Pomerans and Erica Pomerans. New York: Persea, 1995.

Friedman, Norman L. "Social Movement Legacies: The American Jewish Counterculture, 1973–1988," *Jewish Social Studies* 50, nos. 3–4 (Summer 1988–Fall 1993): 127–146.

Fulford, Robert. *The Triumph of the Narrative: Storytelling in the Age of Mass Culture*. Toronto: House of Anansi Press, 1999.

Frank, Furedi. *Therapy Culture*. London: Routledge, 2003.

Furedi, Frank. "The 'Second Generation' of Holocaust Survivors," *Spiked*, January 24, 2002, accessed March 16, 2013, http://www.spiked-online.com/Articles/00000000545B.htm.

Gerson, Judith. "Family Matters," in *Jewish Masculinities*, ed. Benjamin Maria Baader, Sharon Gillerman, and Paul Lerner, 210–231. Bloomington: Indiana University Press, 2012.

Gerson, Judith, and Diane L. Wolf, eds. *Sociology Confronts the Holocaust: Memories and Identities in Jewish Diaspora*. Durham, NC: Duke University Press, 2007.

Gewen, Barry. "Holocaust Documentaries: Too Much of a Bad Thing?" *New York Times*, June 15, 2003.

Giddens, Anthony. *Modernity and Self-Identity*. Stanford, CA: Stanford University Press, 1991.

Gilbert–Lurie, Leslie and Rita Lurie. *Bending Toward the Sun*. New York: HarperCollins, 2009.

Gilligan, Carol. "Mapping the Moral Domain: New Images of Self in Relationship," in *Reconstructing Individualism: Autonomy, Individuality, and the Self in Western Thought*, ed. Thomas C. Heller, Morton Sosna, and David Wellbery, 237–252. Stanford, CA: Stanford University Press, 1986.

Gilroy, Paul. *Postcolonial Melancholy*. New York: Columbia University Press, 2005.

Gilroy, Paul. *The Black Atlantic: Modernity and Double Consciousness*. Cambridge, MA: Harvard University Press, 1993.

Gitlin, Todd. *The Sixties: Years of Hope, Days of Rage*. New York: Random House, 1993.

Glenn, Susan A. "The Vogue of Jewish Self-Hatred in Post-World War II America," *Jewish Social Studies* 12, no. 3 (Spring–Summer 2006): 95–136.

Goffman, Erving. *Stigma: Notes on the Management of Spoiled Identity*. New York: Touchstone, 1986. Originally published as *Stigma: Notes on the Management of Spoiled Identity* (New York: Simon & Schuster, 1963).

Goodwin, Jeff, James Jasper, and Francesca Polletta. *Passionate Politics: Emotions and Social Movements*. Chicago: University of Chicago Press, 2011.

Gordon, Avery. *Ghostly Matters: Haunting and the Sociological Imagination*. Minneapolis: University of Minnesota, 1997.

Gordon, Mordechai. "The United States and Israel: Double Standards, Favoritism, and Unconditional Support," in *The Miseducation of the West: How Schools and the Media Distort Our Understanding of the Islamic World*, ed. Joe Kincheloe and Shirley Steinberg. Westport, CT: Praeger, 2004.

Govrin, Michal, "The Journey to Poland" in *Second Generation Voices: Reflections by Children of Survivors and Perpetrators*, ed. Alan L. Berger and Naomi Berger, 141–152. Syracuse, NY: Syracuse University Press, 2001.

Greenberg, Douglas. "Historical Memory of the Shoah: The Use of Survivor Testimony," conference on The Shoah and Mass Violence in the 20th Century, Florence, Italy, 2008.

Greenspan, Henry. *On Listening to Holocaust Survivors*. Westport, CT: Praeger, 1998.

Greenspan, Henry. "Lives as Texts: Symptoms as Modes of Recounting the Life Histories of Holocaust Survivors," in *Storied Lives*, ed. George Rosenwald and R. Ochberg, 145–164. New Haven, CT: Yale University Press, 1992.

Grogan, Jessica. *Humanistic Psychology, Sixties Culture, and the Shaping of the Modern Self* (New York: Harper Perennial, 2012).

Gross, Netty. "Finding the Words," *The Jerusalem Report*, May 26, 2008.

Gruber, Ruth. *Virtually Jewish: Reinventing Jewish Culture in Europe*. Berkeley: University of California, 2002.

Haaken, Janice. *Pillar of Salt: Gender, Memory, and the Perils of Looking Back*. New Brunswick, NJ: Rutgers University Press, 1998.

Haas, Aaron. *In the Shadow of the Holocaust: The Second Generation*. London: Cambridge University Press, 1990.

Hacking, Ian. "Memory Sciences, Memory Politics," in *Tense Past: Cultural Essays in Trauma and Memory*, ed. Paul Antze and Michael Lambek. 67–88. Thousand Oaks, CA: Sage, 1996.

Hackstaff. Karla. "Who Are We? Genealogists Negotiating Ethno-Racial Identities." *Qualitative Sociology* 32, no. 2 (2009), 173–194.

Halbwachs, Maurice. [1950]. *The Collective Memory*. New York: Harper and Row, 1980.

Hartman, Geoffrey. *The Longest Shadow: In the Aftermath of the Holocaust*. Bloomington: Indiana University Press, 1996.

Hartman, Saidya. *Lose Your Mother: A Journey along the Atlantic Slave Route*. New York: Farrar, Strauss and Giroux, 2007.

Hass, Aaron. *In the Shadow of the Holocaust: The Second Generation*. London: Cambridge University Press, 1990.

Heinze, Andrew. *Jews and the American Soul: Human Nature in the Twentieth Century*. Princeton, NJ: Princeton University Press, 2004.

Heizer, Robert F., and Theodora Kroeber, eds. *Ishi the Last Yahi: A Documentary History*. Berkeley: University of California Press, 1981.

Heller, Thomas C., Morton Sosna, and David Wellberry, eds. *Reconstructing Individualism: Autonomy, Individuality, and the Self in Western Thought*. Stanford, CA: Stanford University Press, 1986.

Helmreich, William. "Don't Look Back: Holocaust Survivors in the US." Jerusalem Center for Public Affairs, 1991.

Henry, Marilyn. *Confronting the Perpetrators: A History of the Claims Conference*. London: Vallentine Mitchell, 2007.

Herman, Ellen. *The Romance of American Psychology: Political Culture in the Age of Experts*. Berkeley: University of California Press, 1995.

Herman, Judith. *Trauma and Recovery: The Aftermath of Violence from Domestic Abuse to Political Terror*. New York: Basic Books, 1997.

Hertzberg, Arthur. "The First Encounter: Survivors and Americans in the Late 1940s." United States Holocaust Memorial Museum, Washington, DC, 1996.

Hirsch, Marianne. *The Generation of Postmemory: Writing and Visual Culture after the Holocaust*. New York: Columbia University Press, 2012.

Hirsch, Marianne. "Marked by Memory: Feminist Reflections on Trauma and Transmission," in *Extremities*, ed. Nancy K. Miller and Jason Tougaw, 71–91. Urbana: University of Illinois Press, 2002.

Hirsch, Marianne. *Family Frames: Photography, Narrative, and Postmemory*. Cambridge, MA: Harvard University Press, 1997.

Hirsch, Marianne, and Valerie Smith. "Feminism and Cultural Memory: An Introduction," *Signs* 28, no. 1 (2002): 1–19.

Hochman, Edward S. Letters, *New York Times*, October, 8, 2012.

Hochschild, Arlie. *The Managed Heart: The Commercialization of Human Feeling.* Berkeley: University of California Press, 1983.

Hochschild, Arlie. "Emotion Work, Feeling Rules and Social Structure," *American Journal of Sociology* 85 (1979): 551–575.

Hoffman, Eva. *After Such Knowledge: Memory, History and the Legacy of the Holocaust.* New York: Public Affairs, 2004.

Hollander-Goldfein, Bea, Nancy Isserman, and Jennifer Goldenberg, eds. *Transcending Trauma: Survival, Resilience, and Clinical Implications in Survivor Families.* New York: Routledge, 2012.

Hollway, Wendy, and Tony Jefferson. *Doing Qualitative Work Differently.* London: Sage, 2013

Holstein, James A., and Gale Miller. "Rethinking Victimization: An Interactional Approach to Victimology," *Symbolic Interaction* 13 (1990): 103–122.

Homans, Margaret. "Adoption Naratives, Trauma and Origins," *Narrative* 14, no. 1 (2006): 4–26.

Huyssen, Andreas. *Present Pasts: Urban Palimpsests and the Politics of Memory.* Stanford, CA: Stanford University Press, 2003.

Huyssen, Andreas. *Twilight Memories: Marking Time in a Culture of Amnesia.* New York: Routledge, 1995.

Igo, Sarah. *The Averaged American: Surveys, Citizens, and the Making of a Mass Public.* Cambridge, MA: Harvard University Press, 2008.

Illouz, Eva. *Saving the Modern Soul: Therapy, Emotions, and the Culture of Self-Help.* Berkeley: University of California Press, 2008.

Ingall, Marjorie. "My Generation: New Identity," *The Jewish Daily Forward*, August 11, 2006, 25.

Irwin-Zarecka, Iwona. *Frames of Remembrance: The Dynamics of Collective Memory.* New Brunswick, NJ: Transaction, 1994.

Jacobs, Janet. "Women, Gender, and Memory: The Ethics of Feminist Ethnography in Holocaust Research," *Gender and Society* 18 (2004): 227.

Jacobson, Matthew Frye. *Roots Too: White Ethnic Revival in Post-Civil Rights America.* Cambridge, MA: Harvard University Press, 2006.

Jaggar, Allison M. "Love and Knowledge: Emotion in Feminist Epistemology, *Inquiry* 32, no. 2 (1989): 151–176.

Janaczek, Helena. "Joemi's Table," in *Nothing Makes You Free: Writings by Descendants of Jewish Holocaust Survivors*, ed. Melvin Bukiet, 255–262. New York: W. W. Norton, 2002.

Kahane, Claire. "Dark Mirrors: A Feminist Reflection on Holocaust Narrative and the Maternal Metaphor," in *Feminist Consequences: Theory for a New Century*, ed. Elisabeth Bronfen and Misha Kavka, 161–188. New York: Columbia University Press, 2001.

Karafilly, Irena F. *Ashes and Miracles: A Polish Journey.* Malcolm Lester Books, 1998.

Karpf, Anne. *The War After: Living with the Holocaust.* London: Minerva, 1996.

Kaufman, Debra. "Ethnicity, Collective Memory and Post-Holocaust Identity Narratives," in *De-ghettoizing the Holocaust: Lessons for the Study of Diaspora, Ethnicity, and Collective Memory*, ed. Judith Gerson and Diane Wolf, 39–54. Durham, NC: Duke University Press, 2007.

Kessel, Barbara. 2000. *Suddenly Jewish: Jews Raised as Gentiles Discover their Jewish Roots.* Hanover, NH: University Press of New England, 2000.

Kestenberg, Judith. "Psychoanalytic Contributions to the Problems of Children of Survivors from Nazi Persecution." *Israeli Annals of Psychiatry and Related Sciences* 10 (1972): 311–325.

Kidron, Carol A. "Toward an Ethnography of Silence," *Current Anthropology* 50, no. 1 (February 2009).

Kidron, Carol A. "Surviving a Distant Past: A Case Study of the Cultural Construction of Trauma Descendant Identity," *Ethos* 31, no. 4 (1999): 513–544.

Klatch, Rebecca. *A Generation Divided: The New Left, the New Right, and the 1960s.* Berkeley: University of California Press, 1999.

Klawans, Stuart. "Europa, Europa." *The Nation*, February 16, 2004, 34.

Kluger, Ruth. *Still Alive.* New York: The Feminist Press, 2003.

Kolin, Andrew. *One Family: Before and During the Holocaust.* Lanham, MD: University Press of America, 2000.

Kroeber, Theodora, and Karl Kroeber. *Ishi in Two Worlds: A Biography of the Last Wild Indian in North America.* Berkeley: University of California Press, 2002.

Krystal, Henry, and William Niederland. "Clinical Observations on the Survivor Syndrome." In *Massive Psychic Trauma*, ed. H. Krystal, 327–348. New York: International Universities Press, 1968.

Kugelmass, Jack. "The Rites of the Tribe: American Jewish Tourism in Poland," in *Museums and Communities: The Politics of Public Culture*, ed. Ivan Karp, Christine Mullen Kreamer, and Steven D. Lavine, 395–453. Washington, DC: Smithsonian Institution Press, 1992.

Kugelmass, Jack, and Jonathan Boyarin. *From a Ruined Garden: The Memorial Books of Polish Jewry.* Bloomington: Indiana University Press, 1998.

Kuhn, Annette. *Family Secrets: Acts of Memory and Imagination.* London: Verso, 1995.

Kushner, Aviva. "Donors Open Pockets for a Cambodian Museum," *The Jewish Daily Forward*, January 7, 2005.

Lancaster, Roger. *Sex Panic and the Punitive State.* Berkeley: University of California Press, 2011.

Landsberg, Alison. "America, the Holocaust, and the Mass Culture of Memory: Toward a Radical Politics of Empathy," *New German Critique* 71 (Spring–Summer 1997): 63–86.

Langer, Lawrence. *Holocaust Testimonies: The Ruins of Memory.* New Haven, CT: Yale University Press, 1991.

Lasch, Christopher. *The Minimal Self: Psychic Survival in Troubled Times.* New York: Norton, 1984.

Lasch, Christopher. *The Minimal Self: Psychic Survival in Troubled Times.* New York: Norton, 1985.

Laub, Dori. "The Empty Circle: Children of Survivors and the Limits of Reconstruction," *Journal of the American Psychoanalytic Association* 46, no. 2 (1998): 507–529.

Lerner, Paul, and Mark S. Micale. "Trauma, Psychiatry, and History," in *Traumatic Pasts: History, Psychiatry, and Trauma in the Modern Age, 1870–1930*, ed. Mark S. Micale and Paul Lerner, 1–30. Cambridge, UK: Cambridge University Press, 2001.

Levinas, Emmanuel. *Entre Nous: Thinking of the Other.* Trans. Michael B. Smith and Barbara Harshav. New York: Columbia University Press, 1998.

Levi, Primo. *The Drowned and the Saved.* New York: Random House, 1989.

Levitt, Laura. *American Jewish Loss after the Holocaust.* New York: New York University Press, 2007.

Levy, Daniel, and Natan Sznaider. "Memory Unbound: The Holocaust and the Forma-tion of Cosmopolitan Memory," *European Journal of Social Theory* 5, no. 1 (2002): 87–106.

Levy, Daniel, and Natan Sznaider. *The Holocaust and Memory in the Global Age.* Philadelphia: Temple University Press, 2006

Leydesdorff, Selma, Graham Dawson, Natasha Burchardt, and T. G. Ashplant. "Introduction: Trauma and Life Stories," in *Trauma: Life Stories of Survivors*, ed. Kim Lacy Rogers and Selma Leydesdorff (with Graham Dawson), 1–23. New Brunswick, NJ: Transaction, 2004.

Leys, Ruth. *From Guilt to Shame: Auschwitz and After.* Princeton, NJ: Princeton University Press, 2009.

Lifton, B. J. "The Adopted Self," in *Trauma and the Self*, ed. Charles B. Strozier and Michael Flynn. New York: Rowman and Littlefield, 1996.

Lifton, B. J. *The Adoption Experience.* New York: Harper and Row, 1979.

Lifton, Robert Jay. *The Protean Self.* New York: Basic Books, 1993.

Lifton, Robert. *Home from the War: Learning from Vietnam Veterans.* Boston: Beacon Press, 1973.

Linenthal, Edward. "The Boundaries of Memory: The United States Holocaust Memorial Museum," *American Quarterly* 46, no. 3 (September 1994).

Lipstadt, Deborah. *Denying the Holocaust: The Growing Assault on Truth and Memory.* New York, Plume, 1994.

Lorde, Audre. *The Cancer Journals.* Aunt Lute, 2006.

Louie, Andrea. *Chineseness across Borders: Renegotiating Chinese Identities in China and the US.* Durham, NC: Duke University Press, 2004.

Ludsin, Steven A. Letters, *New York Times*, October 8, 2012.

MacCannell, Dean. *The Tourist: A New Theory of the Leisure Class.* New York: Schocken, 1976.

Mannheim, Karl. [1928]. "The Problem of Generations," in *The New Pilgrims: Youth Protest in Transition*, ed. P. Altbach and R. Laufer, 101–138. New York: David McKay and Company, 1972.

Margalit, Avishai. *The Ethics of Memory.* Cambridge, MA: Harvard University Press, 2002.

May, Elaine Tyler. *Homeward Bound: American Families in the Cold War Era.* New York: Basic Books, 1988.

Maynes, Mary Jo, Jennifer L Pierce, and Barbara Laslett. *Telling Stories: The Use of Personal Narratives in the Social Sciences and History.* Ithaca, NY: Cornell University Press, 2008.

McAdams, Dan. "Identity and the Life Story," in Catherine A. Haden, John W. Dimmick, and Robyn Fivush, 187–207. *Autobiographical Memory and the Construction of a Narrative Self.* Mahwah, NJ: Lawrence Ehrlbaum, 2003.

Miller, Nancy K., and Jason Tougaw, eds. *Extremities: Trauma, Testimony, and Community.* Urbana: University of Illinois Press, 2002.

Minow, Martha. *Between Vengeance and Forgiveness: Facing History after Genocide and Mass Violence.* Boston: Beacon Press, 1998.

Mitscherlich, Alexander and Margarete. *The Inability to Mourn.* New York: Grove Press, 1984.

Misztal, Barbara A. *Theories of Social Remembering.* Philadelphia: Open University Press, 2003.

Mitchell, W. J. T. *On Narrative.* Chicago: University of Chicago Press, 1981.

Moeller, Susan D. *Compassion Fatigue: How the Media Sell Disease, Famine, War and Death*. New York: Routledge, 1999.

Niederland, William G. "Clinical Observations on the 'Survivor Syndrome,'" *International Journal of Psycho-Analysis* 49 (1968): 313–315.

Nora, Pierre. "Between Memory and History: *Les Lieux de Memoire*." Trans. Marc Roudebush. *Representations* 26 (Spring 1989): 7–25.

Novick, Peter. *The Holocaust in American Life*. New York: Houghton Mifflin, 1999.

Nussbaum, Emily. "Tune in Next Week," *The New Yorker*, July 30, 2012.

Ochs, Elinor, and Lisa Capps. *Living Narrative: Creating Lives in Everyday Storytelling*, Cambridge, MA: Harvard University Press, 2001.

Odenheimer, Micha. "Jerusalem Is Still Burning," in *Guilt and Pleasure* 4 (Spring 2007).

Olick, Jeffrey K., Vered Vinitsky-Seroussi, and Daniel Levy. "Introduction," in *The Collective Memory Reader*, ed. J. Olick, V. Vinitsky-Seroussi and D. Levy, 3–62. New York: Oxford University Press, 2011.

Orgad, Shani. "The Survivor in Contemporary Culture and Public Discourse: A Genealogy," *Communication Review* 12, no. 2 (2009): 132–161.

Passerini, Luisa. *Autobiography of a Generation: Italy, 1968*. Hanover, NH: Wesleyan University Press, 1996.

Peled-Elhanan, Nurit. "At the Gates of Gaza," http://www.jewishvoicefor peace.org/publish/article_955.shtml.

Phelan, Shane. *Getting Specific: Postmodern Lesbian Politics*. Minneapolis: University of Minnesota Press, 1994.

Plummer, Ken. *Telling Sexual Stories: Power, Change, and Social Worlds*. New York: Routledge, 1995.

Polletta, Francesca. *It Was Like a Fever: Storytelling in Protest and Politics*. Chicago: University of Chicago Press, 2006.

Pols, Hans. "War Neurosis, Adjustment Problems in Veterans, and an Ill Nation," *Osiris* 22 (2007): 72–92.

Power, Samantha. *A Problem from Hell: America and the Age of Genocide*. New York: Harper Perennial, 2007.

Prager, Jeffrey. "Lies, Deception and False Memory: Self-States in their Social Context," in *The Psychic Life of Sociology*, ed. John Andrews and Lynn Chancer, Basingstoke: Palgrave Macmillan, 2014.

Prager, Jeffrey. "Beneath the Surface of the Self: Psychoanalysis and the Unseen Known," *American Journal of Sociology* 112, no. 1 (July 2006): 276–290.

Prager, Jeffrey. "Lost Childhood, Lost Generations: The Intergenerational Transmission of Trauma," *Journal of Human Rights* 2, no. 2 (2003): 173–181.

Prager, Jeffrey. *Presenting the Past: Psychoanalysis and the Sociology of Misremembering*. Cambridge, MA: Harvard University, 1998.

Prell, Riv-Ellen. *Struggling to Become Americans*. Boston: Beacon, 1997.

Rabinowitz, Dorothy. *New Lives: Survivors of the Holocaust Living in America*. New York: Knopf, 1976.

Raj, Dhooleka. "Ignorance, Forgetting and Family Nostalgia: Partition, the Nation State and Refugees in Delhi," *Social Analysis* 44 (2000): 30–55.

Raphael, Lev. *My Germany: A Jewish Writer Returns to the World His Parents Escaped*. Madison: University of Wisconsin Press, 2009.

Raphael, Lev. *The German Money*. Wellfleet: Leapfrog Press, 2003.

Remnick, David. "Letter from Jerusalem: The Apostate," *The New Yorker* July 30, 2007.

Report to the Annual Meeting of the United Service for New Americans, New York City, January 11, 1948.

Richmond, Theo. *Konin: One Man's Quest for a Vanished Jewish Community.* New York: Vintage, 1996.

Rogers, Annie. *The Unsayable: The Hidden Language of Trauma.* New York: Random House, 2008.

Rogers, Kim Lacy, Selma Leydesdorff, and Graham Dawson, eds. *Trauma: Life Stories of Survivors.* New Brunswick, NJ: Transaction, 2004.

Rose, Daniel Asa. *Hiding Places: A Father and His Sons Retrace Their Family's Escape from the Holocaust.* New York: Simon & Schuster, 2000.

Rosenfeld, Alvin H. "The Americanization of the Holocaust," *Commentary* 6 (June 1995): 35–40.

Rosenthal, Gabriele. *The Holocaust in Three Generations.* London: Cassell, 1998.

Rosenwald, George C., and Richard L. Ochberg. *Storied Lives: The Cultural Politics of Self-Understanding.* New Haven, CT: Yale University Press, 1992.

Roth, Philip. *The Plot Against America.* New York: Houghton Mifflin, 2004.

Roth, Philip. "Eli, the Fanatic," in *Goodbye, Columbus, and Five Short Stories.* New York: Bantam, 1970.

Rudd, Mark. *Underground: My Life with SDS and the Weathermen.* New York: Harper Collins, 2009.

Rudof, Joanne Weiner. "A Yale University and New Haven Community Project: From Local to Global," Fortunoff Video Archive for Holocaust Testimonies, New Haven, CT, October 2007.

Salime, Zakia, and Arlene Stein. "Mediating Homophobia and Islamophobia: The 'Paranoid Style' Revisited," unpublished paper.

Saltzman, Toby. "The Birds of Auschwitz: Walking Through Poland in the Footsteps of Ancestors," travelterrific, December 2003, accessed March 15, 2013, http://www.travelterrific.com/dec2003/europeauschwitz_dec03.html.

Scott, Joan. "The Evidence of Experience," *Critical Inquiry* 17, no. 4 (Summer 1991), 773–797.

Schuman, Howard, and Jacqueline Scott. "Generations and Collective Memories," *American Sociological Review* 54 (June 1989): 359–381.

Scheff, Thomas. "Shame in Self and Society," *Symbolic Interaction* 26, no. 2 (2003): 239–262.

Scheff, Thomas, and Suzanne Retzinger. "Shame as the Master Emotion of Everyday Life," *Journal of Mundane Behavior* (2000), http://www.mundanebehavior.org/issues/v1n3/scheff-retzinger.htm.

Schwartz, Mimi. *Good Neighbors, Bad Times: Echoes of My Father's German Village.* Lincoln: University of Nebraska Press, 2009.

Sedgwick, Eve Kosofsky. "Shame, Theatricality, and Queer Performativity: Henry James' Art of the Novel," in *Gay Shame*, ed. David M. Halperin and Valerie Traub, 49–62. Chicago: University of Chicago Press, 2009.

Seidman, Steven, Chet Meeks, and Francie Traschen. "Beyond the Closet? The Changing Social Meaning of Homosexuality in the United States," in *Sexuality and Gender*, ed. Christine L. Williams and Arlene Stein, 427–445. Cambridge, UK: Blackwell, 2002.

Shaechter, Rukhl. "Remembering the Hair Tangle of the 1960s," *The Jewish Daily Forward*, May 11, 2007, B3.

Shandler, Jeffrey. *Jews, God, and Videotape: Religion and Meaning in America.* New York: New York University Press, 2009.

Shandler, Jeffrey. *While America Watches: Televising the Holocaust.* New York: Oxford University Press, 1999.

Shteyngart, Gary. *Absurdistan*. New York: Random House, 2007.

Simon, Andrea. *Bashert: A Granddaughter's Holocaust Quest*. University Press of Mississippi, 2002.

Siraganian, Lisa. "'Is This My Mother's Grave?': Genocide and Diaspora in Atom Egoyan's *Family Viewing*." *Diaspora* 6, no. 2 (Fall 1997): 127–154.

Slezkine, Yuri. *The Jewish Century*. Princeton, NJ: Princeton University Press, 2006.

Slipp, Samuel. "Intergenerational Transmission of Psychic Trauma," in *Object Relations*, 163–173. New York and London: Jason Aronson, 1991.

Smith, Dinitia. "For the Holocaust 'Second Generation', an Artistic Quest," *New York Times*, December 23, 1997.

Solnit, Rebecca. *The Faraway Nearby*. New York: Vintage, 2013.

Sontag, Susan. *Regarding the Pain of Others*. New York: Picador, 2004.

Spence, Jo, and Patricia Holland, eds. *Family Snaps: The Meaning of Domestic Photography*. London: Virago, 1991.

Spiegelman, Art. *Maus I: A Survivor's Tale: My Father Bleeds History*. New York: Pantheon, 1986.

Staub, Michael E. *Torn at the Roots: The Crisis of Jewish Liberalism in Postwar America*. New York: Columbia University Press, 2002.

Steedman, Carolyn. *Landscape for a Good Woman*. London: Virago, 1986.

Stein, Arlene. "Therapeutic Politics—An Oxymoron?" *Sociological Forum* 26, no. 1 (March 2011): 187–193.

Stein, Arlene. "Trauma and Origins: Post-Holocaust Genealogists and the Work of Memory," *Qualitative Sociology* (October 2009).

Stein, Arlene. "'As Far as They Knew I Came from France': Stigma, Passing, and Not Speaking of the Holocaust," *Symbolic Interaction* 32, no. 1 (Winter 2009): 44–60.

Stein, Arlene. "The Photographs Near My Father's Bed," *Bridges: A Jewish Feminist Journal* 14, no. 1 (March 26, 2009): 31–40.

Stein, Arlene. "Trauma Stories, Identity Work, and the Politics of Recognition," in *Sociology Confronts the Holocaust: Memories and Identities in Jewish Diasporas*, ed. Judith M. Gerson and Diane L. Wolf, 84–91. Durham, NC: Duke University Press, 2007.

Stein, Arlene. *Shameless: Sexual Dissidence in American Culture*. New York: New York University Press, 2007.

Stein, Arlene. *The Stranger Next Door: The Story of a Small Community's Battle over Sex, Faith, and Civil Rights*. Boston: Beacon Press, 2001.

Stein, Arlene. "Whose Memories? Whose Victimhood? Contests for the Holocaust Frame in Recent Social Movement Discourse," *Sociological Perspectives* 41, no. 3 (1998): 519–540.

Stein, Arlene. *Sex and Sensibility: Stories of a Lesbian Generation*. Berkeley: University of California Press, 1993.

Steinitz, Lucy Y., and David M. Szonyi, eds. *Living after the Holocaust: Reflections by Children of Survivors in America*, rev. 2nd ed. New York: Bloch Publishing Company, 1979.

Strozier, Charles B., and Michael Flynn, eds. *Trauma and the Self*. New York: Rowman and Littlefield, 1996.

Sturken, Marita. *Tourists of History: Memory, Kitsch, and Consumerism from Oklahoma City to Ground Zero*. Durham, NC: Duke University Press, 2007.

Sturken, Marita. *Tangled Memories: The Vietnam War, the AIDS Epidemic, and the Politics of Remembering*. Berkeley: University of California Press, 1995.

Swartz, Sarah Silberstein. "Return to Poland: In Search of My Parents' Memories," in *From Memory to Transformation: Jewish Women's Voices*, ed. Sarah Silberstein Swartz and Margie Wolfe. Toronto: Second Story Press, 1998.

Sykes, Charles J. *A Nation of Victims: The Decay of the American Character*. New York: St. Martins, 1992.

Taube, Tad. "March of the Living Must Embrace Life," *Forward*, May 5, 2006.

Taylor, Charles. "The Politics of Recognition," in *Multiculturalism and The Politics of Recognition*, ed. Charles Taylor and Amy Guttman, 25–73. Princeton, NJ: Princeton University Press, 1992.

Tompkins, Silvan S. *Exploring Affect: The Selected Writings of Silvan S. Tompkins*, ed. Virginia E. Demos. New York: Press Syndicate of the University of Cambridge, 1995.

Torgovnick, Mariana. *The War Complex*. Chicago: University of Chicago, 2005.

Tumarkin, Maria. *Traumascapes*. Melbourne: Melbourne University Press, 2005.

"U.S. Immigrants Tape-Record Grim Memories of Nazi Holocaust," *New York Times*, May 11, 1976.

Van Gelder, Lawrence. "Groundbreaking in Warsaw for Jewish Museum," *New York Times*, June 25, 2007, accessed March 15, 2013, http://www.nytimes.com/2007/06/25/arts/25arts.html.

Van Ijzendoorn, Marinus H., M. Bakermans-Kranenburg, and A. Sagi-Schwartz, "Are Children of Holocaust Survivors Less Well Adapted?" *Journal of Traumatic Stress* 16, no. 5 (October 2003): 459–469.

Wardi, Dina. *Memorial Candles: Children of the Holocaust*. New York: Routledge, 1992.

Waynryb, Ruth. *The Silence: How Tragedy Shapes Talk*. Crow's Nest, New South Wales: Allen & Unwin, 2001.

Waynryb, Ruth. "The Holocaust as Unspeakable: Public Ritual Versus Private Hell," *Journal of Intercultural Studies* 20, no.1 (1999): 81–94.

Weinberg, Werner. *Self-Portrait of a Holocaust Survivor*. Jefferson, NC: McFarland, 1985.

Whittier, Nancy. *The Politics of Sexual Abuse: Emotion, Social Movements, and the State*. New York: Oxford University Press, 2009.

Wieviorka, Annette. *The Era of the Witness*. Ithaca, NY: Cornell University Press, 2006.

Wolf, Diane. "Holocaust Testimony: Producing Post-memories, Producing Identities," in *Sociology Confronts the Holocaust: Memories and Identities in Jewish Diasporas*, ed. Judith M. Gerson and Diane L. Wolf, 154–175. Durham, NC: Duke University Press, 2007.

Woocher, Jonathan. *Sacred Survival: The Civil Religion of American Jews*. Bloomington: Indiana University Press, 1986.

Wylie, Philip A. *A Generation of Vipers*. New York: Holt, Rhinehart, and Winston, 1942.

Wyman, David. [1984] *The Abandonment of the Jews: America and the Holocaust 1941–1945*. New Press, 2007.

Yagoda, Ben. *Memoir: A History*. New York: Riverhead Books, 2010.

Yanay, Niza. *The Ideology of Hatred: The Psychic Power of Discourse*. New York: Columbia University Press, 2013.

Young, Alan. *The Harmony of Illusions: Inventing Post-Traumatic Stress Disorder*. Princeton, NJ: Princeton University Press, 1995.

Young, James. *Writing and Rewriting the Holocaust*. Bloomington: Indiana University Press, 1988.

Young-Bruehl, Elisabeth. "The Biographer's Empathy With Her Subject," in *Subject to Biography: Psychoanalysis, Feminism, and Writing Women's Lives*. Cambridge, MA: Harvard University Press, 1998.

Zeitlin, Froma. "The Vicarious Witness: Belated Memory and Authorial Presence in Recent Holocaust Literature," *History & Memory* 10, no. 2, Fall (1998): 5–42.

Zelizer, Barbie. *Remembering to Forget: Holocaust Memory Through the Camera's Eye.* Chicago: University of Chicago Press, 1998.

Zerubavel, Eviatar. *The Elephant in the Room: Silence and Denial in Everyday Life.* New York: Oxford University Press, 2006.

Zerubavel, Eviatar. *Time Maps: Collective Memory and the Social Shape of the Past,* Chicago: University of Chicago Press, 2003.

Zerubavel, Eviatar. "Social Memories: Steps to a Sociology of the Past," *Qualitative Sociology* 19, no. 3 (1996): 283–299.

Zussman, Robert. "Picturing the Self: My Mother's Photo Albums," *Contexts* 5, no. 4 (2006): 28–34.

INDEX

immigrating to, 22, 52, 160
second generation in, 77, 78, 83, 93, 95, 133, 188
survivors finding one another in, 2, 29, 42
New York Times, The, 83, 113, 167
New Yorker, The, 1
Newman, Paul, 64
Nicaragua, 91
Niederland, William, 69
nightmares, 3, 66–67, 89, 109
Norich, Anita, 76–77, 98
North Africa, 26, 65
Novick, Peter, 14, 168

Oberlander, Wendy, 154–55
Odenheimer, Micha, 173–74
Oradea (concentration camp), 55
Orgad, Shani, 126–27, 129

Palestine, 14, 64, 169
Palestinian experience, 170–72
passing, 38
as French, 32–33, 35–36, 55
as Gentile, 38, 66
as non-survivors, 34–36
pathologization
created by repressed memories, 85
of Holocaust survivors, 11, 69, 70, 73, 93, 105, 188
Phelan, Shane, 92
photographs, 134, 159, 189
absence of, 134, 140
family, 2, 43, 48–50, 133, 157, 161, 163, 174, 180
as memory triggers, 6, 61
searching for, 19, 132, 133, 139
Piatka, Naava, 149, 151–52
Plummer, Ken, 90
Poland, 21, 22, 39, 63, 71, 85, 149, 157, 161, 162, 167, 177
Jewish communities in, 36, 173
as nation of origin, 2, 21, 32, 39, 52, 54, 62, 66, 85, 123, 133, 152, 178
returning to, 2, 15, 42, 57, 134, 139, 141–46, 148, 153, 156, 164
Polish (language), 21, 97, 158, 159, 160
Polish accent, 15
Pollin, Teresa, 160–61

Pols, Hans, 51
post-traumatic stress, 175, 177
post-traumatic stress disorder (PTSD), 3, 47, 69, 98
Power, Samantha, 178
psychiatry, 7, 18, 28, 68–71, 73, 83, 105, 111, 177
distrust of, 51, 54, 78, 188
See also clinicians; mental health; mental health professionals; psychology; social work
psychology, 7, 8, 10, 47, 68, 69, 76, 81, 83, 93, 94, 98, 101
distrust of, 68, 111, 118
feminist, 125
growth of psychological expertise, 53
humanistic, 80, 81, 83, 92, 105
See also clinicians; mental health; mental health professionals; psychiatry; social work
psychotherapy, 81, 83
group therapy, 190

Rabinowitz, Dorothy, 6–7
rape, 5, 152
survivors, 12, 175
as weapon of war, 178
Raphael, Lev, 148
recognition, 8, 17, 27, 40, 47, 70, 74, 87, 88, 104, 115
refugees, 6, 23, 29, 104
Bosnian, 179
Cambodian, 182
German, 73, 156
German-Jewish, 109, 147
Hungarian, 33
Jewish, 5
hotels, 29
Punjabi, 180, 181
Viennese, 156
reparations, 70–73, 170
resilience, 6, 7, 46–47, 93, 98, 121, 189, 190, 193
Response, 75–76, 79
resistance (to Nazism), 26, 39, 46
commemorations of, 13, 60
See also Warsaw Ghetto Resistance Organization
resisters, 40–43, 129. *See also* Warsaw Ghetto Uprising